The Economics of Poverty

THE ECONOMICS OF POVERTY

Thomas Balogh

Second Edition

Weidenfeld and Nicolson
London

© 1966, 1974 Thomas Balogh
Second Edition 1974

First Published by Weidenfeld and Nicolson Ltd.
11 St John's Hill London SW11 1XA

Printed in Great Britain by
REDWOOD BURN LIMITED
Trowbridge & Esher

ISBN 0 297 76694 5 cased
ISBN 0 297 76702 X paperback

Contents

Acknowledgements

I wish to express my gratitude to Dom Mintoff and to (the late) Norman Manley. It has been a great privilege to serve them and an invaluable opportunity to gain experience, under a microscope so to speak, of the varied problems facing countries whose production and income have lagged behind those of the privileged, mainly North Atlantic, regions of the world. Also I am greatly indebted to Dr Sen. The opportunity of working at the FAO during his director-generalship provided me with great intellectual stimulus; equally so in respect of my stay at the Economic Commission for Latin America under Dr Prebisch and Louis Swenson, and with CEMLA in Mexico. To my work with Professor Mahalanobis and Pitambar Pant now both dead and René Dumont I owe more than can be acknowledged. Dr Sir S. Ramgoolam and Mr Boollel of the government of Mauritius gave me an opportunity to study yet another problem area, as did the United States Special Fund, and especially Paul Marc Henry. I have received much encouragement from Professor Saraceno and his eminent team in Svimez who were responsible for first bringing the problem of regional handicap to the attention of the world and for securing action. I am equally grateful to Mr Dhusis and M. Couvelis of the constitutional Greek government, and to Professors Perroux and Weiller. My debt to Paul Streeten and Dudley Seers, with whom I worked for almost a score of years, transcends the limits which can be accurately acknowledged. Miss T.C. Cooper very kindly helped to select and edit these essays. Without her help this volume could not have been published and I most gratefully acknowledge my debt to her.

Preface to Second Edition

In preparing this second edition of *The Economics of Poverty* I have omitted all of the reprints of my various country reports ranging from the Mediterranean, to Africa and India. Although the basic problems which I then analysed still remain, alas, and while I am fully confident in my anti-mechanistic approach to the economies of the less developed countries, these reports would need to be brought up-to-date. This, however, is not a task that can be accomplished satisfactorily from afar, nor on the basis of the lightning visits to airports to which more fashionable experts now seem to be restricted.

Although two of the newly included chapters (6 and 7) reflect my continued conviction of the importance of agrarian and educational reform, most of the new material in this volume (chapters 10, 11 and 12) concerns what I regard as having become the most urgent of questions, the reform of planning for development and aid administration. These points are also taken up in a new and lengthier Introduction.

I wish to express my gratitude to Queen Elizabeth House and to its Warden, Paul Streeten, who provided me with a research home; to my colleague, Mr Peter Balacs, whose editorial work well exceeded the limits connoted by that term and who helped to clarify obscure passages; and to the Social Science Research Council, whose grant enabled me to undertake much of the work embodied in this volume. The Leverhulme Trust, the ODA and the Fund for Studies in Social and Economic Change generously enable me to continue this work. I owe grateful thanks to them.

Introduction to Second Edition

3

THE TIDES OF FASHION

For well over a century and a half it has been taken for granted by most economists that 'qualitative conclusions about the effect of an economic cause upon economic welfare will hold good also of the effect on total welfare'.[1] But even Pigou restricted this to 'nations with a stable general culture'[2] and placed severe limitations upon the relationship between welfare and national income (including its distribution) as conventionally measured.[3] In the end, most economists adopted the size and growth of national income as a valid criterion for policy.

Lately, however, there has been a multiple reaction to this view. Not only have the implications of inequality in the distribution of consuming power been stressed far more forcefully than before,[4] but the need for a greater regard for employment has also been given its due priority in shaping overall policy. Moreover, the appropriateness of measuring general welfare and progress on the basis of the conventional criterion of net national income (or even gross national product for that matter) has been questioned. Criticism has been rightly directed at the potentially destructive consequences of failing to take due account of the deleterious impact on the environment of the uncontrolled sway of the private profit motive. This is especially relevant in the case of the extractive industries (including agriculture)[5]

---

[1] A.C. Pigou, *The Economics of Welfare* (4th ed), Macmillan, London, 1960, p 20.
[2] *Ibid.*, p 21.
[3] I hope to deal with this problem in greater depth in a forthcoming essay on the limits of economics.
[4] This excludes the LSE/Chicago School whose advice would entail increased inequality in the hope that the 'rich' gainers would increase their savings and domestic investment. As I argue (chapters 1 and 3) it is all but certain that this will not happed in areas of feudal character and may not happed even in tribal systems.
[5] For example, agricultural 'mining', which causes soil erosion by wind and water, or salination (see chapter 1).

4

which play such an important part in less developed areas.

Beyond that, the effect of 'development', as conventionally measured, on social institutions had been almost completely neglected. It was hopefully postulated that the only sure way to 'prosperity' lay in the imitation of North Atlantic – and especially British – institutions.[6] From Macaulay to the misconceived East Africa Report and the constitution of universities, wrong advice was confidently expounded and put into effect, with disastrous consequences. The same sort of attitude was reflected in official British constitution-mongering, which resulted in the proliferation of parliamentary regimes and federations, both of which either stood in the way of progress[7] or failed to survive.[8] The various presidential regimes, laced with one-party states and military dictatorships, reflect the consummate ignorance of the former colonial powers of the needs of independence and the complete lack of preparation for it. As we shall see, this was especially so in respect of education and in the imitation of the expatriate mode of living by the new African (and, to a lesser extent, Asian) governmental, civil service, and commercial elites, which has brought about a class apartheid to a degree hardly equalled even by very old-fashioned imperial expatriates.[9] It must be admitted, however, that even in those cases where independence was granted after a bloody and prolonged rebellion or civil war – as in Algeria – the same elitist deterioration can be observed.

---

[6] For example, the transformation of Mohammedan tax relationships into large, quasi-feudal property relationships, as in Bengal and other parts of India, the Sudan, Iraq and parts of Africa.

[7] Beginning with the Canadian and Australian constitutions, each of which in its way made government intervention virtually impossible.

[8] The Colonial Office often used economic arguments (e.g. the advantage of large markets) to foster the most outrageous combinations, not the least unfortunate of which was the Central African Federation sponsored by Sir Andrew Cohen. See also my paper 'Making a Customs Union', *Social and Economic Studies* (University of the West Indies), March 1960, on another equally inane and reactionary experiment; also 'Jamaican Future', chapter 17 in the first edition of this volume.

[9] Presidents Nyerere and Kaunda are rare exceptions to this depressing scene. Mrs Ghandi has introduced important reforms in India but their effect is yet to materialize.

While these criticisms are important and valid, the violent change in emphasis now fashionable must be deprecated. No doubt it would be essential for progress to be more evenly spread — with safeguards for traditional social relations, including security on the basis of the (extended) family or tribal coherence — so long as 'modern', money-based, social services cannot be introduced. These qualifications must not, however, lead to the deprecation of material advance *per se* as conventionally measured. Without such progress resources would not be available for putting an end to the misery of the masses,[10] although if it is the rich who alone or mainly benefit from this progress, and if there is no impulse towards its broadening and self-perpetuation, the political consequences of 'development' might be disastrous.

THE AID CONTROVERSY

This leads me to a second basic attack on the view, which I had not dealt with in 1964 when the first edition of this volume was being prepared by Miss Cooper. This attack is based neither on the notion that economic progress might have serious drawbacks, nor that it might not be measurable in the traditional fashion, but on the denial that it can be accelerated by means of foreign assistance. In this matter *les extrêmes se touchent.* Mr Griffin, the most downright of the progressive critics of aid,[11] suspects that aid is almost invariably used with definite and nefarious ends in mind,[12] and that therefore it will in the end sustain a socio-political structure which is the cause of stagnation and poverty and which still also inhibits development. He also assumes — at least implicitly — that aid in this framework will result in an increase in consumption and a fall in domestic savings; thus, aid would not achieve even its most direct aim of fully

---

10 See chapter 2.
11 Cf. K. Griffin, *Underdevelopment in Spanish America: an Interpretation*, Allen and Unwin, London, 1969, and 'Capital Imports and Domestic Savings in Under-developed Countries: A Comment on Mr Papanek's Views', mimeo, Oxford, 1972.
12 A suspicion very much aggravated by the downgrading of the aid-administering agencies both in the United States and Britain to the status of a division within their respective Foreign Departments.

speeding investment. Indeed, if 'aid' takes the form of direct investment or fixed loans on conventional terms, it might ultimately have a negative effect. On both points Mr Griffin has been able to find good supporting evidence, especially in Latin America, the Caribbean, and the Far East, notably Indo-China. There is, however, no inevitability even about these cases. An increase in consumption, provided that it is not permitted to benefit solely those who are already affluent, might play an important and beneficial part in the effort to mobilize, without the need for drastic compulsion, manpower which might then be able to perform heavy work on development projects on the basis of an improved diet.[13] In these, as in other economic matters, it would be rash to lay down general rules, although deterrent examples should alert both contributors and recipients to the various severe pitfalls in the way of development; I shall return to this important point.

The right-wing critics of foreign assistance, on the other hand, point to its deleterious moral effects — in much the same way as those who in the nineteenth century advocated reform of the Poor Laws, and their linear successors, the critics of unemployment benefit, attacked the rise of the Welfare State for encouraging 'malingerers and scroungers'. Further, they argue that aid would increase the size of the public sector relative to the private sector, allow wasteful public expenditure, and distort the structure of the economy. The bureaucracy would be permitted to lord it over an upward-thrusting entrepreneurial class labouring under a progressive tax system destructive of incentive. The upshot — and the direct consequence of aid — would be decay. The irresponsible bureaucracy would then wreak vengeance on the innocent would-be entrepreneurs: compulsion would follow control, and poverty and suffering would be aggravated.[14] If only aid had not been given, and power thus

13 Timely foreign assistance to President Allende might have made his policies, which almost inevitably depressed production, more acceptable to large parts of the Chilean population (see also chapter 5).
14 Similar ideas were expressed in respect of Britain by Mr Jewkes in his book *Ordeal by Planning*, not one of the more scientific or sensible contributions to policy-making to have been made by economists.

been handed over to the private sector, development might have occurred along those lines which brought flowering to the industrializing countries of the North Atlantic and Japan. *Laissez-faire* and all would be done!

History does not bear out these 'hypotheses' — if one can so compliment prejudice. For more than a hundred years the less developed territories existed in a state of economic *laissez-faire*. The rich paid no direct taxes; nor were they restricted by laws or administrative controls. And there was no industrial protection to 'distort' development. The result has been, over much the greater part of the globe, the creation of a slum of poverty, ignorance, disease and misery. The nostra of Chicago and the London School of Economics have been tried and they have failed abysmally. Despite the loss of trained manpower that followed on independence, even the most miserable of the less developed countries have made faster 'progress' (though not always leading to a better life) than ever before.

No doubt — and mainly for short-term and short-sighted political reasons — some regimes have been supported which are cruel, corrupt and wasteful, and thus condemned their countries to continued stagnation, if not worse. No doubt, also, the woollier do-gooders, who would wish to accept as of right the demands of the less developed areas without any political or economic strings attached, are exceedingly silly. This does not, however, justify the wholesale condemnation of the concept of the international transfer of resources from the rich to the poor. Potentially at least, it expresses the noble inspiration of accepting responsibility for re-distributing the world's income and wealth, beyond the confines of national territory. Yet most economists would take such redistribution for granted in the domestic field, despite the protests of the survivors of last century's orthodoxy.

AID AND DEVELOPMENT

However that may be, it is plain that, in our effort to promote co-operative development in the miserable, tradition-ridden areas of the world, we have run into a deep-seated intellectual and emotional crisis. This effort was conceived during and after the Second World War with the object of achieving self-sustaining progress in those areas, but also of establishing a more equitable balance in the world — between the rich and the poor, the trained and the untrained, the educated and the ignorant, and between the industrialized and the primary-producing countries. It would be wearisome to repeat the mass of quantitative evidence and to try to argue as to whether international inequality has increased only in absolute terms, or whether, worse still, there has been also a widening of the disparity of the overall rates of growth of national income. The disappointment and disillusionment are unmistakable, and they themselves create additional problems and obstacles in the path of bringing to fruition this experiment unique in peacetime: the experiment of redistributing resources and knowledge with a view to mitigating global inequality and reducing privilege.

After twenty years or so of striving, both recipients and donors alike find themselves confronted with grave socio-economic and political questions, which will have to be resolved if better progress is to be made in future.[15] The most ominous consequence of recent developments is that the very basis of collaboration is now in jeopardy. On the one hand there is the danger of a change in attitude on the part of the industrialized countries with regard to international socio-economic co-operation, an attitude which has not been seriously challenged since the war. On the other hand, and in consequence, this stimulates bitterness and suspicion in the poor countries.[16]

The magnitude of the postwar achievement in terms of international economic relations must not be underestimated. Never before have countries, in time of peace, subsidized on a large scale the development of backward areas and assisted actively in their progress. For all the criticism that

[15] This occurred towards the end of what had been officially designated the International Development Decade and in the first years of the Second Development Decade, the latter being itself a testimony to the failure — perhaps self-inflicted — of the former.
[16] See chapters 1 and 3.

can be brought against the giving of aid, this has represented an inestimable advance; it should be remembered that, even within the vast and wealthy European empires, policy before the war was to maintain a strict 'financial purity' as between the metropolis and the dependencies — although this was, in fact, a disguise for actual exploitation in the sense that a very large part of the surplus obtained in the dependencies through economic development accrued to the metropolis. Indeed, the need for grants-in-aid was regarded as reflecting a failure on the part of the colonial administration. Moreover, in most colonies, direct taxation or the levying of export duties on the products of foreign enterprise were non-existent. In addition, the whole 'modern' infrastructure — such as it was and is — in the colonial regions was fashioned to the convenience and profit of the metropolis, i.e. in favour mostly of the enterprises of the metropolis itself.[17] It is against this background that the greatness of the advance since the war is to be perceived. Nor should it be forgotten that the alleged 'failure' of aid is in fact compounded of an unprecedented rate of material improvement — far higher than anything achieved during the colonial era — but grievously offset by a frightening acceleration in the rate of growth of population. This latter explosion was the consequence in turn of a fall in mortality rates, which was not entirely unconnected with — though not mainly due to — the general advance in material welfare.

No doubt a certain proportion of bilateral aid has been besmirched by the political and military ambitions of the donor countries. Nor is there any doubt that, mainly as a result of these mixed, ulterior motives, in many countries — such as Ayub Khan's Pakistan, Colombia and Brazil, which have been singled out for praises and prizes in the development stakes by the high priests of *laissez-faire* — the social implications of such material progress as there has been — and in some it was spectacular — are far from satisfactory, not to say disastrous. Indeed, the distribution of income has worsened to such an extent that it is questionable whether the poorest, instead of benefiting at all, have suffered a

---

[17] See chapter 3.

further depradation even of their material standards. It follows, moreover, that the implications flowing from all this also remain uncertain.

It has been suggested that one of the reasons for the present disenchantment and unrest has been the growing realization by the poor countries that per capita — that is the individuals in — the rich countries are advancing more rapidly than they, and that it is their faster per capita enrichment which is creating the dissatisfaction.[18] But it must be doubted whether poor 'countries' adopt such an anthropomorphic view of rich 'countries'. What is much more likely is that it is the growing inequality, together with the rapid increase in the standard of life of the rich, including the expatriates, in the poor countries themselves (and not of the rich countries *per se*), which lies at the root of the dissatisfaction. This growing inequality is given a considerable stimulus by the greater mobility of the new elites emerging in the less developed countries. This generates pressures aimed at equalizing the incomes of the educated and skilled with those in the rich countries.[19] The fate of the rest is aggravated.

It is not only the implications and efficacy of bilateral aid which arouse misgivings. Multilateral aid, also, has often proved futile or been frustrated by the lack of relevant expertise, especially in regard to its phasing and co-ordination in planning. Nor is multilateral aid always free from the political pressures which donor countries exert in their bilateral activities. Nor is there any doubt that some, perhaps a considerable number, of the institutions and a lot of the know-how that have been transplanted in the process have been a hindrance rather than a help in furthering develop-

[18] Thus, the postulation by Professor Hirschman of the so-called 'tunnel effect', which blurs the internal problem of market economies and the increasing inequality which results from the operation of the market system, represents in effect an attempt to rationalize the classical hypothesis of the existence of a basic harmony of interests between nations, with but the rider that should such harmony be disrupted it will only be for fortuitous reasons quite unconnected with the fundamental nature of international economic relations.
[19] This, again, is praised by relentless propagandists as an increase in 'world income', a wholly meaningless phrase if there is no redistribution internationally.

ment, because of their secondary effects in the aided countries. Nevertheless, the core of achievement remains, supported as it has been by purposive action in the field of international trade, where attitudes have moved away from those strict canons of orthodoxy, the principle of non-discrimination, which worked so much to the detriment of the underprivileged areas and so much to buttress the position of the rich, educated, skilled and clever.

Politically, the failure to achieve a decisive acceleration in per capita rates of growth, despite the well-publicized triumphs of the Green Revolution, has had a momentous effect. In the rich, donor countries, there has been a tendency to lay blame on the recipients of aid, and to couch discussion of the failure in terms of their weak 'absorptive capacity'. There has also been a revulsion from some of the uses to which aid has been put, and more especially in the case of those less developed countries in which, racked by military revolts, leading to brutal and brutish dictatorships, civil wars and mass exterminations,[20] the most elementary human rights are being steadily eroded. For reasons of political expediency, and the fear that other competing powers might steal a march on the more squeamish, this disturbing factor has been much underplayed, and the blame shifted on to general economic rather than political reasons for limiting aid. This has certainly been so as far as the United States is concerned. On the other hand, in the rich countries the professional humanitarian sponsors of international aid are unwilling to speak out, for fear of giving a handle to their opponents (whatever the latter's case may be); the several donor governments, meanwhile, for reasons of state, were only too glad to support this evasiveness. It is not surprising that, with all this shuffling about, its desired result was not in the end achieved. Meanwhile, at the receiving end, the disappointed expectations of the less developed world made for bitter recriminations, only to be further exacerbated by the discovery of politically actuated moves and interventions (such as happened only too often in south-east

---

[20] The contrast between the reaction to such barbarities as occurred in Indonesia, Bengal, Sudan, Uganda, Congo and Burundi, and those committed by the colonial powers is striking.

Introduction

Asia and Latin America) on the part of donor countries.

THE ADMINISTRATION OF AID

To judge from past experience, we seem to have arrived
at yet another intellectual and emotional turning-point in the
ceaseless cycle that has characterized attitudes in this matter
since the war: a cycle whose fluctuations are, if anything,
of an even greater amplitude than that reflecting attitudes
towards the relevance of orthodox economic theory in the
context of fully industrialized economies. The optimism
and self-satisfaction of the 1950s gave way in the early
1960s to despair, only to be superseded again by an
undistinguished and untenable optimism with the onset of
the Green Revolution. Now, with the resurgence in the
developed world of a primitive monetarist and anti-trade-
union view, combined with some obsolete free-trade propaganda, there has been a corresponding, but equally unjustifiable, revival in 'liberal' attitudes towards the less developed
world, which, based on the 'successful' development of
Hong Kong, Taiwan, Singapore and South Korea, would
leave everything to the tender mercies of the multi-national
companies, acting partly through the medium of home-grown
entrepreneurs (see, for instance, the article by H. Kahn in
Development Forum, vol 1, no. 2, March 1973). As yet,
the damage which they have wrought has not been too great.

It is an ominous fact, however, that the sudden acceptance
by the conservatives, in Britain, in the United States and
elsewhere, of the virtues of the multilateralization of aid
should have coincided, at least in the United States, with a
reduction in the total amount of aid granted. My own views,
as can be seen in this collection of papers, have not undergone
any such startling fluctuations. I had not expected too
much from the International Development Decade and was
not deeply disappointed by what I do not consider to have
been a total failure. I have always been an adversary of the
political use of bilateral aid,[21] but I also never thought that a

21 I was chairman of a group, reporting to the leadership of the Labour Party on
the question of reorganizing the administration of aid, which recommended the
establishment of a separate ministry to be presided over by a minister of cabinet
rank.

deus ex machina, such as a diversion of aid into multilateral channels, would solve all the problems of the less developed countries.

Multilateral channels have their problems too. Their political organization (or, rather, disorganization) and lack of integration are grave drawbacks which are in turn largely responsible for the inadequacies and inefficiency of distributing aid in this way. This, again, is a theme which seems to be taboo, both to the national and international bureaucracies which profit directly from the present system, and to the international woolly-goodies who make a living by it.

A large proportion of the new material in this volume,[22] in contrast with the earlier hardback edition, deals with this problem and, especially, with the question of the recruitment and training of experts. While making all allowances to the principle that the recruitment of personnel should conform to some reasonable geographical distribution, it is surely possible to insist that objectively ascertainable and relevant knowledge of conditions in the less developed countries and the capacity for leadership should decide the choice of international civil servants. I discuss at length the need for thorough training, especially of the personnel which ought to serve (but which does not) as the backbone in the system of channelling multilateral aid, that is, the Resident Representatives of the United Nations Development Programme: this with particular emphasis on their relationship with planning staffs at the sub-regional level. Such training must comprise a socio-political element; without this, the present unacceptably high rate at which technical reports are being completely wasted will persist and, perhaps even be accelerated.

THE RECORD REVIEWED

A number of factors have been responsible for the disappointment of those brave hopes and aspirations of the early 1950s and early 1960s. Some have been inevitable, because

---

[22] Especially chapters 11 and 12.

Introduction

deeply embedded in the socio-economic structure of the developing countries themselves; others indicate a failure of political leadership in both donor and recipient countries. Some, further, hint at the less than perfect co-ordination of the various aid channels; and yet others point to the difficulty in the timing of the various aid processes and of the infusion of technical knowledge and resources.

Population explosion

By far the most important reason for the failure of the growth of income per capita to accelerate (if it did not actually slow down) and, to a very large extent, consequently for the failure to mitigate absolute poverty in the developing world, has been the explosive increase in population. This has been the result, principally, of the deep disturbance to ecological balance brought about by the chemico- and antibiotic-therapeutic revolution in the highly developed areas of the world, which, during and after the Second World War, was transplanted to the less developed areas. In most cases this contrasts very sharply indeed with the impact of economic development on population growth in the nineteenth century,[23] which was based on general, humane (educational) progress and linked organically with higher productivity and improved living standards. Thus, the decline in the rate of mortality was followed by a sympathetic fall in the birth rate as the increased probability of their children surviving becomes apparent to prospective parents. The current population explosion has been due mainly to discoveries made outside the areas affected by them and, hence, has been independent of their economic and social development. Not only could there be no immediate hope of a decline in birth rates but, with the

---

[23] One of the most hopeful signs of a change has been the halving of the rate of population growth in Malta. This has happened despite the continued resistance of the Catholic Church against mechanical, chemical and biochemical methods of contraception. *Coitus interruptus* combined with the rhythm method, impracticable as these are, seem to work in that peculiar island.

abatement, if not the eradication, of certain parasitical diseases, those factors which reduce mortality rates have also resulted in an often rapid, and in some cases explosive, increase in fertility. Thus, the economic impact was redoubled.

The problem of agriculture

On the other hand, there has as yet been relatively little success in increasing output in the traditional sectors of agriculture. It is still uncertain, for example, to what extent recent increases in agricultural output have been associated with the cycle in climatic conditions rather than with new techniques of production, although much has been made of the spectacular success in some countries, such as South Korea, Mexico, Taiwan, and parts of Pakistan and India. Such success in increasing agricultural output has been attributed to the responsiveness of the traditional sector to 'market' stimuli and it is argued as a consequence that it is the absence of such stimuli which has been at the root of the trouble elsewhere — as well as the excessive attention being given to industrialization. The inference to be drawn, supposedly, is that it is a relatively simple process, even in the agricultural sector, to achieve success by 'freeing' the economic system from its socio-economic constriction.

The success of this propaganda, combined with exaggerated notions of the success of the Green Revolution, resulted in the repudiation of continued food aid by the government of India and in the adoption of economic 'independence' as a planning priority. Ever since 1955, and particularly so in my reports to the government of India in 1961 and 1971, I have criticized this policy, a policy which, if it has not caused, has contributed to suffering in periods when the monsoons have failed.

The so-called Green Revolution with its miracle seeds has obviously had an important impact on agricultural productivity in certain areas. The application of the new seeds, however, is limited by their heavy technical require-ments. Moreover, as with other transplanted techniques, it is possible that, given unfavourable circumstances, even their direct effects might be deleterious. Drought, disease and the burning of crops (as a result of excessive use of fertilizers) might turn a technical advance into a catastrophe. Further technical advance — the development of drought- and disease-resistant strains — in the end may well diminish these dangers. Much more difficult is the task of dealing with the social impact and political consequences of the new seeds. These may prove calamitous, in that the income of the more fortunate larger peasants and landowners might increase, while prices fall under the pressure of increased yields to the detriment of the poorer peasants; while the still poorer deficit farmer and landless labourer will be crippled by increased land prices and mechanization, which reduces opportunities for rural employment and so also the income of the poorest, despite the fact that some of the new produce or seed might require a considerable increase in labour input.[24]

To some extent the spread of better techniques which are already available and of the resources needed for a self-sustaining breakthrough will depend on institutional reforms and a new approach to education. In principle, therefore, there is no reason why progress should not be generalized, but it would be entirely fallacious to draw the conclusion that self-sustained growth is likely to ensue automatically.

Industrialization

The failure in agriculture, in turn, has contributed to the lagging development of industry after the brave start that had been made and which had been connected mainly with the introduction of protective policies in the wake of independence. Unfortunately, however, the newly created 'independent' markets were so small and fractured that, in conjunction with their poverty, import-replacement has been unable to provide a sufficiently large impulse, a

[24] The case of Mexico is important, where the capital-poor co-operatives (*ejido*) have not benefited from the 'revolution' which has increased social imbalance in the country.

sufficiently wide front, for industrialization. Moreover, savings available for domestic use have failed to increase rapidly enough, despite the frightening inequality in the distribution of income and wealth in the less developed areas.[25] In many cases, such savings as there have been have found their way into hoards in Switzerland and other havens or, almost as barren, have been squandered on luxury building or in the acquisition of land (this partly because of fears of depreciation). This latter tendency, moreover, has helped to aggravate the problem of agricultural progress, by driving up the price of land (see above).

This failure of what has been christened 'linkage' (surely a double linkage in this case) is far more important than the much-discussed problem of the choice of industry, that is, whether one wants to achieve a broadening of industrial activity 'upwards' (i.e. towards capital goods) or 'downwards'. In my opinion the latter choice is not to be made on the basis of simple calculations, because of the side effects and the non-marginality of individual projects in this context. It is akin to the old problem, or pseudo-problem, of 'balanced' versus 'unbalanced' growth. What is certain is that industrialization — with the exception of Britain — has never been promoted without the help of protection.[26]

Export earnings

The consequences of this failure, already grave, have been aggravated by the fact that the exports of the less developed countries have grown at a slower rate in terms of value than those of the developed countries. The restrictions which the latter have placed on imports from 'low wage' countries (and to which so much attention has been devoted) can

[25] The 'liberalization' of capital movements under these circumstances amounted to an impediment to domestic development. The conventional reaction of economists was to blame protection and 'inward-looking development strategies' for the failure. Yet the 'liberal', 'outward-looking' policies which obtained under colonial or quasi-colonial rule were no more successful.

[26] 'Protection' of indigenous industries in less developed areas might take the form of banning imports from highly developed areas.

only be a partial explanation of this trend. The inability of the less developed countries to produce suitable manufactures efficiently (partly because of the uneconomic size of industrial units and of the lack of skilled manpower at all levels) was surely also to blame. The failure of the expansion of trade between less developed countries is a pointer in this respect. The examples of Hong Kong and other far eastern countries (and certain special exports from India, e.g. electric fans) on the other hand also show what can be done, despite the pressure of protection from labour-intensive industries in the developed areas.

Productivity

In retrospect, what investment there has been seems to have been rather less effective than had been hoped in bringing about an expansion of incomes, despite all the planning and analysis that had been undertaken with the reinforced (with aid) help of both the rich donor countries and the multilateral agencies.[27]

---

[27] The dissatisfaction felt with the results of industrial development as based on import-substitution has led to a general condemnation of economic 'nationalism' or protectionism (see I.M.D. Little, T. Scitovsky and M.F.G. Scott, *Industry and Trade in Some Developing Countries: A Comparative Study*, Oxford University Press for OECD, London, 1970, and I.M.D. Little and J.A. Mirrlees, *Manual of Industrial Project Analysis in Developing Countries; Volume II, Social Cost Benefit Analysis*, Development Centre of OECD, Paris, 1968). To this (i.e. economic nationalism) are now attributed all the ills afflicting the less developed countries – and there are many – including, surprisingly enough, urbanization and dilapidation. It is, therefore, proposed that any project should be evaluated on the basis of the ruling world prices of inputs and outputs. In the first of my essays reprinted here ('Economic Policy and the Price System'), I have analysed the limitations of the price system, especially as it operates in backward areas, and its inability to reflect social needs and costs sufficiently closely for the purposes of development. These areas, after all, have been exposed to the relentless and unimpeded functioning of the price mechanism, both under competitive conditions and in the first half of the present century when it became increasingly subject to oligopolistic influences and changes. The results have not really been satisfactory. If one contrasts even the more maddish postwar example (say) of Ghana under President Nkrumah in his last stages with prewar, it must be said that progress did accelerate, however one might wish to measure it. And more

Introduction

An impressive plea has, however, been made to the effect that the developed countries should liberalize the import of manufactures or (labour-intensive) components from the less developed countries — even if such a course entailed serious unemployment. However well-meant or morally admirable this plea, I fear that, in a democratic country at any rate, such a policy would be politically inadvisable, not to say wrong. From an economic point of view, moreover, it neglects the fact that a sudden crisis in an important (labour-using) industry in a fully developed country will have a secondary impact on imports. Now we know from experience that such a recession is likely to affect the price of primary products (the main export items of less developed countries) far more than the price of manufactures. Thus while in these matters it behoves us to be very cautious, it is at least not unlikely that such a move might hurt the less developed countries indirectly far more than it would help them directly to increase exports, since primary products comprise a very high proportion of their total exports, whereas manufactures are relatively insignificant.

There is a further important argument. The stimulus to the exports of manufactures from less developed countries would redound mainly to the advantage of the urban

forcefully, in the case of India or that of Jamaica under Prime Minister Manley (see *The Economics of Poverty* (1st ed), chapter 17), the superiority of 'nationalistic' protectionism over the unfettered forces of colonial free trade is striking.

The neglect of such convincing experiences has brought with it its own refutation, and attempts have been made to accommodate the obvious and large divergences between social and private costs. This can, of course, be accomplished by the use of shadow prices, wages and interest rates, which can, in principle, take into account the existence of unemployment, market imperfections and, especially, the inapplicability of the marginal principle (i.e. because of the 'lumpiness' of investment projects). All this is evident; but if all these amendments have been introduced into the calculations, the exercise becomes a wholly arbitrary and tautological substitution of quantified personal political judgements for the outcome of the 'free' play of market forces. Worse still, it gives a completely unjustified impression of scientific exactitude which, in fact, it utterly lacks. Cf. F. Stewart and P. Streeten, 'Little-Mirrlees Methods and Project Appraisal', *Bulletin of the Oxford University Institute of Economics and Statistics*, February 1972.

population, including skilled workers in manufacturing industry, who are in any case highly privileged in relation to the unskilled urban (and much more numerous rural) masses.

The plea of aiding the less developed countries by means of trade liberalization, to the extent that it carries with it the threat of unemployment in fully developed areas, therefore would not in fact achieve the aim claimed for it. Even if the receipts of the exports of (labour-intensive) manufactures from the poorer areas were spent on the purchase of manufactures of the 'rich', political pressures would remain unless the displaced workers were smoothly absorbed. Thus the emphasis on the primary importance of maintaining or restoring full employment at home, is both economically and morally justifiable. The 'liberal' view on the other hand amounts simply to an inefficient method of subsidizing the developing countries at the expense of the unemployment of relatively poor and unprotected workers in the more developed countries.

Sub-contracting and specialization

The establishment of subsidiaries or long-term contractual suppliers by giant (often not-so-giant), technologically advanced, multi-national firms in less developed countries in order to make use of the availability of cheap labour is one of the ways in which the liberal dream of 'spreading' the benefits of technical 'progress' can be achieved. It is not an unmixed blessing. It does, of course, open up opportunities for employment at wages far higher than the average national income (per family); it also transfers know-how, skills and resources. If this leads to the growth of indigenous entrepreneurial (or public-sector) capability – which can ultimately be controlled and taxed – then this might well accelerate development.

But there are grave risks, which are generally either over-looked or wilfully ignored, attaching to the unduly powerful position of such 'guest' firms, especially if they are manu-facturing rather than extractive or plantation industries, which depend on the goodwill of the host government as a result of the eclipse of gunboat diplomacy. The former might be supported by their governments and can move their activities to other areas; indeed, the strength of the multi-nationals is enhanced if their governments contribute a certain amount in aid, while at the same time trying to make such donations dependent on good behaviour.[28] As a result the guest firm may be able to exact tax or other concessions, or a gradual lowering of the purchase price, which together may prevent the 'host' country from duly benefiting in the surplus created. (Even in the worst case, employment income would rise. It is the indirect effects, the rise of privileged elites and the exacerbation of inequality, which represent the gravest dangers of this phenomenon.)

It should be said, however, that under present conditions, and even in areas which are not favourably situated strategically (e.g. as Latin America is in relation to the United States, compared with the Middle East where Russian countervailing power has at times been effective), not only larger, but quite small and *per se* powerless countries have defied large firms from strong aggressive countries. Admittedly, this happened more in those cases where the host country possessed natural resources such as oil or metals which the guest firm or country needed, than in those involving manufacturing activity where marketing know-how and the complementarity of the product as a component of the multi-national's end product made in the host country prevented an alternative to tied working for foreign firms.

Integration

The difficulties facing the backward areas are well illustrated by the fact that their trade with each other had not expanded with the vigour that one might have expected. It is significant from this point of view that neither in Latin America nor in Africa have efforts at establishing common markets prospered.

---

[28] For example, British policy in Tanzania. Also the 'Hickenlooper' amendment − cutting aid to defaulters and nationalizers − was (unsuccessfully) invoked in the case of Peru.

On the other hand, and for reasons which are deeply
embedded in their social structure (including their poverty
itself), primary-producing countries have been persistently
unable to obtain price increases for their exports comparable
with those gained by the rich industrialized countries for their
essential manufactures.[29] This cannot be taken as reflecting
some 'natural law'; as neither does its opposite, the
'permanent' worsening of the terms of trade of the
industrialized countries as a result of the 'law' of decreasing
returns, so sedulously propagated after the First World War
and, more recently, during the Second World War.[30] The
trend is unlikely to be changed in the medium-short term,
however, although cumulative crop failures have recently
benefited primary producers.[31] The continuous inflation
which raises the money price of primary products (though
less than that of manufactures) does not represent a
sufficient alleviation. The fact that expansion in the highly
developed areas of the world tended to slow down after
the rapid advance in the 1950s, and that in a number of
countries there has been increased — and unsuccessful —
reliance on general, indirect, policy weapons or monetary
restrictions which have a greater impact on the more highly
organized world markets in primary commodities than on
the managed markets for manufactures in the developed
areas, has been one more factor militating against the less
developed countries.

Colonial legacy

The intimate connections between most of the former
colonies and their late metropolitan countries, their respective
capital structures, and the extreme difficulty involved in
the finance of anything but international trade, all this must
have played an important part in preserving colonial patterns

[29] See chapter 8.
[30] For example, Colin Clark, *The Economics of 1960*, Macmillan, London, 1942.
[31] The formation of the enlarged EEC will aggravate the problem. Only a sharp
change in the foreign-trade policy of the Soviet Union offers the possibility of
relief in the short run: but this is unlikely.

of trade and economic structures.[32] Neither the United Nations and its agencies nor the World Bank have been able to mitigate this condition of post-imperial dependence.

As a consequence of this, outflows connected with direct foreign investment in the developing countries, together with the added burden of international fixed-interest debt, have both increased and threaten to offset inflows in respect of foreign aid. The latter burden in particular has been augmented both by inflation and by the effects of the system of direct taxation in the rich countries: interest rates have risen considerably, not the least because their nationals can offset interest charges against their direct-tax liabilities. Thus, the poor countries are sharply penalized by the operation of market forces in a modern framework.

Lack of skills

Progress in the underdeveloped world has not least been retarded by the acute shortage of skilled manpower, especially in the vital rural sector; this again is an interacting consequence of poverty, but also of tribal, feudal or religious attitudes which are incompatible with collective and individual social responsibility, cohesion and economic incentives. Again, in many countries this reflects the continuing influence of the neo-colonial or pseudo-colonial relationship which subsists between rich and poor: this because the educational system in these countries has been fashioned in such a way as to increase the mobility and prosperity of the few and the misery and helplessness of the many. For this reason there is imposed upon the less developed areas an internal inequality of income distribution which at the same time increases the burden of development. It is in this lop-sided evolution that the Chinese can hope for increased credence and support for their propaganda efforts. It is a sad reflection on the ways of human society that, as we have already pointed out, even in those countries to whom independence was not granted by a disillusioned colonial power wishing to rid itself of its obliga-

[32] See chapters 1 and 3.

tions, but which was fought for and won after bloody battles (as for example, in Algeria), the resulting elitism is nonetheless revoltingly evident.

Institutional and social factors

It should be said that many of the above-mentioned problems are the consequence of deep-seated institutional and social factors, which had themselves been at the root of past failures. The conquering Europeans and Americans have merely accentuated rather than created the causes of stagnation.

THE BLIGHT OF IRRELEVANT ECONOMICS

In a great many cases — and especially in the pre-Kennedy era and, again, under Nixon — it has been the influence of the United States, supported by its overwhelming predominance in providing aid, which prevented in fact the institutional changes necessary for the liberation of progressive domestic forces and for the creation of a social framework in which development would be practicable. It is one of the more disillusioning and dispiriting facts of life that a great many economists still insist on the benevolence of market forces and on the basic (or long-run) harmony of interest between rich and poor, advanced and backward, sophisticated industry and primitive peasant agriculture. This view remains the fervently held belief of the ruling political party in the United States (despite its various tergiversations and shifts in policy) and was shared, even before 1951,[33] by ruling official opinion in Britain (and increasingly so again now).

Accordingly, there developed a proclivity towards simple mechanistic explanations, based on general (historical or mathematical) models, while the computers — those Delphic

---

[33] On the policy of the Labour government under Attlee, see my paper 'Britain and the Dependent Commonwealth', in A.C. Jones (ed), *New Fabian Colonial Essays*, The Hogarth Press, London, 1959, esp. pp. 97-209; also my essay 'The Apotheosis of the Dilettante: the Establishment of Mandarins', in Hugh Thomas (ed), *Crisis in the Civil Service*, Anthony Blond, London, 1968.

oracles of the modern era — readily came up with the required answers. Their advice was nearly always the same: devalue the currency; stop inflation; let the market-mechanism take over — and all would be well. In Asia and Latin America there have been numerous political victims of this approach. The IMF under Dr Jacobsson had been a great exponent of these policies, as had been the World Bank at an earlier stage.[34] Backed by the American and British governments, their influence has been pervasive — as anyone can testify who tried to work in this field during the second half of the 1950s, and again more recently.

The attitude underlying this approach, of course, reflects a fallacious belief in the applicability of the neo-classical model of perfect competition to traditional or dual economies, beset with rigidities, and riven into non- (or barely) communicating sectors.[35] Perfect competition implies the absence of festering social bondage; it implies perfect knowledge, mobility and flexibility; it implies social integration and equality (or a justifiable, or at least a tolerable, degree of inequality); and finally, but no less important, it implies the absence of cumulative advantage from mass-production,[36] so that competitive superiority does not necessarily accrue continuously to the rich advanced countries and that increasing inequality is not inevitable. In the framework of the underdeveloped world, the *status quo,* the partial dominance of market forces, means the perpetuation — indeed, as Latin America shows, the aggravation — of the co-existence of misery and opulence, a condition in which the hewers of wood and the drawers of water are condemned to remain, both nationally and internationally, in a state of perpetual inferiority.

A similar approach has also been used — rather more innocently — to 'measure' the 'need' for aid of the underdeveloped areas: to wit the notorious 'gap' calculations.[37]

---

[34] See the scathing remarks of Arthur Schlesinger, Jnr., in his book *A Thousand Days: John F. Kennedy in the White House*, Andre Deutsch, London, 1965, pp. 174-8.
[35] See chapters 1, 3 and 8.
[36] The whole basis of the neo-classical theory of international trade rests on the negation of increasing returns.
[37] This was the method used, politically quite rightly, by Professor Rodan in his

However laudable in intent, these calculations were also based on the desire to 'de-politicize' and to sterilize sociologically the problem of development. Aid simply appears as a mathematical formula leading to a dollar sum, thus eliminating the uncomfortable need to consider radical reforms or changes in social structure and attitudes.

Savings gap. Calculations of the savings gap were based at first on the fundamental hypothesis that increases in productivity are related in a certain predetermined (and similar, if not identical) way to investment.[38] On the basis of historical examples it was possible to show, by means of a quick calculation, the 'need' for capital investment arising from the 'deficiency' in domestic savings. A certain savings ratio was assigned to each level of per capita income; the difference, or 'gap', in turn was equated with the amount of aid required.

On the historical analogy of the territories under the sway of the Protestant North Atlantic ethos, it was axiomatic that savings would unfailingly increase with income. In time, destiny would bring about a 'take-off', or what have you, and

---

effort to interest and influence President Kennedy in intensifying United States aid, but with a less overt *laissez-faire* bias. It was also used more recently, and unforgivably, by a United Nations committee preparatory to the debates on the Second Development Decade (see chapter 11).

[38] These sort of calculations resembled the so-called Harrod-Domar growth 'models'. Professor Domar must of course be absolved from any claim that his calculations – which were designed to show certain quantitative interrelationships, based on what he knew to be quite arbitrary, extremely simplified and unrealistic assumptions – could possibly be taken as a picture of historical development. His followers were less discreet. Professor Kindleberger, whose ingenuous enthusiasm for mathematical relationships is matched only by his artlessness in handling and interpreting them, tries to associate development 'of the Harrod-Domar type' with movements in the terms of trade. This is, of course, wholly illegitimate. No development ever took place on the basis of rigid technical relationships.

The neo-classical 'model' itself completely ignores the consequences of inequalities in the economic strength of trading partners. Thus: 'While land and labor remain relatively unchanged in the short and intermediate run, capital accumulation proceeds at a steady pace. The theory is readily adjusted to accommodate this change. As capital accumulation proceeds faster in one country than another, the factor endowments underlying comparative advantage, and comparative advantage itself, change. The basis for trade is altered. *But a new basis exists*'. See Charles P. Kindleberger, *Economic Development*, McGraw-Hill, New York, 1958, p. 239.

with it an automatic diminution in the need for aid. All this
was wholly illegitimate as applied to the overwhelming portion
of the Third World.

Trade gap. Another, rather more pessimistic, result was
derived on the basis of projections of less developed countries'
export earnings in relation to their import requirements,
calculated on the basis of the rate of investment that would
have to be maintained if a certain target rate of 'growth' was
to be achieved. Fundamental to these exercises again, of
course, was the assumption of a fixed ratio between investment and imports and between output and imports.

It was in this way that discussion was divorced from
political and sociological problems. The objective was equated
with an inflow of capital; policy decisions to alter the
functioning of the system and the implementation of structural reforms so as to release internal economic forces were
topics excluded from purview. What a contrast to the pre-
mathematical, politically and sociologically alive analysis of
the middle-aged Keynes! He realized with conviction 'the
intensely unusual, unstable, complicated, unreliable, temporary nature of the economic organization by which Western
Europe [had] lived for the last half century'.[39] Thus it came
about that:

> Europe was so organized socially and economically as to
> secure the maximum accumulation of capital .... If the rich
> had spent their new wealth on their own enjoyments, the
> world would long ago have found such a regime intolerable.
> But like bees they saved and accumulated, not less to the
> advantage of the whole community because they them-
> selves held narrower ends in prospect.[40]

There was no inevitability about it.

To mistake tribal chiefs or feudal lords, elitist civil
'servants' or sergeants transformed into jumped-up generals,
for puritan entrepreneurs; to apply quantitative relationships derived either from purely implicit theorizing or from

[39] See J.M. Keynes, *The Economic Consequences of the Peace*, Macmillan,
London, 1919, p. 1.
[40] *Ibid*, p. 16.

irrelevant historical examples, is to rob economics of all value in actual decision-making.[41] It is tantamount to applying the example of those countries, where the activity of fierce entrepreneurs resulted in the transformation of imbalance and discontinuous development into a process of relentless, if not unbroken, growth, to those areas where development has failed to occur as a spontaneous result of the unco-ordinated interaction of individual effort, and where it will necessarily depend on the balanced elimination of those institutional, social, motivational and functional obstacles that stand in its way.

This artless theorizing has been, in my view, motivated by a snobbish desire to match the rigorous methods and abstract purity of the natural sciences. I would admit that the Marxist explanation of the self-interest of economists, in providing a moral justification for the existing (or rather an idealized picture of the pre-1914) system, has a slightly more solid basis with the faithful, the respectable and the orthodox supported on all sides by private foundations and research contracts, being tempted by lush pastures and global peripatetic opportunities. But some crumbs are falling into less 'deserving' laps, and I suspect that the widening and increasingly interesting opportunities to help the weak are a more important motivation than material advantage.[42]

41 A very similar fallacy underlies the quantitative approach to manpower planning based on the distribution of employment in countries which have successfully developed at an earlier stage of their expansion, an approach on which much of the World Bank's present policy is based.

42 I would also assert that economists, having some (albeit extremely dubiously) quantifiable phenomena to interpret in their abstract system, have made less fools of themselves than either the psephologists or sociologists. One of the nicest examples of the latter is found in a paper by T.L. Blair, 'Social Structure and Information Exposure in Rural Brazil', *Rural Sociology*, March 1960. We are told that 'the field research was conducted in a rural community on the edge of Lake Tapes in eastern Rio Grande do Sul, Brazil (p.66) . . . [that] the research data were collected by questionnaire, case histories, and participant and non-participant observation over two one-month periods (p.67) . . . [that] each operational hypothesis assumed that significant differences among the average ranks for each occupational group would occur and stated the hypothesized direction and pattern of difference. These hypotheses were arranged so that it was possible to treat each initially as independent indices of the dependent variable to which they were related (p.68) . . . [that] agricultural workers had a low degree of exposure to new information; they did not possess the necessary pre-

However that may be, the fact remains that classical economic theory was especially pernicious when it came to analysing and explaining the interrelation between strong, highly developed and intensely dynamic countries with poor, weak, primitive and therefore stagnant economies — that is, the problem of unequal partnership. In my analysis of this historically typical relationship, I concluded that:

> In analysing problems pertaining to international economic relations the details of the particular situation, the character of the countries concerned, the historical context, the general monetary position, cannot legitimately be disregarded. They form the essential basis for any prediction of probabilities . . . A completely new approach [is] obviously needed and [is] equally obviously impossible on the basis of 'traditional' foreign trade theory.[43]

The fact that, apart from the example of Japan in the post-war period, no non-Atlantic country has attained full industrial maturity, has imparted a bitter racial flavour to the classical argument. The hewers of wood and the drawers of water who were supposed to benefit from trade, and who were in fact kept automatically down-trodden, happened to be non-white. Thus was the acrimony of the underprivileged redoubled. The fact that the oligarchies of these areas, irrespective of colour, behave far more ruthlessly towards their inferiors, spend an inordinate part of their ill-gotten gains abroad on luxury imports and lush living, thus combining the privilege of mediaeval servitude with the enjoyment of modern durable goods, does not improve matters.

prerequisites [literacy and money for example] for the use of mass media; they were infrequently exposed to the principal means of mass media communication; they were not exposed to new information through social visiting since persons they visited were fellow workers as unexposed as themselves; and they had an extremely low and infrequent degree of contact with bearers of information from the outside world' (p. 69). And the author concludes: 'From the point of view of international relations, the increasing exposure of the people of less developed areas to news, information, opinions and ideas — in short, to new social knowledge — makes it possible to stimulate a proper climate for harmony and understanding among nations' (p. 75). One wonders how it comes about that the author did not suspect that 'two one-monthly interviews and questionnaires' were not needed for this conclusion.
[43] See *Unequal Partners*, Blackwell, Oxford, 1963, vol I, pp. 10-11.

It is in these cases that the 'neo-classical' assumption that inequality of income distribution promotes savings and results in increased investment and accelerated progress is least warranted. We have seen[44] that there is a fundamental objection to regard as 'progress', *any* increase in productive capacity and output, irrespective of whose welfare it serves. In fact in backward areas the increase will almost certainly be appropriated by a small minority. It follows from the preceding analysis moreover that there is not the slightest assurance that inequality will, *per se,* lead to increased savings. It might in fact lead to increased luxury consumption and an increase in the propensity to import. Unfortunately the most straightforward alternative, the increase in collective saving through budget surpluses, might not in all cases prove feasible because of the weakness of the fiscal machinery. Given the scarcity of entrepreneurial ability, moreover, the deterrent effect of (relatively) high taxation might prove in the event unfavourable. Direct controls on imports, together with an investment-licensing system preventing the burgeoning of luxury import-substituting industries, could in certain cases be more conducive to promoting industrial development. Public sector savings and fringe loans could be channelled through a development bank. Protective measures will also be required even though they will for an interim period depress real income in the poorest sectors. No 'infant' country, not to say industry, has ever succeeded in this difficult operation without them. The grave problem is how to avoid picking eternally retarded 'infants'. Once development is under way, however, taxation and an accentuation of public sector investment is probably the most effective way of mobilizing productive resources for accelerated development.

Thus the hotly disputed problem of whether greater equality is necessarily in conflict with accelerated growth, just as the problem of whether 'balanced' or 'unbalanced' growth should be striven for, turns out to be impossible of a straightforward answer − or is rather a faulty posing of an important question. It will depend on the social structure, therefore on the history of any given territory, whether a self-sustained 'unbalanced' expansion based on rather greater

[44] See above pp. 4-6, and chapter 2.

inequality will in the end produce a faster rise of the income and social well-being of the less favoured or ill-favoured classes than one relying on more equality and collective effort. One of the important considerations will be the length of the horizon contemplated and the capacity and willingness of the population to endure sacrifice for a desired political aim. Which of the ways would seem preferable is in the end not an 'objective' but a political or moral choice.

THE ROLE OF PLANNING IN AGRICULTURE, INDUSTRY AND EDUCATION

Some of the disillusionment felt with regard to the progress made by the less developed countries stems from the fact that vast amounts of both bilateral and multilateral aid have been wasted because of the lack of appropriate planning.[45] Inasmuch as bilateral aid has tended, indeed has been used consciously, to propagate the *laissez-faire* approach to development, it has rightly come under attack. The parliamentary and governmental machinery needed to process bilateral aid has constituted a further difficulty. The inevitable political overtones and undertones attaching to bilateral aid, indeed its express aims, and hence its tendency toward the spectacular in order to impress both donor and recipient, all militate against the appropriate distribution of funds, because they are allocated on the basis of irrelevant criteria. This ostentation (or the need to display the extent of one's generosity) has resulted in bilateral aid being tied to grandiose projects, when there existed an equal or greater need for more general aid in the promotion of overall programmes of development, or in the furtherance of a programme of social change coupled with less impressive physical contributions, such as small hydrological works rather than huge dams. However, the fact that it is easier to tie large projects has been an additional reason for this misdirection. In addition, the chances that bilateral aid will be efficiently planned are reduced for the reason that in most donor countries budget appropriations have to be renewed annually.

45 See chapters 8, 9 and 10.

In the circumstances it was to be expected that there would be a sharp, if ill-considered, reaction away from bilateral and in favour of multilateral aid (chapter 11). Yet it could also have been anticipated that this too would turn sour as the shortcomings of multilateralism in turn became apparent. While at first my gravest misgivings concerned the problem of applying conventional economic analysis to the field of monetary policy (chapter 1), agriculture (chapter 5), education and labour relations (chapter 7), I became increasingly worried by the misdirection of effort characterized by the organization and structure of the various multilateral agencies.

It should be noted that, despite its numerous faults, bilateral aid does have certain inherent advantages: it is probably easier for it to be increased or maintained at a high level[46] (even discounting the effects of its being tied), and it permits not only harmful and illicit, but also beneficent and helpful intervention on the part of donor countries.[47] By contrast, the organization of the United Nations and the specialized agencies has been characterized by certain defects which have in my opinion contributed to the failure to eradicate, or even mitigate, poverty and inequality, an aim which had been laid down by both developed and less developed countries alike. Nor is multilateralization a guarantee of freedom from political pressures. Depolitization of aid through multilateralization has often been an illusion. The present analysis is the more important because the various strenuous efforts made at co-ordinating and unifying if not the purpose then at least the activities of the United Nations organs, have not been wholly successful. Indeed, the very fact that these efforts have been so repeated, and undertaken by such a great number of diversely composed committees and special bodies, shows that, while the need for reform is

---

[46] Because of the political forces lined up behind it — often based on a feeling of moral obligation, such as was felt, for instance, in Britain with respect to the sugar islands and New Zealand.

[47] The rise of immoral, beastly, rapacious and cruel (military) dictatorships suggests that *the right kind* of political strings — impossible to enforce in multilateral connections — might be needed only too much. The goody-woolly brigade in opulent communities has had a disastrous influence in this respect.

recognized, the obstacles to its achievement from the inside are difficult to overcome.

The Committee on the Reorganization of the Secretariat and the Review Team appointed to investigate the organization of the FAO were both equally unsuccessful.[48] Their respective Reports seem to have been based on a complete misunderstanding, if not downright ignorance, of the nature of the planning process, particularly in predominantly traditional agricultural areas, in which the fundamental prerequisite is for development programming to be organized as one coherent whole.

The failure of the conventional approach to the three supremely important and closely interlinked problems of agriculture, labour relations and education has demonstrated the need for a fresh effort; otherwise there is the danger that ultimately the adverse effects on these three areas combined might stifle progress altogether, regardless of any amount of aid.

Agriculture

A radical reform of the system of land tenure or at least the introduction of a progressive system of taxation would seem to be essential requirements in large parts of the world, if the forces of stagnation are to be weakened.[49] These must, however, be followed up by a reform of the supporting infrastructure, including education. However, the introduction of individual property in land in a number of countries might merely bring about its abuse.[50] In others, while it might effect an increase in output and in the marketed surplus, so too might it aggravate inequalities and, therefore, rural misery – although such experiments tended to attract high praise from the United States before these aspects became apparent, as for instance in Colombia and Pakistan. On the other hand, the taxation of cash crops (whether by means of export duties or through the use of statutory marketing

[48] See chapter 12.
[49] See chapter 1.
[50] As happened in Sierra Leone and parts of Ghana and Brazil.

boards), which has been so harshly attacked by the adherents of conventional theory,[51] would seem an essential device for the accumulation of capital. At first marketing boards were merely supposed to stabilize the revenue of farmers, by means of equalizing prices over bad and good seasons. As they became more experienced, however, the boards began consciously to accumulate rather large reserves, a policy which was alleged by their critics to have hindered the adaptation and, especially, the expansion of production in accordance with the 'requirements' of the market. Generalization is dangerous in this field, in which the impact of divergent social attitudes and institutions induces vast differences in the motivations of producers. The income derived from export cash crops, for instance, diverges fundamentally from crops also produced for domestic consumption.

The stage of economic development and the system of land-tenure have an obvious, but only too often neglected, impact on the problem. The prices of cash crops produced in the traditional peasant sector often fluctuate *within* seasons, and more so *within* production periods (which, in the case of tree crops might be as long as seven or eight years), to an equal and sometimes greater degree than *between* production periods or in the longer run. In such cases this argument seems rather feeble. Moreover, it is *technically* feasible vastly to expand the production of most cash crops. In the case of cocoa, for instance, the experimental farms produce an output as much as ten to fifteen times as large as that of the average farmer. Finally, cash crops seem to yield several times the value of the alternative food crop, in which case it seems that it is socio-technical, rather than strictly 'economic' reasons that explain the restriction of the volume of crops. Indeed, the experience of a number of countries, notably Ghana, has shown in fact that conscious efforts directed at promoting technical advance, financed by a central agency such as a marketing board, are a far more effective means of increasing production than the impact of price fluctuations.[52]

[51] See, for instance, *East Africa Royal Commission, 1953-55, Report*, HMSO, London, Cmd 9475, 1955, and my review paper, 'Primitive Economies and Primitive Economics', *Venture*, January 1956.
[52] This is, of course, not the case with the products of large-scale plantation industry.

Even in rich industrializing countries (e.g. Australia) we have seen that agricultural production may respond 'perversely' to price changes.[53]

But these niceties of pure theory neglect the most important aspect of marketing boards. By smoothing short-term price fluctuations, marketing boards banish ignorance and uncertainty as to prices and hence remove from the hands of the large-scale buyers (or their agents), and of money-lenders and landowners, their most powerful weapon with which to exploit the peasant. As soon as price levels and commission charges have been laid down for long periods, the peasant can be assured of the value of his crop. Comparisons of the receipts of peasants, based on world market prices prior to the establishment of the marketing board, with those based on the buying price of the latter once established, are thus irrelevant.

While fluctuations in primary-product prices seem to depend mainly on rapid changes in expectations about demand conditions rather than in output, crop fluctuations in turn have obviously had catastrophic effects on prices and, consequently, on the receipts of farmers. In a number of cases, especially in those of export cash crops which are not consumed domestically, it would only be possible to deal with this problem by means of controlling output. But, as we have seen,[54] the implementation of such a solution is hindered by differences in social attitudes and economic development which in turn create a difference of interest as between dynamic and sluggish countries.

The impact of large bumper harvests may be especially disastrous, particularly of domestically consumed food crops in countries with an explosively expanding population. In India, for instance, the fall in the prices of food grains in 1955, and again more recently, had destructive effects in the longer run. It encouraged speculation, hoarding and the exploitation of weak producers. The obvious solution, again, would seem to be the maintenance of stable prices, either

---

[53] Such a reaction is, of course, the natural one. Only if leisure or own-consumption are excluded would it be perverse: the perversity is in the eye of the beholder.

[54] See *The Economics of Poverty* (1st ed), chapter 12.

through the operation of a national marketing monopoly, or at least through the appropriate geographical distribution of buffer stocks, which could be refilled whenever prices threatened to fall.

Labour and industrialization

The laying down of international rules to encourage the enactment of minimum-wage legislation and the establishment of trade unions can be based on perfectly sound reasoning. Not only do they promote equality of opportunity in industrialized countries; they might prevent wage-dumping from areas in which an export-led boom in labour-intensive industries is not the most obvious way to prosperity and development. But, if applied to primitive traditional economies, such rules might become the deadliest menace to progress, especially in those countries which possess some outstanding natural asset ready to be exploited by modern technological methods. Income tax was unknown in the colonies before independence,[55] and royalty arrangements were always biased in favour of the metropolis. Thus, the only way in which a colony could retain the purchasing power generated within its boundaries was by means of a strong trade union movement to force up wages.

After independence the revenues from the same natural resources increased, sometimes spectacularly by as much as thirty or forty times, as in the case of bauxite in Jamaica or in almost all of the oil-producing areas. Income tax was introduced and royalty agreements were revised. In the new situation, therefore, *accumulation henceforth depended on the maximization of revenue from royalties and taxes;* disproportionately high wages in the 'modern' sector would only create a further (semi-) privileged minority and impede accumulation.

High wages, relative to the traditional sector, since they are only feasible in the context of capital-intensive techniques, would also hamper industrial development and the maximiza-

[55] This includes the countries of Latin America, at any rate before the Second World War, even though they were nominally independent.

tion of employment growth, since the adoption of such techniques is only practicable in sectors where the existence of exceptional natural resources (including climate) provides an absolute, or a very substantial comparative, advantage – a condition which is not available on a broad front. Consequently the practice of sectional trade-union bargaining based on monopoly power detracts from balanced development and threatens to aggravate inequalities in income distribution and opportunity. Countries endowed with mineral wealth, or with a climate especially suited to the production of certain crops on large-scale plantations (such as sugar or palm oil) have often been prevented from using their natural advantage to the full for precisely this reason, such as in the case of the copper mines in Chile. The labour market, already fragmented for historical reasons, becomes further riven by the creation of sectional vested interests thus constituting a growing impediment to the expansion of the 'modern' sector beyond that of the favoured industry.

The conventional Western, i.e. highly developed, industrialized, approach, as embodied in the doctrine that compulsory national service is only permissible for military purposes, is equally inimical to development. There is no doubt that national service in colonial times was in fact often tantamount to forced labour, whether indentured or worse, the effects of which redounded to the benefit of the great concessionary metropolitan plantation or mining companies, or simply to the feudal landlords. Nor is there any doubt that even after independence 'national' service might be, and has been, exploited by a greedy elite, as has been the case in Latin America.

But there can equally be no doubt that accelerated development (and the assurance of equality of sacrifice in the process) will depend on the ability of the less developed countries to mobilize their own manpower for purposes of capital investment in schools, roads, irrigation and other related public works.[56] Indeed, unless such an effort is successfully made, the large majority of the population in these countries, particularly in the rural areas, will be condemned to continue indefinitely in the miserable bondage of

[56] See chapters 7 and 12.

primeval poverty. Obviously, if receipts of aid in kind or money permit governments to provide incentives to effort or to induce voluntary participation, this would be all to the good. But aid in kind, especially food, is not always practicable[57] and, even more often, may not be available in sufficient quantities. This, however, must not be allowed to stand in the way of the organization of public works for economic development.

It should be noted, in addition, that without a system of general national service, the construction, by means of public works, of the kind of capital projects mentioned above, and more especially if they take the form of relief operations in the event (say) of a natural disaster, might instil a feeling of inferiority among the beneficiaries. It is essential that the privileged and educated youth of the less developed countries be mobilized and their advancement made dependent on periodic stints of national service in rural areas. Unfortunately, such a proposal is far from acceptable to them, and Western doctrine continues to be exploited for the purpose of maintaining aristocratic educational precepts, particular stress being placed on oligarchic prerogative.[58]

Education

Not surprisingly it is in the field of education that the conventional wisdom of economic theory has been applied with the most notable extravagance. For it was here that it suited both orthodox economists and educationists to join forces in defence of their respective callings, in which, moreover, they could rely on the approbation of the conventional administrator. The suggestion that education should be modelled consciously to serve the task of social transformation and adapted to the means and needs of the less developed world was as repugnant to the *bien-pensant* as it was to the privileged,

[57] Whether for nutritional reasons or because of the pattern of production in the recipient country. President Nyerere of Tanzania has provided a conspicuous and stirring example of leadership in this respect.
[58] One of the problems involved is the intolerably unequal distribution of land-ownership, or pseudo-feudal or tribal system of land-tenure. No national labour service will prove practicable if it merely aggravates the inequality of wealth.

exploiting the national revulsion against foreign domination for the protection of their own advantages. The actual history of de-colonization has in most cases resulted in the rise of a new elite, which is as hostile to change in this respect as had been their predecessors and adversaries. Once more it has been shown that no vested interest is as dangerous and ferocious as that of the intellect.

It is in this field that any reconsideration of past follies has been slowest. Indeed, the number of institutions, whether academic, governmental or multilateral (e.g. in the United Nations family) established in the last ten years has fostered a vested interest in the sort of naive econometric manipulations which I tried to combat[59] and which now prevents a saner approach. It is without any doubt the most constrictive growth industry in the academic jungle, pouring out meaningless correlations, thriving on intellectual simplicity, and prospering through pandering to the Establishment.

In my essays no place is given to the 'social' and 'private' returns on 'investment in humans'. They try to explore by far the most important task ahead, the organization of a cheap and pervasive system of rural education, directed towards increasing agricultural productivity, which would be so designed as to co-exist in the closest of mutually supporting (one might say symbiotic) relationships alongside the agricultural extension service. But success in this cannot be hoped for on the basis of a classical, literary training: it requires a direct attack on agricultural ignorance, founded on a system of self-supporting school-farms in conjunction with a programme of rural national service. The starting age for schooling and training could with benefit be raised in the poorest of areas.[60] Children who begin their education at the age of six and then 'drop out' from eight onwards can hardly derive any advantage from such experience. The most valuable period would be from the age of fourteen onward,

[59] See J. Tinbergen and H.C. Bos, 'A Planning Model for the Educational Requirements of Economic Development', in *The Residual Factor and Economic Growth*, OECD, Paris, 1964, pp. 147-69, and my comments thereon, ibid., pp.180-7.
[60] It is astonishing that Lord Shaftsbury's success in raising the legal minimum age for child labour to ten, hence keeping down the school-leaving age in nineteenth-century England, should now prevail in the tropics.

followed by two years of national service. The date of school-entry, and not that of school-leaving, should be determined by what the country can afford. The inane insistence on 'excellence' in higher education, buttressed by living standards which the vast majority would not be able to enjoy for decades, perhaps centuries, is neither economic sense nor is it socially equitable. But unfortunately it pays off — that is, for the new elite, who are eagerly supported by the *ci-devant* colonial administrators who knew (and know) no better.

THE LESSON FOR THE FUTURE

Much the most urgent task in the field of international action is to reform the international agencies in charge of multilateral aid and to provide their personnel with adequate training. Without such reforms there can be no hope for any improvement in the effectiveness of aid. Yet well conceived and administered aid is needed both for progress towards the elimination of undue, mainly indirect, political influence, and for a steady pressure in the direction of the kind of internal reforms in the countries aided that are required if the basis of continued, self-sustaining, balanced progress is to be created, consistent with greater equality and less political abuse. But we must accept that such reforms cannot be other than politically inspired. It is for governments to see that they are inspired in a spirit of compassion and charity. The lesson that is taught by the experience of more than a quarter of a century's political and intellectual struggles in this field is the futility and foolishness of simple explanations and of formulae based upon them. Economics in this field especially must accept a far more modest role than the protagonists of the various 'scientific schools' claim for it. Painfully detailed analysis and not facile but completely wrong-headed quantification is in order.

Part One
Theory and Reality

1

Economic Policy and the Price System*

THE IDEAL

Much of the current discussion of economic policy in Latin America and, even more, of particular measures or institutional arrangements such as the proposed Latin American Common Market or Latin America Payments Union, is couched in terms which suggest that the main, if not the sole, problem of these countries is the restoration of the 'free' play of the price mechanism and the elimination of inflation. Thus economic restoration is viewed exclusively as aiming at the removal of artificial interferences with the working of the price mechanism.[1] There seems to be no recognition of the fact that an acceleration of growth and optimal progress might, in the circumstances confronting these countries, demand positive, systematic and discriminatory policies.

It is clear that the underlying and implicit hypothesis is that most, if not all, of the distortions in the economic system, at any rate in Latin America, are the result and not the cause of inflation. The inference is that with the elimination of inflation these distortions would also disappear, or at any rate

* Reprinted from *U N Economic Bulletin for Latin America*, March 1961. This analysis applies with some variation to the whole of the less developed world.
[1] See the memorandum on payments systems submitted by the IMF to the Meeting of Government Representatives of Central Banks, held in Montevideo, reproduced in the *Revista de Ciências Econômicas*, No 2, Sao Paulo, June 1960. With the increasing popularity among central bankers of the monetarist approach and of vulgar econometric and cost-benefit analyses, the severely restricted applicability of appreciations based on current prices should be re-emphasized. It is interesting that Professor Kahn's basic essay on 'Ideal Output' laid down that severe divergences from the Walrasian riskless static model invalidate optimal policies which are based on that model. In developing countries these divergences are especially severe; the Chicago-LSE approach in these matters is therefore totally fallacious.

that there will be such a net reduction of distortion that it would make possible an optimal increase in the rate of growth. The implicit character of the hypothesis dispenses with the need to demonstrate that the rather stringent conditions in which this view might be valid do in fact exist in the circumstances to which it is being applied.

Thus no answer is given to the question whether the relative price system, once inflation is eliminated, can be expected to revert to something corresponding to the ideal pattern that would lead to what is implied to be an 'optimal' allocation of resources and, therefore, also an optimal rate of growth. Nor is it clear whether measures of monetary stabilization are themselves thought to have any impact on relative prices, other than restoring their 'natural' level.

Hence it would seem useful to recall the assumptions on the basis of which such claims were originally put forward for a self-contained system, assumptions which are apparently forgotten when the conclusions are applied to current economic issues.

There must be full employment, since anything less would vitiate *inter alia* the allocative efficiency of the price system from a social point of view. The distribution of income must be desirable or at least politically tolerable. Consumers' tastes must be independently determined, that is they must not be influenced by the policies chosen. Both product markets and factor markets must be perfectly competitive. The capital market must function in accordance with the assumptions of the model, i.e. allocate capital at negligible cost among projects according to their relative social profitability. There must be a significant response by either savings or investment to changes in the rate of interest. There must be no considerable divergence between, on the one hand, private money costs and returns and, on the other, social real costs and returns. In particular, investment projects must be marginal (not 'lumpy') and should not significantly affect the returns of other investment projects (external economies). Cumulative movements – favourable or unfavourable – diverging from the original position must also be ruled out.

A further complication arises with the introduction of international economic relations into the simple, closed or self-contained model. In an open economy with foreign trade relations, the rules of the 'free' market would apply only if the terms of trade were independent of the policy pursued. But most countries in Latin America are specialized exporters, the demand for whose produce is not infinitely elastic. Thus, as will be seen, any liberalization of imports would, in fact, tend to result in a worsening of the terms of trade and therefore a fall in real income. Since Latin America is relatively poor and its income grossly maldistributed, such 'monopolistic doctoring of the terms of trade' as would be implied by a restriction of imports can hardly be rejected on welfare grounds.[2]

The efficient operation of the price mechanism is thus dependent on the full social (income-distribution) and economic integration of the economy. In this article an attempt will be made to show that these conditions for the successful working of a market economy are not fulfilled in the economic framework of countries at the stage of development reached in Latin America. Both factor and produce markets are fragmented, and there is not even a tendency towards equalization of factor remuneration. In addition, given the great difference in the degree of imperfections, the monetary measures enforcing stability might, because they can only operate through the creation of increased unemployment, further undermine the validity of the assumptions on which they are based.

Moreover, monetary measures ought not to distort relative prices and thus factor allocation: the maintenance of the complete integration needed for the optimal functioning of the price system is compatible only with measures which are neutral in this respect, i.e. those which operate in a diffused general way and do not impinge with different severity on different sectors of the system. This is generally accepted by

---

[2] Even though the alternative, an equivalent free grant from the fully developed countries, if available, might be preferable, provided always that the pattern of imports is not the result of an intolerable distribution of wealth and income. It is, of course, possible that protection will be granted to those industries that are totally, and even potentially, lacking in international competitiveness where the infant-industry argument does not apply and where proprietors and workers are prosperous relative to the rural sector.

the critics of direct controls, who base their attacks on direct regulation on the fact that they have severe directional or sectoral effects and thus disrupt the harmony of the system. It is not so generally realized that, unless they act on marginal demand for capital through a rise in the cost of borrowing, monetary measures might equally have such strong directional effects. They will impinge on construction and possibly the consumption of durable goods. They will act by rationing borrowers rather than by reducing the desire to borrow: the impact of interest as a cost element has become extremely weak, even in fully developed areas, as a result of the need for speedy depreciation and of modern direct taxation. In less developed areas there are in addition the problems which arise from the concentration of economic power and its exploitation by the feudal-plutocratic controllers. Thus, restrictive monetary measures might cause new distortions, even in a well-integrated system, rather than remedy distortions caused by previous monetary imbalance. It is unlikely that directional effects would happen to coincide with and offset the existing disequilibria.

Monetary policy will impinge on projects which are particularly vulnerable to the pressure it generates. Apart from the creation of unemployment, certain prices and incomes will prove especially sensitive, and the sectoral differences will be further accentuated in a way that harms the most vulnerable parts of the economy. Within these sectors, the restriction will be most effective against those least able to defend themselves by monopolistic practices. In an underdeveloped area, where there is strong monopoly market power, this means that the sector of labour least able to protect itself, i.e. unskilled workers, will be most affected. The general upward pressure on wages and prices (that is profits) in the rest of the economy need not be − and historically has not been − affected sufficiently to stop their upward tendency immediately. The fragmentation of the economy, combined with an exclusive reliance on monetary policy, results in stability having to be purchased at the cost of significant unemployment, because the degree of employment and investment compatible with stability in the most monopolistically protected sector will, *ipso facto*, mean much more severe pressure and unemployment elsewhere. These phenomena, which are apparent even in the United States and the United Kingdom, assume much greater importance in less developed areas with the sort of social and economic structure found in Latin America. Under these circumstances, monetary restriction, instead of restoring a perfect price system, is likely to increase the degree of monopoly and sectoral unbalance.

It should not be concluded that policies involving direct government intervention and control exercised in a milieu of limited administrative capacity, under intense and conflicting pressures from political power-groups and general corruption, might not seriously aggravate economic unbalance. If such measures are intended to check incipient inflationary pressure and are applied without sufficient vigour or scope, it is only too likely that new disequilibria and bottlenecks will be created, hampering a policy of balanced development and stability. However, monolithic explanations of the problems of underdeveloped areas, especially of a demand-inflationary character, and a therapy based on them, must be severely scrutinized as being *a priori* suspect of illicit simplification and exaggeration. Relations between economic factors are seldom anywhere reversible or symmetrical, in these areas least of all.[3]

THE REALITY

Even in highly developed communities, socially and economically integrated, sectoral problems tend to defeat what might not unfairly be called the 'negative liberalizing approach'[4] as a means of restoring the efficient working of the economic system through the 'free' price mechanism. In underdeveloped countries, the failure of this approach is immensely aggravated by the fact that the inherent defects of that mechanism are greatly magnified in such a framework.

These defects are due, in the first place, to large-scale unemployment, especially in agriculture. In the second place, they are the consequence of the deep-rooted lack of

---

[3] This problem has been exhaustively analysed by K. Griffin, *The Green Revolution*, UN Research Institute for Social Development, Geneva, 1972.
[4] For example, that of the Chicago-LSE School, which is made worse by insidious propaganda, not for an improvement in aid, but for its cessation.

integration between the various important sectors of the economic structure, parts of which are only imperfectly linked with the market — or money — economy. Within each of the sectors of the economy there are faults no less deep in the markets both for productive factors and for products. All this is aggravated by extreme differences in monopolistic market power, and also in the capacity for exerting political pressure. Thus there is neither mobility nor even a semblance of unified markets.

Consequently, short-run money costs and prices fail to express long-run relative social opportunity costs, even more than they fail to do so in better integrated and more competitive economies (i.e. leaving aside the problem of external economies, which are not taken into account in the theoretical systems). As this failure is more far-reaching in certain sectors than in others, the present short-cut recommendation to restore the 'free' play of existing market forces would not promote, or even permit, an efficient allocation of scarce resources. It might well perpetuate and further aggravate their present inappropriate use. In particular, since the problem of unbalance between agriculture and industry is grave, it would leave labour in what is, taking the long-run social view of classical comparative costs, an inferior employment.

It should be noted that, in the case of economies at an early stage of their development, the failure of current money prices to reflect the immense potentiality of external economies, both of production and of consumption, is far more detrimental to welfare than in richer countries.[5] The 'lumpy' character of investment makes itself much more felt at a low absolute level of accumulated capital, and the reduction of costs with the increase in the scope of markets might be of a dramatic nature in poor countries.[6]

[5] Mr Streeten and I have adduced reasons why external economies are of much greater importance even in rich countries than is usually assumed (see 'Domestic versus Foreign Investment', *Bulletin of the Oxford University Institute of Statistics*, August 1960).
[6] This is almost entirely lost sight of in the fashionable approach to 'project evaluation', cf. I.M.D. Little and J.A. Mirrlees, *Manual of Industrial Project Analysis in Developing Countries, volume II, Social Cost Benefit Analysis*, Paris, Development Centre of the Organization for European Co-operation and Development, 1968; and for a critique, F. Stewart and P. Streeten, 'Little-Mirrlees

Hence, it seems entirely unjustified to single out one factor, usually the monetary one, in an attempt to explain the failure to achieve greater progress. If we are looking for the reasons why, in some cases, accelerated development has not been achieved, why it has not, in others, been compatible with monetary stability, we must investigate the sectoral structure of the economy and the precise relations of these sectors to one another. In this way, the historical uniqueness of each case can be recognized, while some restricted general features of the mechanism of instability can be established. The precise nature of this mechanism in fully developed countries will obviously differ from that in underdeveloped areas, even though some common factors might be discovered. The same monetary and fiscal policy gives very different results in countries with different basic structures (e.g. even as between the United States or the United Kingdom and the Federal Republic of Germany, and far more so as between one of them and either Argentina or Chile). From this analysis, one might hope to gain some insight into the conditions needed to ensure accelerated growth while maintaining stability. Short-cut recommendations are not likely to succeed.

Special features of Latin America include its rapid population growth, its dependence on exports, which are in the main rather unfavourably placed, its singular social structures, and its distorted productive patterns. These features will obviously influence, if not determine, the character of the problem of how to make the price mechanism work in such a way as to achieve optimal growth.

The defective integration of the economy

Professor Williams, in his celebrated article,[7] pointed to the imperfect domestic mobility of labour as a serious limitation on the applicability of the classical analysis, since this analysis postulated the equalization of factor incomes on the basis of perfect domestic factor mobility, in contrast to the absolute immobility of factors assumed to characterize international

Methods and Project Appraisal', *Bulletin of the Oxford University institute of Economics and Statistics*, February 1972.
[7] J.H. Williams 'The Theory of International Trade Reconsidered' *Economic Journal*, June 1929.

trade. Imperfection in labour mobility exists in a more severe and dangerous form in underdeveloped countries.

As a rough approximation, the economy of most under-developed areas, especially in Latin America, might be conceived as being divided into four parts:

(1) The fully developed, mostly foreign-owned and managed, sector mainly producing minerals or agricultural produce[8] for export and often with an extremely high output per head, relying for capital and technical knowledge on foreign markets and resources.

(2) Traditional agriculture, often monoculture, producing cash crops for markets rather than representing a self-sustained subsistence economy, of low output per head, and usually showing extreme inequality in the distribution of land-ownership,

(3) Domestic industry, under heavy protection against foreign competition and sometimes in a consciously-created position of monopoly, confronted with a fragmented labour market in which the skilled workers in a number of trades form strong unions, while unskilled workers partly drawn from agriculture are virtually unprotected, except by laws which are often not effectively enforced,

(4) Services, especially distribution, banking and finance are again in a closely-knit structure of monopoly or oligopoly. Transport and public utilities are often state enterprises working at heavy losses and, if privately owned, at times controlled with prices at a lower level than the general level of profits would seem to justify. Thus these sectors tend at times to become severe bottlenecks.

This fractioning of the economic structure produces two equally unfavourable results. It leads, in the first place, to an unsuitable allocation of factors; and, in the second place, it renders the system inelastic and incapable of responding to economic stimuli considered 'normal' in more highly developed countries.

---

[8]   And lately, in a very restricted number of countries (such as, for example, Hong-Kong, Taiwan, South Korea and Singapore), labour-intensive components or other manipulation.

Unsuitable allocation and factor prices

The problem of agricultural labour. The real consumption of individual members of a peasant family is determined by the earnings of the family as a whole. It is, even in Latin America with its relatively rich endowment of land relative to labour, likely to be higher than the productivity of the marginal member of the family. There is, generally, and except for peak periods, severe underemployment. In contrast, urban wages are relatively high because of the much higher cost of urban existence and partly because of trade-union pressure. In between there exist the squatters, essentially unskilled, and leading a precarious existence, who are only occasionally employed. Thus the expansion of industry is impeded by its high money costs, even though from a national point of view a faster absorption of agricultural labour would raise productivity. There is a fatal discontinuity in the structure of costs between agriculture and small handicrafts, on the one hand, and large-scale enterprise, on the other. Its paralysing effect in some countries of Latin America is increased by the absence of an industrial leadership which could begin to bridge it. The mercantile tradition of the urban areas and the large monopoly profits which can be obtained from trading and finance constitute further obstacles to industrial expansion. Employment in various service industries, especially trade, is far higher in Latin America than would be justified by the average national productivity. In Argentina, Venezuela, pre-revolution Chile and Cuba it was between three-quarters and nine-tenths of the United States ratio. The consequences of this are discussed below.

In those countries of Latin America in which industrial development started as a result of the two world wars, subsequently only comprehensive protection was able to maintain, let alone expand, industrial employment. Unfortunately the process was neither carefully thought-out nor consciously managed. Thus it took place mainly during foreign-exchange crises when import substitution became imperative and at the same time difficult to achieve in an economic manner. Whenever the pressure ceased, the relief was not used for a systematic development of industry. Hence, the real income of agricultural workers, already miserably low, tended to be reduced further by increases in industrial prices due to protection.

It is unlikely that the situation of the peasant can be much improved without securing a decisive improvement in the distribution of land-ownership, either through land taxation or through agricultural reform. This is likely to take a considerable time. It is also essential to improve production techniques and, in particular, to decrease the seasonal character of agricultural work: the peak sowing and harvest requirements will otherwise prevent a shift of a large portion of the work force.

In the short run, rural public works with the accent on irrigation might be the best way to tackle the problem. Such rural works might also encourage co-operative organization and, by injecting additional incomes, accelerate rural re-organization. They could, in addition, help to create the infrastructure investments needed for increased output and reduced seasonal strain on manpower.[9]

The problem of non-rural labour. The scantiness of budgetary means for education, attributable partly to insufficient and regressive tax structures, and partly to the high proportion of unproductive expenditure on administration and defence, has left even non-rural labour divided into sharply differing groups of utterly different education, technical skill, and capacity for organizing themselves. As a result, extreme divergences appear, reflecting inequalities in bargaining and political power, as between salaries and wages and as between different sectors in each income group. This necessarily distorts the international comparative-cost position of the country. Consequently, there will be introduced into the system a strong deterrent to expansion, with, on the one hand, firms of varying degrees of monopolistic and oligopolistic power using their market strength to increase profit margins, and, on the other hand, certain privileged groups of fully employed labour continuously pressing their wage demands. However justified these may seem to be from a humanitarian point of view, they cannot but further reduce

9 Unfortunately this tactic was not employed either in Cuba or in Chile. Cf. R. Dumont, *Cuba est-il socialiste?*, Editions du Seuil, Paris, 1970.

the prospect of a proper integration of the economic system as well as of sound industrial development.

The problem of the unsuitable capital infrastructure. The character of much of the present social infrastructure capital is a further influence militating against both balanced economic growth and a shift from primary production, even where relative social opportunity costs indicate that such a shift would be desirable. Historically the evolution of this capital structure has been dominated by the distortion of costs and prices in favour of primary exports and the import of manufactures.[10] The banking and transport systems in underdeveloped areas thus became a potent influence in helping to perpetuate the existing patterns of production in those areas, however uneconomic they may have been in terms of classical analysis on the basis of long-run social comparative costs. [11] Because they can be financed internationally, export and import activities are artificially stimulated, to the detriment of domestic production, and an immense further stimulus is given to industrial monopoly, since only enterprises which are able to shift the burden of high rates of interest on to the consumer can survive.

All this contrasts sharply with the beginnings of banking in the United Kingdom and United States in the eighteenth and nineteenth centuries, when local bankers provided the financial basis of the industrial and agricultural revolution by undertaking local commitments, often incurring great risks. Their influence and activity deserve study in poor underdeveloped areas and will provide pointers to banking reform.

The problems of the inelasticity of the productive structure.

The rigidity of agriculture. At present the conventional working of the market mechanism is often impeded in considerable parts of the agricultural sector because of the inequality of the distribution of land and of the inappropriate land-tenure systems.[12] It would be far from accurate to say

10 See chapter 3 below, especially pp. 83-7

11 Even if these could be analysed at all on those terms, having regard for the prevalance of increasing returns, especially those arising from the general dynamism of the economic system (and their failure in less developed areas).

12 In the first edition of this volume I included a sardonic review of Professor

that the owners of large and tiny estates (the latifundia and minifundia) are not activated by rational or economic motives. It would be more appropriate to assert that their motivations differ considerably from what is assumed in the instantaneous-profit-maximization model of perfect competition (which has become highly inaccurate also in the fully industrialized areas largely dominated by oligopolies). The owners of the vast feudal land-holdings which characterize certain parts of Latin America have no interest in improving the land, or even in maximizing output in the short run. They are interested in the maximization of their incomes over time, with the constraints of being able to maintain the most effective supervision of the work of their labourers and of incurring as little effort and risk, both economic and political, as possible. Thus in a large part of Latin America there is a heavy concentration on crops and animals that need relatively little care and enable the holder to absent himself for the maximum of time. Moreover, modern techniques would necessitate education, and education might encourage change. The aversion to change thus contributes to the continuance of outmoded production techniques.

The inequality in the distribution of land, which permits the landlord to be sure of a large income, also reduces the marginal utility of increments in terms of effort. Thus the traditional assumptions about the working of the system, assumptions on which important policy recommendations are based, are undoubtedly vitiated.

The minifundia, on the other hand, lack both the capital and, what is more important, the technical knowledge to react in the conventional way to price changes. Their owners are often subject to the power of merchants and money-

Schultz's booklet *Transforming Primitive Agriculture* (*Economic Journal*, December 1964). In that work Professor Schultz ascribes rural misery to the fact that 'the price of the sources of income streams from agricultural production' are too high. The deep socio-political defects in the system are not mentioned. Thus: 'There are many farms in parts of South America that certainly qualify in terms of size [for innovatory activity] ... Why they have not done better is a puzzle'. What is no puzzle, to me at any rate, is that the influence of the United States in that part of the world, because of its insensate and insensitive attude has, apart from violent military coups, suffered a steady erosion. So much was predictable, and I did predict it: the Chicago approach is the best weapon in Castro's hands to subvert the influence of the United States in Latin America.

lenders, whose reaction to improvements might well be to increase their charges. Thus the interest of the small farmers — and also of sharecroppers — in improvements is much reduced, if not entirely eliminated. Their lack of capital and access to credit at reasonable terms make risks connected with improvements unbearably high. Should anything go wrong, even their wretched existence would be jeopardized.

A further problem arises in this context. In traditional agriculture the share of monetary inputs (as opposed to those which are independent of the market) is relatively low. The money cost of crops on land let on a sharecropping basis approaches zero; the share of the landlord becomes pure rent. Thus, irrespective of the superior alternative possible use of manpower in modernized agriculture or industry, its traditional use for agricultural products, including exports, remains possible. A large part of the proceeds serves to buy the supplies and services which the landlords desire, to a considerable extent imported luxuries and travel. With the increase of population, and often merely on account of monopoly market power, the share of the crop which can be exacted for rent increases. Thus the impulse to higher production is further decreased. The market mechanism certainly does not, and cannot, force landlords to alter the productive structure by eliminating the inefficient.

The situation differs only slightly in cases where the owner works his land through managers or stewards. The need for supervision remains. Money inputs, are, as before, not high enough to compel productivity improvements. A large part of the wage is in terms of land-use or its produce. And productive inputs bought for cash — such as machinery, fertilizers and the like — are kept traditionally at a minimum.

Two influences have raised land values above all relation to the yield of other forms of assets: one is that land-ownership is a social status symbol; the other, that land is bought as a guarantee against possible monetary instability because of century-long experience of steady appreciation of land values. The high prices for land represent an additional obstacle to its better distribution and, together with the existing monopolistic conditions in the financial markets, militate against medium-sized commercial agriculture.

Thus the traditional system of land tenure, in its inequality, prevents the full mobilization of resources. The consequence is an extreme rigidity in the agricultural framework and output.

In some Latin American and Asian countries, however, landowners have shown an elastic response to price stimuli. In Mexico, Brazil, and a number of countries in Central America and northern South America, latifundia owners and a newly emerging class of often smaller-scale agricultural entrepreneurs have achieved considerable successes in increasing output and adapting it to changes in demand. In some countries, moreover, of which Brazil is perhaps the most important, there still exist large tracts of free land, which might be thought to limit the inequality in the distribution of income by providing alternative opportunities for tenants and landless labourers. Yet, for political reasons the extension of quasi-feudal land tenure (the mechanism of which merits further research), and even the existence of this (in principle) free land has not, in contrast to the experience of the United States in the nineteenth century, set a limit to the inequality. of income.

Thus the double handicap to industrial development deriving from the poverty of the rural population, which has been discussed earlier, remains even in these countries. An additional problem stems from the fact that the supply of certain protective foodstuffs (e.g. meat, fruits and vegetables) is held back by the difficulty of securing a more equitable distribution of land, and thus productivity is cut for physical reasons.

All these difficulties are much augmented by the defective organization of marketing, which is only partly attributable to those deficiencies in the organization of domestic transport, to which allusion has already been made. When the middleman is able, partly because of his power as a money-lender (and often, also, landlord), to exact an undue share of the price paid by consumers, the response of production to changes in demand will be imperfect and sluggish. The establishment of a marketing organization giving security from abrupt price fluctuations and enabling producers to obtain credit at reasonable rates might therefore help in increasing the elasticity of supply and the efficiency of grading, thus securing better returns.

It should be noted that land reform in the sense of a complete redistribution might not be able to achieve a full mobilization of agricultural resources, even though it might be beneficial from the point of view of income distribution and social balance. On the share-cropping estates there would be hardly any change in traditional methods of production. On large estates in owner management, there might be a fall in production. On the other hand, partial land reform might well cause the landowner to farm his remaining holdings more effectively, especially if he receives compensation or credit. The total effect will depend on the circumstances in which the land reform is carried out.[13]

If pressure for land reform is not extreme, a progressive land tax, based not on actual but on potential yield and accompanied by suitable taxes on water resources, might, in the short run, produce more favourable results, in the sense of increasing the elasticity of agricultural supplies. Such tax reforms must be accompanied by the establishment of an effective agrarian credit system, providing both long-term credit, enabling the acquisition by cultivators of the land entering the market, and supervised medium- and short-term credit to help create economically sound cultivation. The provision of extension services, supplemented by the introduction of improved seeds and fertilizers and advice on the effective use of water, is a further condition for success. The rigidity of the agricultural structure might also be loosened, as already mentioned, by undertaking rural public works in conjunction with these reforms. The increase of rural incomes will put pressure on landowners, thereby speeding the sale of uneconomic units and spurring them to adopt better productive methods and to accept less onerous terms for tenants.

Should land reform be enacted, the same institutional changes will be required, but extending over far larger areas, since the change in ownership will be far more widely spread. One possible method of effectively infusing new technical knowledge into the countryside might be the formation of

---

[13] These conclusions have been confirmed in both Cuba and Chile.

co-operatives, to which the surrendered land would be in the first instance entrusted. This would enable scarce expert knowledge to be used in improving growing practices, introducing better seeds, adequate fertilization, and the organization of irrigation. These might be severely impeded, or indeed made impossible, by a fragmentation of land-ownership. Support for these co-operatives for the farmers might be secured by entrusting to them the execution of the rural public works. [14]

In different countries the solutions that will prove politically acceptable and technically efficient will vary. A pragmatic approach is therefore essential. The aim should be to restore or maintain the growth and elasticity of production while achieving a less uneven distribution of ownership and income.

Non-agricultural rigidity. The classical mechanism of readjustment is, of course, based on the existence of a large area of marginal choices imperceptibily merging into each other. 'Marginal' in this sense means divisible and small, not *grosso modo* choices between ways of life or modes of production.

Such marginal choices can only exist where the organic growth of the industrial structure had already been achieved, and increased mobility of labour and capital has led to a certain degree of equalization of factor remuneration. As a picture of the conditions in underdeveloped areas this could not be further from reality. In these areas, individual projects usually bring about large-scale changes. The whole development process is violently changing the relations of the various factors of production to each other. Any one investment decision is likely to lead to substantial changes in the markets and supply conditions of other firms. The price mechanism is inherently incapable of assuring optimal allocation unless it is assisted and modified by conscious and discriminating measures, which can either consist of physical control or be financial in character i.e. taxes and subsidies.

The highly developed foreign-export sector. A number of Latin American countries possess a fully developed foreign-

[14] See chapter 5 below.

export sector which is an enclave, a state within a state, and which has no organic relationship with the rest of the economy. The capital needs of this sector are met from foreign sources at rates of return which are independent of those in the domestic sector.[15] Marginal productivity in the export sector is not related to marginal productivity in the other sectors and will often be far higher than average productivity in the metropolitan area which controls it. The pattern of transport facilities and the supply of energy have been traditionally shaped by its needs and help to perpetuate its superiority.

The very superiority of its productivity has certain important consequences. The relative taxability of the developed foreign sector has obvious political and economic advantages, but dependence on it implies the danger of not having any effective alternative on hand should any unfavourable development slow down or reverse the rise in exports. Even stationary foreign-exchange receipts from the fully developed export sector involve, *ceteris paribus,* an appreciable fall in real income per head from this source, if the population is growing as fast as it is in most Latin American countries.

Government revenue is only too often dependent on taxing the exports of the developed foreign-export sector, while domestic vested interests, even when successful in the export field, effectively prevent the imposition of a corresponding tax burden. So long as the exports of the developed foreign sector rise, and with them government revenues, the elasticity of the economy is safeguarded. An increase in import capacity may have more pervasively favourable effects than an increase in domestic physical productivity, since it permits much greater flexibility in satisfying demand.

Thus the continued expansion of the markets of the foreign sector has a significance for smooth economic growth which cannot be emphasized too greatly. Any actual switch from that sector would involve a very sharp decline in productivity. Even a failure to grow at least at the rate of the increase in population might result in a fall of average national productivity, because the small numbers employed by the

15 Though the yield paid might not be lower. There are often political risks, and the monopoly power of the large mining enterprises secures them high returns, making them disinclined to undertake projects on the basis of lower ones.

sector are offset by the high output per head. At the same time, undue dependence on exports is stimulated if virtually free imports (including luxury goods due to the maldistribution of income) prevent the development of domestic industry, while the service sector, handling imports, expands.

This threat to productivity is the more acute because of the exaggerated size of the mercantile sector. This is one of the consequences of the high productivity in the developed foreign sector. Partly because its contribution to government revenue is relatively much higher than that normally contributed by the domestic sectors, a foreign sector which does not employ many people itself can indirectly maintain a large ancillary establishment. The distribution of employment in a number of Latin American countries between primary, secondary, and tertiary industries is more akin to that in countries of the productivity level of the United States than to that in other areas of the same average income as Latin America.

Thus the availability of goods becomes unduly dependent on export capacity. Shifts to industrial employment are seriously impeded by the monopolistic character of trade, by the lack of training, and so on. The outlets in trade for entrepreneurs are so remunerative, with profits being increased by disproportionately low ancillary costs (e.g. those of transport and banking) that there is little inducement for them to enter productive industry. The impediment to industrialization implicit in the nature of the agricultural sector, which has already been discussed, is further enhanced by the indirect consequences of the existence of a highly developed foreign sector. This must not blind us to the importance of the financial contribution which the fully developed foreign-export sector has made to the standards of living in Latin America. Government expenditure and national income would be far lower without it. The point to be made is that its existence renders conscious action to achieve a balanced development of domestic industry even more necessary than would be the case if that development had been impeded by the distortion of classical comparative costs because of the defective framework of agriculture alone.

Economic Policy and the Price System

The traditional agricultural export sector. In contrast to the mainly foreign mining and plantation enclaves, traditional agriculture is also divided in most countries between a domestic (often subsistence) sector and one which is mainly devoted to exports. As a rule, the export sector, based on the whole on large or medium landholdings, has a higher-than-average productivity but is not intrinsically superior to industry. It is in those countries where foreign mining and plantation ventures do not play an important role that the shift from agriculture to industry is most impeded by the distortion of classic comparative advantage. Here no loss of real income would be implied in a shift towards industry. Traditional exports are important in this case because foreign exchange is needed to pay for imported capital equipment. The importance of the terms of trade is evident in this case too: the less favourable these are, the greater the justification for a shift to industry, but the greater the difficulty of securing such a shift.

The terms of trade and industrial development. The importance of this ineluctable fact is much enhanced by the uncertain prospects of primary exports, both those produced by the fully developed foreign-export sector and those produced by traditional agriculture. After wars, especially after such a devastating one as the Second World War, economists usually foresee an increase in the relative price of primary commodities, i.e. worsening terms of trade for manufactures. This is strictly in accordance with the classical model of static balance, which assumes that costs of production rise as demand and production increase.

After the last war, these predictions seemed more nearly borne out than in earlier periods. The improvement in primary-commodity prices encouraged the hope that the consequential increases in production and income might produce a sufficient bases for sustained growth,[16] especially

16 Not all writers shared this expectation. See, for example, Raul Prebisch, ECLA, *The Economic Development of Latin America and its Principal Problems* (E/CN 12/89/Rev. 1), United Nations publication (sales No. 1950, II, G.2);*Economic Survey of Latin America*, 1949 (E/CN 12/82), United Nations publication (sales No. 1950, II, G.1); and H.W. Singer 'The Distribution of Gains between Investing

if judiciously supported by foreign aid; it also deeply influenced thought on the strategy of economic development.[17]

With the end of the boom consequent upon the hostilities in Korea, the postwar trend abruptly changed. The terms of trade of the manufacturing countries improved by some 30 per cent. It was perhaps even more ominous that the further rise in the relative price of manufactured goods in the 1957–8 recession was not fully reversed in the subsequent recovery; thus the deterioration cannot be entirely attributed to short-term and reversible fluctuations in demand. And the vital question arises whether and how far a further worsening should be anticipated in determining the strategy of development. The matter is of the utmost importance. Any deterioration in the terms of trade necessitates an acceleration of import substitution. If a further worsening of the terms of trade is expected in future this would demand a completely different, far more domestically orientated, investment programme.

This is not the context for a lengthy analysis of the actual export prospects of Latin America. There is, of course, no natural law governing these matters. The terms of trade of primary commodities against manufactures will be determined by relative demand and supply, and these, as has been learnt in the last ten years or so, can change with astonishing violence. They are especially influenced by the market structure of the two types of products in the fully industrialized countries and the prevalence of cost-push inflation.[18]

There is little doubt that the rate of economic expansion in relation to productive capacity in the rich industrial part of the world has been, and will remain, the main determinant of the outlook for the products of primary-producing countries. A slowing-down of growth represents the gravest danger to the poor areas. The rate of progress of Latin

and Borrowing Countries', *American Economic Review*, Papers and Proceedings, May 1950, p. 478.

[17] Underdeveloped countries, such as those of Latin America, have been periodically advised not to industrialize, even in recent years. See, for example, F.C.C. Benham and H.A. Holley, *A Short Introduction to the Economy of Latin America*, Oxford University Press for the Royal Institute of International Affairs London, 1961.

[18] See chapter 8, below.

America's foreign market is not encouraging.[19] Advertising and innovation are likely to change the pattern of demand to the further disadvantage of goods with a relatively high content of primary commodities. Thus the general tendency of the demand for these commodities to grow more slowly than income will be reinforced.

The relationship between commodities and manufactured goods is likely to be affected by the fact that the former are sold on organized world markets while the latter are supplied directly by the producers. Primary producers may be organized or constitute an oligopoly, as is the case among the great base-metal-producing firms and petroleum companies, or regulated by governments, as is the case with sugar and coffee. Nevertheless, the existence of free markets on a worldwide scale seems to destabilize and depress primary-commodity prices relative to those of manufactures.

This greater sensitivity of primary-commodity prices to downward pressure is heightened in the case of those products which are grown by small, weak, and remote producers, especially if marketing is manipulated by middlemen. Even when the market is not controlled in this way, the inability of the producers to store and carry stocks will tend to lower the prices they are likely to obtain. When producers are indebted to middlemen, this increases their vulnerability. It would be foolish to assume that this pressure on primary commodities will continue indefinitely. All that is claimed is that, in the present state of the development of the world economy, the risk of a worsening of the terms of trade of primary producers can be appreciable even if we disregarded the mechanism of cost inflation, which has such dire implications in this respect. This deterioration can occur both when the prices of manufactures are likely to rise before those of primary commodities, and also in those periods when the governments in the developed countries try to control the rise in prices by restrictive monetary measures. The relative sensitivity of primary-commodity markets tells against those

[19] The increase in population and the growing exports of manufactures in exchange for imports of primary commodities by rapidly growing industrial countries, such as the Federal Republic of Germany, Japan, and the Soviet Union, might easily reverse the trend.

products unless special countervailing measures are taken. Such measures are difficult to administer.[20]

In addition to these factors, which are quasi-short-term but likely to remain persistent, the poor areas have been beset with rather more structural handicaps, mainly in the biased character of technical advance and growth. The emergence of substitute materials and the reduction of waste through technical progress have played an important role in this respect. More important still has been the rapid technical advance in agricultural production in the highly developed areas of the world, surpassing even the improvement in industrial productivity.

Domestic protected industry. The difficulties and dangers to living standards arising out of even a relative decline in the fully developed foreign-export sector are aggravated by the problem of monopoly. The vicious circle of poverty and lack of investment is a commonplace in development economics. Most underdeveloped areas lack sufficiently wide markets for the establishment of competitive industry. The fact that they are late-comers in industrial development, together with the scarcity of skilled labour and the well-organized character of such skilled labour as exists, further impedes the rise of numerous units capable of facing import competition. The mercantile character of such capitalist classes as exist, and their proneness to tight organization, often implicit, completes the picture.

Important substitution will involve a real loss in income if it is an alternative to a further rise in the production and foreign sales of the fully developed foreign-export sector, because that sector is more productive and it permits supplies to be purchased from the most efficient foreign

[20] In addition, the poorer areas are menaced by the so-called 'whip-lash' effect. Large corporations operating in both the metropolitan territory and elsewhere might be forced by political pressure to cut production abroad rather than at home (e.g. the Canadian experience). Protective measures of the metropolitan area (e.g. the Venezuelan experience with United States oil quotas) have the same effect. The establishment of OPEC and the violent improvement of host-country participation in the proceeds of petroleum production show conclusively the importance of the monopolistic power. But petroleum is an exceptional case — as yet.

sources. This loss can be offset by an increase in the general level of productivity. If the periods of buoyant export markets had been used for a planned increase of investment in import substitution rather than for increases in current outlays, both public and private, the effects of the worsening in the terms of trade could have been easily handled.

This has not happened. In consequence, acute problems have arisen, especially for countries interested in mineral exports. In this field, the domestic market is limited, and manpower cannot easily be switched. In the case of traditional agriculture, the productivity differences are not large between exports and production for internal consumption, and alternative domestic uses for land might be easier to find. The danger in this case is that the increase in internal consumption during a foreign slump might prove politically impossible, or at least difficult, to reverse.

But, as has been seen, the relative cost of industrial production prevents such an orderly process of unprotected import substitution.

In the absence of conscious planning and encouragement, during favourable times, of import substitution, the process is likely to take place in periods of crisis, owing either to the failure of foreign supplies (e.g. as a result of wars) or to balance-of-payments difficulties and heavy political pressure. Thus it will be difficult to prevent the emergence of unnecessarily large profit margins as a result of the exploitation of newly created monopoly power. It is not improbable that the degree of protection granted will be far greater than necessary. If so, the loss in real income attendant on the shift from imports to home production may be accompanied by a redistribution of income from the lower to the higher income classes, i.e. from real wages to profits, as the result of an all-round increase in the degree of monopoly.

It is quite possible that an appreciable part of such investment as is achieved will be frustrated by monopolistic influences keeping output low and prices high. In this way, a large excess capacity would be created. The inelasticity of the supply of manufactures is joined to that of agriculture. Since a large-scale substitution of domestic manufactures for imports will involve not merely a loss of real income but special pressure on non-profit incomes, the conditions are created in which strong unions can press for wage increases. The fractioning of the factor market will then be further aggravated. Thus monopoly power can transmit a cost-inflationary spiral.

A similar influence might be exercised by the interaction of supply rigidities in agriculture and industry. Insufficient expansion in agricultural output, at a time when population and industrial production are rising, can prove particularly pernicious in the case of goods with a fairly high income-elasticity. If agricultural output as a whole does not respond to price stimuli, the tug-of-war between an archaic agricultural sector and a monopolistic industrial one would by itself seem sufficient to start a reciprocating and self-sustaining inflationary spiral.

Given the fragmentation of the product and labour markets, and the varying degree of monopoly, comprehensive measures aimed at an overall balance between monetary demand and supply need not, and probably will not, be effective in ensuring stability. Sectoral unbalance, added to monopolistic rigidity, might be the explanation of inflationary pressures. Monetary, indirect factors under these circumstances might respond to, rather than cause, unbalance. No significant conclusions can be drawn from purely monetary analysis, however tempting that may be because of the relative abundance of monetary statistics. In order to ensure stability by indirect means, sufficient pressure has to be exercised to restrain the least stable and most monopolistic sectors. This would seem to imply heavy unemployment or underemployment in the more elastic or defenceless sectors. The consequent overall discouragement is unlikely to promote growth.

The system in inherently so rigid that it becomes unstable and prone to cost-inflationary pressure. Both cyclical instability and the long-run weakness of export markets constitute a severe strain on such a framework. Given the fact that the rigidities of the system vary in degree, and that the sectoral imbalance might be of a complex yet non-uniform nature, indirect measures, especially monetary restraint, are most unlikely to have a diffuse and neutral effect. Their directional effects might be strong and cannot conceivably be such as neatly and precisely to offset the divergence of sectoral resources from an efficient allocation of scarce productive factors. Decontrol and monetary restraint are most inappropriate. Their unfavourable social effects are much aggravated by the fact that they might and probably will fall with particular force on a relatively restricted sector, while the reaction of the monopolistic sectors would be by way of restriction rather than by reductions of price through cuts in profit margins. The cessation of the growth of income might therefore be accompanied by a further worsening of its distribution. A formula more likely to maximize social tension can hardly be imagined.

Savings, investment and income distribution

In most underdeveloped countries with feudal or mercantile governing classes, a relatively low propensity to save is found together with a high propensity to indulge in luxury imports and foreign travel. Redistribution towards the rich, which is commonly regarded as a means of increasing savings, investment, and economic progress, certainly produces no such results in these countries.[21] It might even lead to a worsening in the balance of payments and to unemployment, as the products of low-quality home handicrafts and industry are displaced by high-grade imports.[22]

In this context it must be recalled that a large part of the so-called savings in underdeveloped areas are used to buy luxury buildings. These should properly be excluded from savings and investment altogether. They represent a kind of durable-goods consumption. The misleading high savings ratios and correspondingly abnormal capital-output ratios, which have no meaning in the context of a discussion of economic growth, would then be corrected, so that they bore a more sensible relation to the growth rates experienced.

An increase in the rate of interest, according to historical

---

21 Inflationary finance which redistributes income towards profits has not in this framework been able to increase the rate of savings and investment appreciably.
22 In countries with a completely rigid agriculture, an increase in the income of the poorer classes might not lead to an improvement in the balance of payments, as imports of food might become necessary.

experience, does not seem to have an influence on the rate of saving. For this reason claims that tight or dear money could expedite economic progress by permitting a higher rate of investment are unfounded. A redistribution of income towards the poorer classes in general would not necessarily lead to a shrinkage in savings. Even if it did, its unfavourable effects might be more than offset by an improvement in the quality of private investment, such as the reduction of luxury building and of investment in oligopolistic excess capacity in industry (especially in industry producing luxury consumption goods). The capital-output ratio would then fall.

Policy, however, might be concentrated not so much on a redistribution of income at this stage as on increasing saving through deliberate budget surpluses.[23] A redistribution towards the poor can be supported on different grounds, which the FAO report on Mediterranean development has tried to bring out.[24] This is that most of these countries have unemployed capacity in the handicraft or coarse consumer goods industries. Thus a redistribution of income towards the poor, if well managed, could bring about a fall in the propensity to import, which in turn would permit an increase in national income without a fall in investment. This would have to be very carefully managed, since it might get dangerously out of hand and cause inflation.

The greater the monopolistic or feudal agrarian distortions of the 'normal' working of the price mechanism (which has, of course, never worked 'normally'), the greater the force of the cost-push factors. Thus the greater will be the degree of unemployment induced by global policies which attempt to offset the upward push on the price level, and the more reliance will have to be placed on the psychological shock-effects of credit policy and on rationing by private bankers. Once the systematic operation of the price system as a selector between investment projects disappears, the justification of the claim that monetary policy automatically secures an optimal factor allocation is no longer valid. No one could

---

[23] This was the conclusion of the Staff Report of the Joint Economic Committee of the United States Congress.
[24] *Mediterranean Development Project, Interim Report*, FAO Rome, 1957 chapter 3.

claim that bankers in the milieu of an underdeveloped country will act on the basis of long-run social considerations. To summarize, the greater the distortions, the less optimal and the more haphazard will be the working of the capital market and of the price system.

2

Equity and Efficiency: The Problem of Optimal Investment in a Framework of Underdevelopment*

In the present paper I shall try to consider the determinants in an underdeveloped economy — an economy with a significant *and increasing* volume of employment at a level of remuneration considerably below the average[1] — of what might be called an optimal policy for investment.[2] In particular I shall review this question with reference to the geographical spread of newly-created employment.[3]

* This chapter comprises a shortened version of a paper of the same title first published in *Oxford Economic Papers*, February 1962.
1 I prefer this expression to the more usual 'underemployment'. In many cases it might be possible to provide more work within the existing framework of employment (as implied in the expression 'underemployment'), in others simple reforms (without much capital investment) might suffice. But in a large number of cases either considerable institutional reforms or investment will be needed for the mobilization of manpower. Thus the grouping of these very different categories of less than effective employment into one all-embracing class seems inaccurate and might be seriously misleading. Cf. the interesting sample studies by Professor Mahalanobis.
2 This definition of the problem is closely related to, but quite different from, that of Mr Horvat ('The Optimum Rate of Investment', *Economic Journal* (1958), pp. 747-67). He tries to show that 'optimum' involves growth at a rate at which no further increase in production is possible by increasing investment. As Mr Sen pointed out ('On Optimising the Rate of Saving', *Economic Journal* (1961), pp. 479-96), there is no reason (if we do not pay attention to the problem of destitution in underdeveloped countries) to neglect the fact that current consumption is of *some* value. Mr Sen's solution, however, neglects the vitally important problems of distribution, which, in my opinion, *should* be (a value judgement) decisive. As I shall try to show, he is also too sceptical about the range of choice in policies (esp. pp. 491-2 and p. 496).
3 The express reference is India's declared policy of favouring the most backward and depressed areas as embodied in her *Third Five-Year Plan* (Delhi, 1961), chapter 9 'Balanced Regional Development'.

So long as a policy of giving preference to the more depressed regions in the provision of new job-opportunities (insofar as it succeeds) does not diminish appreciably the overall rate of progress of the economy, and thus its capacity to provide a cumulative increase in investment, the sentiment is unexceptionable. Equally so would be the expressed desire to limit the concentration of economic power,[4] not only by extending the public sector (which would provide a complete answer — subject to efficient management and an appropriate price and investment policy), but by using licensing powers to spread output not merely geographically but also between a number of firms.

Unfortunately these laudable aims present grave dilemmas which are not always acknowledged. Even if the geographical spread of investment is not initiated and dominated by the political needs of the various regional parties, expressive of local provincial interests, this might still reduce its present effectiveness and, therefore, stunt the future growth of domestic savings and, hence, the permissible expansion of investment in the longer run. Not only might regional considerations demand increased ancillary investments, especially in transport capacity, but they might retard productivity growth in view of the scarcity of skilled manpower and lack of training facilities in the depressed regions.

Now it is obvious that the lower is national income the greater will be the degree of compulsion required to elicit a given increase in investment. Given the fact that an increase in the rural population results inevitably in greater inequality and a sharpening of the dichotomy of life as between the rural and urban areas, any diversion of resources away from investment is a serious lapse. It is regrettable that this has not altogether been appreciated. It is, for instance, assumed that the provision of more employment, at wages well above the level of average real income, and at the cost of decreasing the productivity of investment, would nevertheless increase equality. This is certainly not the case.[5] *What would happen*

4 *Third Plan*, chapter 1, sec. V, pp. 13-16.
5 More recent investigations tend to reinforce this view. See, for instance, V.M. Dandekar and N. Rath, *Poverty in India*, Ford Foundation, Delhi, 1970 and *Economic and Political Weekly*, 2 and 9 January, 1971.

*is that the basic problem of rural underemployment and
misery would continue to increase, while the number of
quasi-privileged people would grow at the cost of slowing
down relief to the (much more numerous) rural poor.* It is
difficult to assert that there are many whose living conditions
have in fact actually deteriorated since the inception of
India's First Five-Year Plan. The Reports of the All-India
Agricultural Labour Enquiries seem to indicate, however, that
something of this sort may have happened, but available
data are inadequate.[6] In any case, there can be no question
but that a great number of people still remain pressed down
on a level which from all human points of view must be
totally insufficient.

In view of the fact that a large and growing number of
people in most 'less developed' areas still exist in a state of
wretched poverty, it is essential (1) that as large a share of
any increase in national income as is politically feasible should
be devoted to investment;[7] and (2) that much greater care
should be taken to ensure that the increased investment yield
maximum increases in income. I feel, therefore, that policy in
respect of the location of industry, the public sector in general
(and especially price policy in the public sector), taxation,
and the control of monopoly, ought really to be thought
out again, with a view to accelerating both the increase in the
rate of saving and the growth of national income.

Any attempt to divert attention from the consideration of
maximizing the increase in national investment capacity, and
with it the need to provide productive employment, implicitly
reduces the ability to cope with inequality. This ability will
depend either on the possibility of enforced saving or on
increasing the ease with which savings will be voluntarily
forthcoming as incomes rise. So long as there is an immense

[6] Matters have not really changed in the decade since this paper was written.
See A. Vaidyanathan, 'Some Aspects of Inequalities in Living Standards in Rural
India', Planning Commission, Delhi, October 1970 (mimeo).
[7] The limits at which any increase in investment necessarily yields lower
returns, e.g. because of the physically unavoidable shortage of skilled manpower,
have not been reached, in contrast to the fall in yields due to the implementation
of unwise projects or to insufficient manpower planning.

amount of suffering due to the fact that, for lack of capital, people cannot be provided with employment at tolerable rates of income, there is no need to speculate whether or not the overriding of individual preferences for current over delayed consumption is justifiable from a social point of view. *For the increase in the income of those who are already above the subsistence level will be at the cost of prolonging the agony of those who are at subsistence levels.* Those projects must be preferred, therefore, which will produce a greater increase in production, provided that they facilitate further increases in investment over a long period. It is essential, however, that (a large part of) this increase should be capable of being tapped, either by means of taxation or through increases in public sector profits.

Perhaps one of the most important fields in which policy must be reconsidered in deciding on the geographical distribution of investment is the distribution between what might be called spearhead development areas and spreading employment. The choice between these ought to be made in such a way as to maximize advance in the short run while the absorptive capacity of the less favourably situated areas is strengthened, so that when the time comes to concentrate on spreading development more evenly these areas should already be in a position to receive investment.

The inescapable choice between decentralization and the effectiveness of capital investment has been largely ignored. It has been taken for granted that if a balance in regional growth is secured this would *ipso facto* also secure the most advantageous growth. In addition, there has been a regrettable growth of political demands of a regional character for the allocation of industries for which even such justification has not been found. It is evident from the strain thrown on the transport system (in India for instance) and the immense increase in the need for new investment in the railways and roads that the diversification of industrial development has already exacted and threatens to continue to exact a tremendous toll from the available scarce capital resources of the country. The rates policy of the railways has aggravated this strain.

It seems that the onerousness of accelerating economic

development in backward regions has not at all been realized. The advantages of more happily situated industrial centres in a framework of extreme underdevelopment such as exists in India are manifold. Much the most important is the availability of trained manpower, or at least the possibility of arranging for training. In addition, there will be some infrastructure, and its expansion will be far less costly than a completely new start, which would be required in the depressed areas which have seen no development at all. This applies to energy, to transport, and other public utilities, as much as to housing. Expenditure on these is extremely high for the yield in income. This is especially so in India, where distances are vast and where the distribution of natural resources is extremely uneven. By concentrating at first on a few more privileged regions, a greater increase in income can be achieved for any given investment. Thus the time can be hastened at which cumulative growth can be attained. A more rapidly increasing income automatically results in a faster and cumulative expansion which can be put at the disposal of the government for capital investment. Thus, taking into account the prospects of increased population, a balanced growth of the country over a longer period would be more efficaciously secured by concentrating effort.

Admittedly in the short run this would mean an increase in the inequality between the most favoured and the backward areas. It would not increase, however, the degree of inequality because in any case the number of destitute people will increase, and is likely to increase to a much greater extent if investment cannot be speeded up. It should be added that an alternative to such concentration of investment would be a greater increase in relative taxation in the short run to obtain more savings. Yet the smaller the national income the more difficult will it be to obtain a greater amount of resources for investment.[8]

Much the same conclusion applies to the problem of monopoly control in the private sector as it has been practised in a number of important instances. The attempt to reduce monopoly power by spreading industrial capacity over a large

---

[8] In a way, the Chinese, who have a much greater capacity to enforce savings than the Indian government, would be better able to 'afford' spreading investment.

number of firms is likely to reduce productivity, especially in heavy or even in the durable goods industry. Thus it will reduce the possibility of attaining a higher income level in the long run. In addition, it may endanger the future of the balance of payments, for it is unlikely that Indian import needs will be able to be fully covered by the increase in the export of primary commodities if national progress is to be accelerated. If this is so, and if balanced development requires an increase in industrial exports, any measure which decreases productivity would represent a serious threat to Indian economic independence. It is essential that the scale of production should be approaching optimum when it is started. Yet there is an insistent need to reduce or control monopoly. This should be arranged directly through a monopolies commission with effective supervision over costs and pricing policies as well as other conditions of sale. This is especially important when new industries are being started. It is far too optimistic to assume that inequalities that are permitted to emerge can be subsequently muted or altogether abolished by taxation.[9]

From this point of view the determination of a country like India to accelerate the increase and widen the scope of the public sector is to be welcomed. It should be noted, however, that if such a policy is to produce the best results in promoting a balanced and integrated society, the pricing policy in that sector will have to be appropriately formulated. There has often been a general reluctance to increase prices under the direct control of the government. This has been defended with the plea that national welfare demands the supply of products and services at low prices. There is no justification for this view. If the economy is a mixed one, as in India, and if the bulk of the supply of goods originates in the private sector, whose prices incorporate profits (including profits used for accumulation) then the maintenance of relatively low prices in the public sector implies a subsidy to the private sector. Unless there are specific reasons which justify such a subsidy from the point of view of social considerations, this will result in a misallocation of resources

---

[9] The problems caused by the affluent classes in India are similar to but even more dangerous than those of the affluent societies analysed by Professor Galbraith.

in favour of the consumers of the goods and services in question, and a reduction in the community's capacity to increase investment. The consequences of this policy are serious if, as a result of the pricing policy, the public sector cannot easily meet the demand for its products. This has happened in a number of instances. It is absolutely essential, if the increase in the public sector is to make as large a contribution as possible to the welfare of the country, that the public sector should contribute its due share of resources directly in furthering the accumulation of capital.

It is also essential that pricing policy, both in the private and public sector, should be entirely subordinated to the need to ensure maximum production and investment. This means that in the agricultural sector prices should be stabilized, lest the peasant, for fear of a fall in his income, should refuse to increase his effort (i.e. in the rural sector, *ipso facto* his investment) in increasing production. In the urban sector care should be taken to stabilize the price of all essentials so as to avoid cost-push inflation, as well as an increase in the burden of the poorest elements of that sector. Pricing policy with respect to non-essentials should be guided entirely by the need to exact as great a toll as possible for the country's investment programme. For this reason, general cuts in prices are entirely out of order.

Beyond prices, both import and investment licensing should be co-ordinated so as to exclude Western consumer-durables, and the temptation that goes with them. The persuasive pressure to buy large cars and labour-saving household devices has been one of the weakest points in a number of countries: it has given an additional edge to inequality and has resulted in a formidable pressure on savings. It is usually argued that the purchase of radios, television sets, etc. of ever improving quality and in increasing quantity has given zest and impetus to labour and entrepreneurship alike. Given the wretched standard of living, however, one might have thought that better nutrition and improved housing conditions would have gone a long way as a substitute, and more suitable, outlet for these energies. It is the motivations which need to be changed, rather than the pattern of production in imitation of the prosperous Western countries.

Equity and Efficiency

It is impossible in this context to treat at length the reform of taxation. It is clear from the previous paragraphs, however, that in my opinion indirect taxation must play an important part in increasing the tax contribution. Thus, even in the field of indirect taxation, the principle of progressive taxation could be effectively applied by subjecting non-essential goods to discriminatingly high rates of duty. As regards direct taxation, there seems to be an urgent need for a more direct method, leaving less scope for evasion, of assessing incomes. Alternatively, assessment might be determined on the basis of *expenditure,* as is done in France. At any rate, while a generally low per capita income, combined with inequitable distribution, might hamper efforts to increase direct revenue, there is little doubt that more could be done, particularly in regard to state contributions.

A final word needs to be said about the problem of providing relief in the areas which, on the basis of the above considerations, cannot for the moment be supported by spreading industrial employment. The more determined is the effort to concentrate on increasing production, the greater will be the need for organizing community development projects to augment the standard of living of the rural population and so increase its productive capacity. Not only could the dependence of the country on foreign supplies, especially of foodstuffs, be reduced, but it is the sole way of mitigating rural poverty, which is otherwise going to increase further.

If this is to happen, however, a new philosophy of rural public works will have to be evolved. There has already been a welcome development, in India and elsewhere, away from the original conception of community development, which at first prematurely stressed welfare and social services, when the primary need was for an increase in the income-earning capacity of the rural population. But further changes in attitude are needed for the aim of providing income to the small peasant and the landless labourer to become paramount. This should also determine the choice of technique to be used in the execution of public works.

The first priority in this respect is a reform of rural education. This should combine the teaching of simple requirements for increasing rural productivity while providing for a powerful net by which access to higher education is given to talented children, thus establishing a greater equality of opportunity.[10] The problem of the less-favoured areas should be tackled for an interim period by the provision of public works such as to increase rural productivity rather than by forcing new industries to migrate prematurely, and to develop in unsuitable places in unsuitably sized units.[11] In the end, when a minimum standard of life above subsistence levels can be guaranteed for all, the time will come when social considerations can dictate a deliberate reduction or forgoing of an increase in productivity in favour of greater regional equality. That time has not yet arrived. For the moment there is no conflict between efficiency and equality. Without maximum investment and efficiency it is impossible to achieve the conditions in which equality can be established — or indeed avoid an increase in destitution. The optimum rate of investment in a framework of inequality and widespread destitution is the highest politically[12] feasible rate of investment.

[10] This is discussed at greater length in chapter 7.

[11] See also chapter 5.

[12] From the viewpoint, therefore, of maintaining the desired political system and providing the minimum incentive through increases in the incomes of those who are already above subsistence levels.

3

*The Mechanism of Neo-Imperialism**

THE ECONOMIC IMPACT OF MONETARY AND COMMERCIAL INSTITUTIONS IN AFRICA

Since their liberation from colonial rule most African territories have made accelerated progress. This has happened despite the loss of experienced administrators and technical experts in all fields through the rapid Africanization of public services and the emigration of some entrepreneurial and managerial capacity. This process must also be seen against the background of the systematically damaging impact on the terms of trade of African territories of the development of the world economy in the 1950s and 1960s.The return to the use of monetary controls and the trend towards convertibility and non-discrimination have undoubtedly retarded growth in markets important to Africa and thus contributed to the depressing effect of monetary policy itself on primary-goods prices. The prices of most of Africa's imports − manufactures − are administered and have shown a continuous upward trend during this period.

The record thus seems remarkable and encouraging. It is my view that this acceleration of growth is to some extent exceptional, however, and cannot be relied on to continue. It has been the result of the disappearance of the limitations imposed by the monetary and commercial institutions, arrangements, and policies on the economic evolution of Africa during the colonial period. These were dominated by the relations of African territories with their erstwhile metropolitan countries.

* Reprinted from *Bulletin of the Oxford University Institute of Statistics,* August 1962.

I believe that it can be shown that the automatism which evolved represents in itself a severe limitation on the possibility of the weaker partner in the 'colonial pact' to develop fully, even if there be no conscious policy aimed at its exploitation for the benefit of the metropolitan country. Beyond this, the philosophy of monetary and fiscal soundness itself represents a further handicap to the weaker area. If this analysis is correct, two conclusions follow, both unpalatable to current conventional wisdom. The first is that the present upsurge in the ex-colonial areas provides no guarantee of a stable and steady progress in future unless special efforts are made to substitute positive stimuli for the negative ending of colonial limitations. The second is that neo-imperialism does not depend on open political domination. The economic relations of the United States with South America are not essentially different from those of Britain with her African colonies. The International Monetary Fund has been fulfilling the role of the colonial administration in enforcing the rules of the game favourable to the rich countries.

The theme is fraught with emotional implications. On the one hand, strenuous efforts are made to underline the exploitative aspects of colonial subjection. On the other side, the increasing importance of aid, in terms both of technical knowledge and of resources, is stressed, especially contributions to the budget of African countries, the provision of preferential arrangements in commodity sales, and the provision of capital.

THE RISE OF PREFERENTIAL SYSTEMS
BEFORE THE WAR

Practically all countries of Africa, both those whose independence dates back a long time and those which have only lately achieved it, belong, or belonged until recently, to monetary and banking systems and commercial areas centred in a highly developed metropolitan country and its institutions.[1] All the modern economic organs in Africa

[1] See my article, 'A Note on the Monetary Controversy in Malaya', *Malayan Economic Review*, October 1959; 'Those Sterling Balances', *Venture*, March 1954;

grew up in response to the needs of these metropolitan countries, whose main interest in Africa lay in the supply of food and raw materials from the tropical zone.[2]

There was, until very recently, no autochthonous demand in these areas for modern monetary or economic institutions. Colonial governments were not encouraged to undertake financial operations in the territories for which they were responsible. The large foreign companies operating there had easy access to the capital markets of the metropolis for any financial needs beyond their retained profits. There was thus nothing to deflect the evolution of the monetary and banking institutions of the periphery from responding almost exclusively to the requirements of the centre.

These requirements could best be satisfied by safeguarding the absolute stability of the colonial monetary unit in terms of the metropolitan currency and by encouraging the establishment of banking institutions which would at all times be safe.

Monetary stability

The former aim was achieved by the simple expedient of providing for a 100 per cent cover for the colonial currency. It was immaterial whether the institution in charge was a private bank (as in French Africa) or a currency board (as in British Africa), so long as the assets held against the note issue were metropolitan. In this way, any increase in the currency circulation in the dependent area resulted in a *de facto* loan by it to the metropolis; on the other hand, this arrangement provided an absolute guarantee for the sufficiency of reserves. In a way it reduced the risk of extreme crises. It would incidentally also have prevented conscious policies for economic stabilization and consciously accelerated development in the dependency, if such policies had (or could have) been conceived in this framework before the war.[3]

'Britain and the Dependent Commonwealth', in A.C. Jones (ed.), *New Fabian Colonial Essays*, Hogarth Press, London, 1959.
2 Though the immediate reason for their establishing territorial bases in Africa in the nineteenth century, was, in many cases, their effort to curb slave-trading.
3 It did actually impose limitations to the extension of 'Keynesian' policies in the short period after the war before independence was won.

Banking services

The second requirement, the provision of reliable banking services, was obtained automatically by encouraging the establishment of large (specialized) banking institutions in the metropolis to handle the commerce of the colonial area. These banks became powerful when banking had become stabilized in the metropolitan area and their policies had become impeccably sound and stolid. Their freedom of operation, especially the choice of their investments, was not limited by any regulation such as a *minimum reserve having to be kept in the colonial or peripheral territory.* There was no other agency for handling the slowly emerging domestic savings of these territories at a time when few, if any, liquid assets of the required quality were available in those areas.

It was then a matter of natural 'evolution' that the colonial banking system had to a considerable extent to find uses for its deposits in the metropolis. Under the canons of sound banking, however, they had to confine their lending to 'self-liquidating' purposes. In practice, this meant the finance of the foreign trade of the colonial area, of exports of colonial primary produce, and imports of metropolitan manufactures. A large part of total resources was thus necessarily kept in metropolitan 'reserves', i.e. in liquid sterling or franc assets. Thus a further and increasing flow of (in effect, short-term) lending at low rates of interest originated from the periphery (which was so terribly short of capital) to the centre.[4] In some dependent areas (such as the British) where savings banks and postal saving institutions were legally bound to invest in the government securities of the metropolis, there was an additional loss of savings to the dependency.

The export of liquid savings to the metropolitan area, and the consequent reliance of the dependency on the metropolis for long-term capital for development, secured for the banking system of the latter a useful income, while its control over the financial and economic policy of the dependency (already

[4] They were used especially before the First World War to finance short-term credits (acceptances). After 1920, they served increasingly as the basis of British long-term lending, first to finance European reconstruction after the First World War, and, after the Second, the prosperous developing areas (South Africa, Australia, etc.). It proved to be an embarrassing change.

assured by the hold of the metropolitan administration over the colonial government) was further reinforced, and the participation of the ruling financial interests in its administrations obtained. All long-term expenditure for which long-term loans were needed – and the reluctance to increase taxation, and in particular to introduce direct taxation, in practice reduced the possibility of covering capital expenditure out of current budgetary resources – was thus made subject to financial veto.[5] This made any change in policy difficult, for the 'credit-worthiness' of colonial governments became dependent on their strictly abiding by the limitations imposed upon them. If the metropolis offered special facilities for colonial borrowing (e.g. the concession by Britain of trustee status to colonial securities), this grant did not by any means fully offset the gains secured to the banking system and the capital market by the 'special relationship'.

The provision of cheap facilities for the finance of foreign trade while domestic activity was unable to obtain capital at comparable terms distorted the productive structure of the colonial area. The differential ease with which the international movement of goods could obtain finance at world rates of interest further enhanced the supremacy of the merchandising, mining and plantation operations of large foreign firms, because long-term capital needed for the diversification of the economy and the rise of domestic industry was either not available at all or only on extortionate conditions.[6]

Automatic commercial preference

Thus the divergence in the tropics between private profitability and real social advantage was widened, and the tropical countries' dependence on primary exports was automatically perpetuated. Diversification would have increased productivity and real income. But it was, in the circumstances, practicable only given *positive* economic

5 The history of the establishment of a central bank in Ceylon is a good illustration of the veto.
6 See chapter 1, above. All these problems are disregarded by those who once more advocate policy- and project-evaluation on the basis of what are simple 'free trade' principles.

intervention, and such positive economic intervention for the conscious acceleration of development of the colonial area was not contemplated so long as the territories were not independent. The role of the state was conceived as limited to assuring law and order.

This so-called *pacte colonial,* the exchange of colonial primary produce against metropolitan manufactures and services, was thus in the nineteenth century (in contrast to the eighteenth century) not generally based on explicit restrictive or preferential legislation in favour of the metropolis (the monopoly of French shipping to Algeria and Madagascar represented one of the few exceptions). Over a large part of Africa (e.g. the Congo basin and Morocco) international treaties or agreements enforced free trade, or at least non-discrimination. The free play of the price mechanism (as in the case of the 'independent' countries of Latin America and the Caribbean) was quite sufficient to restrict the less developed countries to a status of permanent economic inferiority. The implicit preference of the colonial administrations for the metropolitan products did the rest. Their orders on public and private account — and these represented a large portion of the total money demand of the colonial area — flowed in the main toward the metropolis.

As this went on and international industrial competition became more acute, these rather informal relationships were increasingly reinforced by preferences explicitly conceded in formal legal arrangements, especially by those imperial metropolitan areas which could not maintain their industrial strength. Even before the war, British Imperial Preference and the French Customs Union brought about a closer integration in those areas in which international treaties did not prescribe free trade or non-discrimination. They were to be reinforced by quantitative restrictions and exchange control. All these arrangements on the whole secured greater advantages for the metropolitan areas than for the periphery, because the preferences granted to the primary produce of the latter was, without quantitative regulation, often ineffectual.[7] The currency disturbance of the interwar period,

7 The export capacity of the areas entitled to Imperial Preference was in excess

during which the dependencies had no option but to share the monetary fate of the dominant country — which meant that the risk of exchange fluctuation was eliminated in the relation of the centre to the periphery — acted as a further bond of some importance. The metropolis continued to secure a large, often overwhelming, share in both the exports and imports of the colonies.

THE IMPACT OF WAR ECONOMIES:
THE RISE OF EXCHANGE AREAS

The war brought fundamental changes, not merely in the economic relations of the metropolis with the dependencies but also in the attitude of the colonial administrations to economic problems. The economic relationship between the metropolis and the periphery was strengthened, while the responsibility of the metropolis for fostering political and economic development became more and more recognized. The fact that the emergent political leaders of the dependencies obtained an increasingly influential voice in the administration of the African territories explains to a large extent, though perhaps not wholly, the recognition of the view that the conscious fostering of economic and social development represents one of the most important functions of the state.

At the same time, the net effect of the change cannot unequivocally be said to have favoured the rapid growth of the dependencies. Even the profound change in the relationship between the prices of primary produce and manufactures which took place during the war and persisted well into the postwar period was insufficient to break the vicious circle of poverty. It is the contrast between the change in government attitude and the improvement of the resources at the disposal of the African territories and the relatively unsatisfactory degree of progress that asks for an explanation.

Already before the war the unrest due to the low prices for colonial primary produce caused by the Great Depression resulted in the appointment of several official committees

of metropolitan import requirements except in the case of a few products, e.g. oil-seeds and tobacco.

to enquire into the problem of the marketing of export produce (e.g. the Cocoa Marketing Enquiry). Their reports questioned for the first time the adequacy and efficacy of a 'free' market in these commodities. They questioned the assumption that bargains between weak peasants lacking knowledge and capital and the indigenous merchants or the agents of the great metropolitan corporations who purchased the produce of the colonies could be said to be between equal partners. They foreshadowd the development of government agencies which, by conscious policy, could secure that balance between the two sides which was supposed to be brought about by the free interplay of market forces in perfect markets.[8]

The outbreak of the war, which disrupted trade in tropical produce, occasioned a change which would hardly have come about without it. On the one hand, the market for colonial produce was guaranteed by the metropolitan countries. This undoubtedly conferred a great advantage on the colonial area, if only or mainly in the sense that claims on the metropolis were accumulated which could at some point in the future be made effective for development. It also served to maintain the distribution of incomes within the colonies which would have been gravely disturbed by a collapse of export prices. At the same time, it might be and has been argued that this guarantee prevented a partial reorientation of colonial production towards food and other products needed in the home market. It is questionable, however, whether in the long run this would have been in the interests of the colonies without effective long-term planning.

The war brought about another important change on the plane of commercial policy. This was the strong reinforcement of the rudimentary preferential arrangements, the grant of privileged treatment to colonial and metropolitan products respectively in each other's market, by the imposition of *direct controls over imports and over foreign payments*, i.e. payments outside the confines of the group. The *de facto* advantage of a stable currency became

---

[8] The critics of marketing boards in their argumentation implicitly and illicitly assume that the peasant obtained a 'perfectly competitive price in the "free" system'. This is nonsense.

consciously and powerfully reinforced by explicit regulation. The loose automatic associations between London and Paris and their respective dependencies were transformed into the powerful groupings of the Sterling Area and the Franc Zone. During this period of monetary and commercial development a series of special connections grew up, which made their interdependence far closer and more purposefully contrived than it had been at any time since the middle of the nineteenth century. The reciprocal possibility of obtaining finance between the metropolis and the dependencies created a unique framework for mutually profitable economic development.

The economic significance of these special relationships is difficult to quantify. They must not be evaluated singly because they are to a large extent interdependent, and their effect on welfare must be judged as a whole. Efforts on either side to show the effectiveness of policy in lessening inequality and promoting development, by pointing to specific measures (e.g. the guarantee of purchases of colonial produce well above the world price level) are obviously beside the point. Nor must grants by the metropolis to the periphery for particular projects, however admirable, be accepted automatically at their face value. It would have to be shown first that a grant was effectively transferred, i.e. not offset by the automatic working of the monetary mechanism through increasing the liquid reserves of the colony at the centre. Even if effective transfers took place, the indirect effects of this expenditure might result in a net burden to the periphery. The advantage gained by some groups of individuals or firms in the periphery or in the centre might well be more than offset by the disadvantages of others.

The advantages and disadvantages, moreover, might be in causal relationship with one another – in other words, either party might be unable or unwilling to grant advantages or suffer disadvantages without some compensation. For instance, it would seem to be beside the point to argue in favour of 'untied', convertible grants when the balance-of-payments position of the donor countries was such as to make a cut in the grant inevitable if convertibility were insisted upon. The cut might more than offset gains due to the possibility of using 'convertible' money in a third and cheaper market. A detailed evaluation, from the viewpoint of welfare, of the special relationships between the metropolitan areas and their dependencies which have by now emerged into full independence is therefore needed if an adequate policy for the social and economic development of the areas is to be worked out, and a suitable international commercial framework established.

To this task we now turn.

THE IMPACT OF PREFERENCE AND AID

The preferential treatment accorded to goods and services in intra-group trade may take the form of commercial preferences — commodity-purchase agreements, tariff preferences, administrative (quota) preferences — or of a discriminatory application of monetary controls. Of the various types of commercial preferences, the first was the most important to the dependent or erstwhile dependent areas, and the second to the metropolitan areas. The monetary arrangements seem to have worked largely in the interest of the metropolitan areas (or, rather, certain groups within those countries) and had the result of diminishing the real equivalent of the money contribution provided for the periphery, i.e. the contribution in terms of resources and technical knowledge. It should be added, however, that in certain cases the net advantage to the metropolitan area would arise not so much through price relationships as through the fact that the periphery was for one reason or another unable to make full use of the purchasing power which resulted from its export sales or which was put at its disposal in other ways.

Commodity agreements

Commodity agreements provided for the purchase of unlimited or of specified quantities of the African territories' produce. The former type was general during the war. As wartime scarcities lessened, and the terms of trade moved against the primary-producing areas, limitation on quantity became the rule.

The Mechanism of Neo-Imperialism

In the *British* territories, the wartime system was continued in the immediate postwar period of shortages. After 1950 — and indeed already under the Labour government — they were first attenuated and their duration shortened, and then purchases at current market price were agreed to. After 1951, most bulk purchases were discontinued. Among the exceptions the Imperial (later Commonwealth) Sugar Agreement was the most notable; it did not affect Africa.

The postwar bulk-purchase agreements seem generally to have worked to the disadvantage of the African colonies, inasmuch as in a period of rising prices, long-term purchases in practice proved to be made below current prices in world markets.[9] Two things need to be said in this context, however. The first is that the relation of prices to the so-called 'world price' is by itself insufficient as a criterion for determining the welfare effects of such agreements; 'world prices' are not independent of the existence of the agreement itself. One of the effects of the agreement might be a benefit far beyond the direct advantage or disadvantage experienced on the sale to the metropolitan country.[10] Nor must the security of market assured by bulk purchases be disregarded.

What might be said to have been really objectionable in British policy from a welfare point of view was the decision to abandon bulk purchases at the precise moment when the world trend in primary prices (and in their terms of trade with manufacturers) turned and when the countries of Africa would have benefited by, and had a strong case for, the continuation of purchases.

In the *French* territories, the provision of preferential markets through quota regulation in the metropolitan market and price guarantees still plays a very important part in the marketing of coffee and groundnuts, and also of cocoa,

[9] See the interesting analysis made by ECE in the *Economic Survey of Europe in 1948*, Geneva, 1949.

[10] This is a significant consideration for the future, e.g. when considering the effects of bulk purchases by the Soviet Union on the world price of surpluses and commodities. If Soviet purchases push up 'free' world prices sufficiently for African countries to obtain the same income from sales of smaller quantities to other countries, they will represent a net benefit. Thus the fact that the Russians may have bought the commodities at less than the world price ruling *after* the agreement cannot be said to prove that they have exploited the African areas.

groundnut oil, palm kernels and palm oil. Their impact is to increase the income of the periphery and to increase its production of these commodities relative to the production capacity of the world as a whole. It should be noted, however (and this qualification is habitually omitted in most treatments of this question), that this relative 'distortion' of the productive structure might in fact not be so significant, because the inherent potential of the periphery might be much greater than actual production, as a result of ignorance, so that 'artificially' high prices might just achieve what would be achieved automatically by the influence of a better-working price mechanism on more knowledgeable producers. This consideration suggests that it is conceiveable that the discontinuance of the provision of preferential markets will *not* have a net discouraging effect on production, because it is quite likely that technical progress will be stimulated by the ending or modification of the favourable commodity agreements, especially since this coincides with greater efforts on the part of FEDOM (the European Fund for Overseas Development) and other 'European' funds, and the international agencies, to channel technical knowledge to Africa.[11]

Duties and quantitative control

The impact of reciprocal *preferential tariffs* seems to have been more effective in securing advantages for the metropolitan country than for the periphery. This follows partly from the fact that the tariffs in force on food and raw materials in the metropolitan area (even in France) were rather moderate and partly (especially in the case of the British territories) because in the case of a number of commodities the metropolitan countries were unable to absorb the whole of the export surplus of the periphery. Since the exports from the periphery were homogeneous this meant that the preferences became inoperative. On the other hand, the preferences granted on metropolitan manufactured exports were substantial in a number of areas and, partly because of the oligopolistic nature of the supply,

---

[11] On the impact of the new arrangements, see my article 'Africa and the Common Market', *Journal of Common Market Studies*, no. 1, 1962.

also effective.

So far as quantitative regulations are concerned, their impact worked more evenly in the British zone until the acceptance by Britain of the GATT principles of non-discrimination reduced the advantages of the periphery. In the French territories, the primary producers continued to enjoy advantages from the discriminatory restriction of imports from outside areas, coupled with price guarantees. Their effect on welfare was offset, and perhaps more than offset, by the discriminatory import controls in the African territories on non-French manufactures. As we shall see (pp. 96-100), the problem resolves itself mainly into one of income redistribution between the various classes in both the metropolitan and the peripheral area.

Monetary and exchange policy

Discriminatory exchange control reinforced the effect on the pattern of commerce of quantitative import regulations. The ease with which payment could be made and finance secured obviously contributed to the strengthening of intra-group trade even where price relationships were not as favourable as they would have been with other parties. More important than this immediate effect on trade was the impact of exchange restrictions in the financial sphere.

Capital movements. Historically, the essence of the functioning of currency areas has been the unlimited freedom of capital movements. This is not necessarily a condition of the functioning of currency areas. Both Australia and India have instituted strict controls on capital, even on transfers within the currency area to which they belong. It certainly has been a feature, until recently, of the relations of both the Franc Zone and the Sterling Area.[12]

It is obvious that a discriminatory ease of capital transfers from the metropolitan area to the periphery would encourage investment there, even if this were not as profitable as investment elsewhere. The assurance of being able to repatriate

---

12 Sharp resistance was encountered by the Governments of Ghana and British Guiana when they introduced controls on capital flight.

purchasing power would be an additional incentive. This may well be reinforced by the advantages secured to these investments by the commercial preference systems discussed above. It should be noted, however, that by and large the establishment of new large-scale productive units was encouraged more *in the centre*[13] than in the periphery and that it would be impossible to assert that the latter did not suffer a relative disadvantage in consequence.

In recent years, with the accelerated movement towards independence, it seems likely that the freedom of capital movements on private account predominantly favoured the centre rather than the periphery. The capital flow was dictated not so much by normal profit incentives as by precautionary motives, i.e. capital was repatriated to the metropolis. This certainly seems to have been the case in the Franc Zone, but it probably played some part in the Sterling Area too.[14] The resultant weakening of the periphery is obvious. It must not, however, be judged without reference to another feature of the functioning of these economic groupings, the grant of aid in terms of loans or outright contributions from the centre to the periphery (see p. 97-8).

The monetary and fiscal policy of the colonial areas continued to be dominated by Victorian canons. The plans prepared — especially in the British territories[15] — were little more than a haphazard collection of departmental investment projects unconnected with one another and decided upon without any analysis of their general economic effects. The reserves which were accumulating were kept in separate accounts in the metropolitan centre and thus could not be pooled for an imaginative use for general development. Balanced budgets and conservative finance, the use of only long-term loan capital for long-term investment, remained the watchword of the administrations. Even when central

[13] Or in other highly developed parts of the currency areas. In the case of the Sterling Area, it was South Africa and Australia which mainly benefited.

[14] Some of the unexplained credit items on the British balance of payments might well be connected with this capital repatriation.

[15] Planning became respectable at a much earlier date in France as a result of the activity of the *Commissariat du Plan.* Young economists and planners were made available to colonial administrations much sooner and in considerable numbers. The British administrations did not encourage such extravagance.

banks were established, against rugged opposition by the
metropolis, their powers remained sharply limited. No
conscious anti-cyclical policies were conceived of for these
areas, even after the victory of Keynesian techniques in the
metropolis. To some extent this was due to the complete
failure to recruit a new type of personnel to devise and
execute policy.

Exchange rates. The rates of exchange fixed for the African
countries, and especially those in the Franc Zone, had
important effects on the relations of Africans with the
metropolitan areas.

   So far as the *British* territories are concerned, the
problem was dominated and modified by the policy of the
marketing boards, which paid less than the world market
price to the farmers, thus limiting incomes in the African
territories and, until after independence, steadily accumulating rather large nest eggs whose real value had been steadily
declining.[16] The fact that the British-African currencies
were devalued together with sterling in 1939 and again in
1949, though their balances of payments were showing
surpluses, may have further slightly worsened the terms
of trade of the African countries in comparison with their
competitors in, say, Latin America. The policy pursued
would have been indefensible had it not happened just before
the violent reversal, in 1951, of the postwar improvement in
the prices of primary products relative to those of
manufactures. Thus the effects of devaluation were
completely swamped by the collapse of primary prices.
Indeed, the African territories under British control may
have benefited by the fact that their currencies were at a
relatively low level at that critical date, while their price
levels were not influenced by the boom because of its
relatively short duration.

   In the case of the *French* territories, the value of the
colonial currency was raised during France's postwar
monetary vicissitudes to a level double that of the metro-

[16] The Ghana government complained in 1961 that the sterling value of the
assets purchased also declined by £15m. The loss in real terms must have been
far greater, perhaps as high as £60m.

politan franc. This decision, together with the structure of commercial relations within the Franc Area, resulted in a violent upward thrust of domestic prices in terms of dollars, since the price levels in the African territories were never revised when shortages became less acute and the colonial franc appreciated. The quantitative control imposed on imports from outside and the preferential relationships which French manufacturers enjoyed within the Area prevented the correction of the anomaly and secured exceptional profits for metropolitan exporters. The producers of those primary products which had preferential markets in France were also shielded from the consequences of the revaluation of the colonial currency on their sale prices. These included the great tribal-feudal-religious chiefs and the metropolitan corporations interested in plantations and ranches. In a number of areas (e.g. Senegal), those who suffered comprised the least privileged part of the population. The policy of high prices (and salaries) also favoured all those whose income and savings accrued in colonial francs but who wanted to spend them in France. Inasmuch as a considerable portion of the money (in contrast to subsistence) incomes in the Franc Area were earned by individuals and firms from France, the high value of the currency tended to enhance the potential claims against these territories on capital account.

Too much, however, must not be made of this, because most of the money incomes provided in the colonies were strongly influenced either by commodity agreements or by direct subsidies granted by France. To that extent the arrangements meant merely that the French consumer of certain colonial produce and the French taxpayer were burdened with the cost of relatively higher payments to French firms trading in Africa and French citizens in the service of the African territories.

Taxes, subsidies, and welfare contributions

Until as late as the last war, it was a general rule in imperial arrangements that the colonies had to 'fend for themselves'. This expression was obviously interpreted by the colonial powers in a rather flexible manner. In the majority of cases, the colonial taxation system precluded the territory from benefiting from a direct contribution from incomes accruing in the territory to the nationals and firms of the metropolitan area, and this income represented a rather considerable portion of the total monetized and taxable income of the country. Even indirect levies and excise did not discriminate to any extent between essential and non-essential goods. This accentuated the regressive character of colonial taxation which, as a whole, was biased in favour of the nationals of the metropolitan and other highly developed areas. This bias was thought to be needed to attract foreign capital. The conventional view is undoubtedly correct that the activities of foreign, or rather metropolitan, firms accounted for an overwhelming proportion of total capital investment in the colonies, and their activity was the major element in such 'progress' in those areas as was made, i.e. an intensification of the contrast between the advanced and the traditional sectors. Whether they would have curtailed their activity if a different taxation policy had been pursued is another question. A different taxation policy could have increased the pace of the development of technical knowledge and domestic markets, and increased the attractiveness of non-export-orientated investment.

The conclusion that the centre exploited the periphery cannot be substantiated by simply pointing to the fact that it was able to earn large profits which were not taxed to any extent. It might perhaps be fairer to say that the share of profits and salaries going to the metropolis was substantial, and that the latter reaped a greater part of the benefits of the development which it initiated and which would not otherwise have taken place. In the framework of taxation as it was, and with a large supply of labour, the forces of the 'free' market alone would have strongly favoured the productive factor in shortest supply, i.e. capital. These forces were massively supported by the fact that the 'free' market implied a strong *monopoly* economic power buttressed by the political influence of expatriate individuals and firms. The resultant distribution of income was far more unequal than that in the metropolitan countries.

The attitude of the metropolitan powers to their dependent territories underwent substantial changes *after the war*. In the British territories, the Colonial Development and Welfare Act made available grants for capital expenditure on education and other social services, such as health, and also for intrastructure investment. In the French territories, FIDES, CCFOM (now CCCE and PAC), and lately FEDOM, made grants on an impressive scale. In addition, the French government defrayed the cost of the metropolitan military personnel and a large proportion of the civilian personnel stationed in former French territories, and in certain instances granted direct contributions to the regular budgets of the new countries.

It has been claimed[17] that these grants represented a complete break with the past, an application to the relation of the metropolis to the dependent territories (soon to be granted independence) of the principles of the welfare state.[18] It would be wrong to discount altogether the importance of the change but its welfare impact can be exaggerated.

In the first place, the grant of these subsidies partly determined the policies of the African countries in question and deflected them from the course upon which the countries themselves might have decided. To some extent, therefore, they might be thought to be objectionable from the point of view of the self-determination of the territory concerned. This rather constitutional argument is reinforced by the fact that foreign grants almost always result in increased expenditure which has to be financed from domestic resources. This is clear in the case of capital grants which imply commitments (as in the case of the British-financed universities) for current and maintenance expenditure outside the scope of the 'welfare' fund. This expenditure might be burdensome and might be for purposes for which resources would not otherwise have been found. In

[17] e.g. Colonial Office White Paper on the U.K., *Contribution to Development*, Cmnd 1308, 1961.
[18] It might be argued, of course, that the sudden willingness of the conservative parties to grant independence ('to preside over the liquidation of empire') is not unconnected with this new relationship. In fact France refused, at first, to make grants or give technical assistance to those countries which did not accept a special 'new' political relationship. There was willingness to purchase 'greatness' by continuing grants to the rest.

many instances the returns were not commensurate even with the direct burden to the country.[19] Moreover, such grants may have general repercussions on the budget and on the distribution of income which might be considered out of keeping with the general situation of the territory.

In the second place, the welfare effects of subsidies or contributions by the metropolitan countries will be strongly influenced if not determined by the geographical distribution of the final expenditure which is undertaken on the basis of these grants. As we have argued above, the very existence of dependent relationships did result in a powerful influence favouring purchases from the metropolitan area. This preferential system has been perpetuated, if not strengthened, by the impact of the system of subsidies. The grants would have been used in the metropolitan country even if currency regulations and other restrictive measures had not meant a very substantial commercial preference between the metropolitan country and the periphery. In addition, capital investment embodied in metropolitan manufactures necessitates purchases for replacement and extension and makes metropolitan goods familiar. Thus, in gauging the net contribution to the recipient countries' welfare of the payments made, the relative terms of trade would also have to be taken into account. These were not favourable to the African countries.

In addition to the assistance or contributions made by the former metropolitan countries, technical and resource contributions were made by the United States on a bilateral basis. These were not large, but increased rapidly. Soviet and (more lately) Chinese contributions to African countries south of the Sahara have been increasing also in volume and geographic scope. These have mostly taken the form of long-term loans on soft conditions, combined with reverse bulk-purchase agreements in order to facilitate repayments.

International institutions were less active in the 1950s in Africa than in other continents. The relative insignificance of their contributions is explicable by the fact that few countries in Africa were independent before the 1950s, and the

[19] This has in fact happened only too often in the case of technical assistance.

metropolitan countries did not favour their activity in dependent areas. With expanding independence, a very rapid increase in the activity of the international institutions has come about.

Unfortunately the experiences which were garnered, especially in South America — which resembles Africa, in the sense of being a continent which has been fragmented into several largely independent regions, whose easiest communication with each other and the rest of the world is by sea — have been ignored. The offices of the United Nations and its specialized agencies (not excluding the Development Bank) are scattered around, thus vastly increasing the difficulties of consistent planning. The dearth of responsible leadership and technical knowledge is aggravated by the relentless and reckless drive for personal aggrandizement and profit by the powerful — mostly undisciplined and uneducated soldiers. The great number of countries (and votes in the United Nations governing bodies) in that unfortunate continent militates against success in achieving any balanced increase in welfare.[20]

Thus in calculating the net magnitude of the contribution of the metropolitan countries to the welfare of the African countries, account would have to be taken of the aid which these latter could have obtained from outside sources, from which they were barred while in a dependent status. This must have been very substantial.[21]

CONCLUSION

In summing up this discussion of the close interrelationship of the now independent African countries with the erstwhile metropolitan countries, two things need to be noted.

The first is the development of their terms of trade, influenced as these were by the special relationships existing, and balance of payments, and, more especially, the changes in their reserves held in the metropolitan centre. The

[20] See chapter 10 on the relative effectiveness of bilateral as compared with multilateral aid.

[21] In the case of the British territories, it can be argued (*ex post* at any rate) that those contributions would have been rather higher than the aid effectively obtained from Britain.

impression one obtains is that the *British* territories on the whole have not been able fully to use the favourable opportunities presented in the immediate postwar period of rising prices, though in certain instances purchases from British territories took place at a relatively higher level. In the case of the main export commodities of Africa, however, the bulk-purchase agreements undertaken by Britain in the immediate past were relatively (if to some extent fortuitously) unfavourable to the African dependencies. The African territories, moreover, did not benefit from bulk-purchase agreements in general after the price trend changed in 1952. The *French* territories, on the contrary, continued to benefit by such agreements. The impression is unmistakable, however, that the quantitative controls did encourage purchases in the metropolitan area even though the metropolitan-area prices were far less favourable to those countries than world prices.

The second criterion is the development of their balance of payments. In this respect, the *British* territories continuously increased their reserves in the metropolitan country. This meant that the subsidies and loans granted to the dependent areas could not be effectively transferred (even though the areas incurred liability for interest payments in the case of loans). On the other hand, the combined effect of the upward trend in prices and the decline in gilt-edged securities, in which the sterling reserves were partly invested, has severely reduced the real value of the reserves thus acquired. This has necessarily meant a heavy loss to the territories concerned.

So far as the *French* territories are concerned, a large portion of the public transfers (in some cases nine-tenths) has been offset by private transfers towards the metropolis. These capital movements were very large in relation to the value of visible trade. Nevertheless, as is shown in the official statistics, the French colonies were at times unable to use the public transfers fully and accumulated unused balances at the Banque de France despite the fact that capital flight from the colonies was very considerable. The effective transfer of capital for use in the colonial areas has thus been small.

If account is taken of the opportunities for obtaining capital and aid from sources outside the metropolitan countries, the view that the African territories benefited by this special relationship to the metropolis must be sharply discounted. Even in the postwar period, the net aid reaching them was more than offset by the concessions or special trading relations granted or obtained for metropolitan firms or individuals. The failure of colonial administrations dominated by the metropolis to use taxation and direct controls consciously to speed development further increased the loss of the dependencies. This perhaps explains how it was possible to accelerate economic progress in a number of areas as soon as independence was gained, despite the loss of experienced administrators and the emergence of depressing political complications.

The implications of this analysis are disturbing. The mechanism of what one might call welfare- or neo-imperialism seems to have artificially restricted the development of colonial areas by preventing viable infant industries from being established. The present surge of activity might simply be the conseqence of making up for this *artificial backwardness.* Once the obvious phase of import-substitution in manufacturing has come to an end, Africa might be in danger of a Latin American or Middle Eastern frustration. Unless the vast primitive agricultural sector can be energized into a response, the upward surge will not become cumulative but, as in Latin America and the Middle East, peter out. There will remain a vast and increasingly dissatisfied ill-employed class in the primitive-subsistence sector confronted with a small privileged class in the cities, unable to provide either supplies or markets for the latter. Only if the rural response were adequate, if productivity and income increased and justified a cumulative increase in industry, could a self-sustaining upward spiral be confidently expected. This has not happened yet, and some of the development plans, with their neglect of agriculture and rural technical education, seem to be disquietingly inept for the exacting task in hand.[22]

---

[22] President Nyerere of Tanzania represents a shining exception to this dismal picture. Cf. R. Dumont, *False Start in Africa*, André Deutsch, London, 1966.

4

The Consumer and Economic Development[*]

All the best economic textbooks at some stage or other make some appealing reference to that shadowy if convenient concept of the average, yet sovereign, consumer. There he stands, steadfast among millions of temptations, surrounded by a host of goods and services from among which to choose. He is alert, and quite determined. He does not look round to see what the Joneses do; his tastes are all his own. The only pointers he looks for are prices. He reacts instantly and intensely even to their smallest alteration, and he is an expert buyer with a quivering knowledge of the last advantage to be squeezed from every deal. It is his buying which rules the economic system. Through the elastic sway of his favours, new firms may spring into being and old ones be instantly eliminated. In this way, what he wants is produced when he wants it and as he wants it. A perfect balance reigns.

This concept of the sovereign buyer and his needs and satisfactions is not, in fact, a very old one. It had, for example, no place in the common-sense system of the great English classics. It was developed simultaneously in Switzerland, Austria and England as late as the early 1870s. Its contemporaneous appearance in these countries is probably attributable to the fact that the classical theory of prices and incomes, based on labour value, was increasingly leading to unfavourable conclusions about the character and prospects of capitalism; and that an urgent need was felt for new assurance and moral justification. Mill, the greatest exponent of the classical doctrine, was turning towards socialism, and Marx used the orthodox Ricardian system to prove to his own and his disciples' satisfaction the fact that the worker was being deprived by capitalist exploiters of his right to the value that he alone created.

The new doctrine contained an element both of optimism and of moral justification regarding the existing state of affairs. It showed clearly that with the relative growth of the stock of capital the share of labour would tend to increase and that nobody got more or less than exactly what he deserved through his contribution to output. Demand and supply were equated at exactly the level at which utility was maximized, and the interaction of prices saw to it that nobody was better off without making somebody else worse off.

Already unreal

This theory was already unreal at the moment of its formulation. On the one hand, it was clear that it could not defend the private ownership of capital or land; on the other, it was equally clear that consumers did not behave in the way assumed. Consumption was, even less than it may have been in earlier periods, the expression of the needs and tastes of the individual. There was a conspicuous competitive element in it which, as the career of Lord Duveen, the most successful art dealer of his time, showed, could be stimulated and played upon to make profit for others. This was clearly recognized by the only wholly American sociological economist, Thorstein Veblen, in his theory of the leisured class, and less consciously by those writers early in the nineteenth century who defended the disproportionate accumulation of wealth by reference to the employment it created.

Artificial needs and social balance

As income increases, both these artificial elements become more patently demonstrable. Not only does income become less essential but the immense importance of *maintaining spending* as a means of *retaining stability* in the system increases. The underconsumption theories of capitalist crises, as well as the growing fears of a running-down of the system and of permanent stagnation, derived from this idea. The Keynesian School, which opted for equality in order to diminish savings, and pleaded for state action to offset them by investment or loan expenditure, was the first scientific expression of this trend of thought.

In his book, *The Affluent Society* (1958), Professor Galbraith has, with his usual brilliance, carried the argument a stage further. He follows to its logical conclusion the critique of the American economic system and points to the struggle by producers, growing more and more desperate, to keep the machine moving by creating needs which are expanding far less vigorously than the capacity to meet them. The fickleness of the consumer grows as income and consumption expand, and the effort to interest him has to be pursued with relentless ferocity. The most modern methods of psychology are used in order to discover a chink in the armour he builds up against the blandishments of the advertiser. Failure means lapse from full employment, collapse of profits, and the diminution of the prestige and power of the firms and managers depending on the successful sales of their product. This obsession with production, this drive for a continued increase in productivity, becomes increasingly absurd. As the intimate connection between real needs and production weakens, it is no longer legitimate to accept all production as being equally urgently needed. We must look to how the composition of production is determined. References to the 'average consumer's sovereignty' or to the 'consistency of choice' as the final determinant of our productive efforts have become absurd in the present situation. In Galbraith's opinion, the neo-classical analysis based on scarcity and want must in present conditions give the wrong answers:

> Keynes did not foresee that the rapid expansion in output which was implicit in his ideas would soon bring us to the time when not total output but its composition would become the critical matter. Had he survived, he would no doubt have been perturbed by the tendency of his followers to concentrate their policy on the single goal of increased output. He did not lack discrimination. But his followers or some of them will almost certainly continue to protect the Keynesian system, with its concentration on aggregate

demand and output, from ideas which Keynes might have been disposed to urge. Such is the fate of anyone who becomes part of the conventional wisdom.

Nor is this all. The preoccupation with production means the abandonment of a balanced approach to society and its requirements.[1] It prevents the setting aside of sufficient resources for those basic needs of the community which cannot conveniently or possibly be satisfied by the market system. Production capacity is pre-empted for the satisfaction of artificially created wants. The mad rush after production even endangers the safety of the state, because taxation for defence is resented and loan expenditure is regarded as ruinous. It destroys amenity because the competitive urge does not embrace collective needs such as education, city planning, rural preservation, the creation of a cultural environment – all these go by the board. They do not yield a greater demand for sales and are thus neglected. At the same time, the affluence of society produces a fundamental change in politics and weakens the opportunity of resolving problems. The great issues rallying the progressive parties, inequality and insecurity, lose their appeal. Left and Right are confronted and menaced by the same problem – that of assuring price stability without unemployment.

Public ownership

Public ownership would, to a considerable extent but by no means wholly, eliminate the motive for pushing production for its own sake. It would have another and hardly less important effect. One of the increasingly awkward problems of a private-enterprise, individualistic system – not merely in America but in all other countries, poor or rich – is the growing (and cleverly stimulated) resentment of (especially direct) taxation. This means that collective needs are difficult to satisfy, because they depend on taxation. But collective needs – for education, for town planning and rural preservation – are of increasing importance. And this ex-

---

[1]   Since this was written the pendulum, as usual, has swung to the other extreme, with employment and the environment (not to say Doomsday) suddenly becoming fashionable and respectable criteria.

pansion is vital to meet the challenge of the communist countries, where collective needs can be met by the profits of
state enterprise or the manipulation of prices.

Professor Galbraith hopes that he can eliminate this particular obstacle in the way of social balance in a free-enter-
prise democratic system by increasing indirect taxes. In this
he merely shows himself to be under the influence of his
American environment, in which agitation has been directed
almost exclusively against direct taxation. But in countries
where a greater proportion of the revenue is obtained through
indirect taxation, we have seen that large corporations wishing
to push their own product inflame their customers against
government policy by indicating how much tax there is in
the total price, and encouraging the consumer 'to write to
his Congressman', i.e. to put pressure on the government to
cut the indirect tax. Even general sales taxes have not been
exempt from this agitation.

Collective consumption

The difficulty of obtaining means for collective consumption
without taxation can only be solved when the public sector
becomes large and prosperous enough to be able to shoulder
an increasing part of the finance of what might be called
'amenity investments', while at the same time meeting its own
needs for maintenance and expansion. It seems clear to me
that balanced progress and stability cannot be achieved
without conscious direct controls, and especially without a
conscious income-distribution policy and a considerable extension of the public sector.

The whole theory of consumer demand is quite inapplicable to poor but quickly developing countries; it is inapplicable because neither needs not tastes can be assumed
as 'given'. The concentration on the consumer's sovereignty
is not less irrelevant, as Professor Galbraith seems to think,
but more irrelevant in that situation than in an affluent society.
Indeed, it is in a poor but rapidly progressing society that
the classical tenets apply least. The problem of the social cost
of change can be disregarded in such a society only at much
greater risk than in a rich and integrated one. Obsession with

'freedom for market forces' would cause far greater distortion and far greater waste of effort with far more ferociously unjust consequences, than in a rich country. Indeed, it might well imperil the whole development programme. After all, in these countries, development is superimposed on a mainly feudal system of land-tenure and agriculture in which the discrepancy between the wealthy and the poor is far more enormous, and where the conspicuous consumption of the former means an immediate impact on and weakening of the balance of payments, as the luxury goods which confer most prestige need to be imported.

Administrative manpower

Some people thought that all this could be remedied by fiscal measures, by a complicated system of taxation. I was always sceptical about this attitude, partly because it implied a disproportionate absorption of scarce skilled administrative manpower on a negative task, to enforce the tax laws. I was also sceptical because of the severe disincentive effect if luxury goods are taxed, and not entirely prohibited. I think it is easier to force people to save and invest by restricting the opportunities for spending than by taxing. In the event, I think my fears have been justified.

I still feel that unnecessary social exacerbation could be eliminated, and imitative competitive spending absorbing scarce resources prevented, if the import, and home production, of certain luxury consumer goods, especially durables, were altogether prohibited. But there is a second, and perhaps equally important, reason for a poorer country in the middle of rapid development controlling the pattern of imports and especially production for consumption. Tastes in these circumstances change quickly, and income and production might be expected to expand rapidly. The free sway of privately stimulated choice would, therefore, bring about the premature introduction of new consumer industries on too small a scale and thus lead to complete mis-investment from a long-run point of view. If new production starts when there is a limited market, it will start on the wrong scale, and eventual rationalization, with the introduction of competitive productive units, might be, if not impossible, extremely difficult. Under these conditions, the country would be condemned to the wrong-sized industry, to the oligopolistic co-existence of a number of wrong-sized units all too inefficient to be able to export.

If the establishment of industries were to be arranged consciously at a point where the scale of production to be started were more or less in harmony with the higher productivity which is eventually aimed at, the industrial competitive power of a poorer country might be revolutionized within a comparatively short period. It was fortunate from this point of view that textile industries have a relatively small optimum size. Otherwise, Japan and India might not have been able to compete, even on the basis of lower, starvation wages. This, unfortunately, is not the case with the industries of the future, heavy engineering, steel, electrical, and the like. The fact that the Chinese motor-vehicle industry, established by the Russians, is on a vastly larger scale than that in India, is as ominous a feature from the point of view of eventual competitive power as the thrust of Chinese agriculture, which has been accomplished by the tremendous compulsory effort towards co-operative investment. Quick achievement depends upon careful and deliberate planning of new products, and not upon their haphazard inception in accordance with the whims induced by foreign examples.

Consumption and investment

Last, but perhaps most important, in the absence of direct controls, reliance on the market will render the direct mobilization of resources impracticable. The large rural and even urban sector of the community that has been and still is suffering from unemployment or underemployment, always contained for poor countries a tantalizing potentiality for expansion. Yet mobilization for investment purposes was prevented by two seemingly insuperable obstacles. The increase in employment, consequent upon additional investment, increased the consumption both of the newly employed and of their families. The newly employed worker had to be paid, and the family which hitherto maintained him not only did not release the food but even increased its consumption. Moreover, an increase in wages of the already employed could not be prevented. The increase in total consumption turned the terms of trade in favour of the peasant and thus further increased his consumption. This, in its turn, limited deliveries to the towns by the rural areas and further accelerated wage demands. The consequential inflation necessarily endangered the investment process, because the increasing consumption prematurely pre-empted all resources available.

Self-help

The underdeveloped areas must do everything possible to help themselves in order to be able to match, without violent totalitarian methods, the efforts of the communist countries. Imports and production must be rationally and directly controlled. The exclusive concentration on highly elaborate machinery must be abandoned. There are some tasks for which high-powered machines are needed but, as the Chinese example shows, immense results can be obtained by the mobilization of idle manpower, without much capital equipment.

For a democratic country even to contemplate such a task a tremendous and conscious educative effort is the most imperative condition; only enlightenment and the conviction that the long-run interests of *all* demand sacrifices *by all*, would be able to stimulate on a voluntary basis what in China is 'organized' collectively.

Finally, powerful incentives must be given to ensure that the organization of co-operatives in the rural areas is rapidly extended, and so to prevent the scattered landownership from impeding the introduction of decisively improved agricultural techniques. In this respect, the Egyptian example shows that much can be done which will be voluntarily accepted, provided a lead is given. More compulsion will not work, as the Russian failure to increase agricultural production has demonstrated. Subsidies and taxes in appropriate doses might smooth the way if a really intense campaign is to be successful. Above all, however, both the rich and the poor countries of the non-communist world must realize the terrible urgency of rapid development away from peasant production and towards the establishment of modern industry and agriculture, if convulsions, and a possible catastrophe, are to be avoided.

Part Two
Agriculture, Education and Development

5

*Agriculture and Economic Development: The Role of Linked Public Works**

Even the most recent schemes or theoretical models of economic development tend to be based on the twin assumptions that the productivity of agriculture cannot be increased except by investment using resources obtained from outside, and conversely, that the pace of industrialization is in some sense dependent on the extent to which supplies can be extracted from agriculture and the agricultural population, helped only by this 'outside' investment.

Agriculture in most of the poor countries of the world is notoriously sluggish, if not completely stagnant. This, indeed, is the main reason for the primeval poverty, since agriculture accounts for the greater part — up to 80-85 per cent — of employment. The standard of life of the peasant is near or at starvation levels. There is thus, in this view, a double limitation on the pace of development, especially in democratic countries which, unlike the totalitarian systems, cannot exact the means of development from a poverty-stricken peasant.

A drastic reform of the taxation of the well-to-do urban classes is held to be one of the ways, if not the sole way, in which the deadlock could be broken.[1] In the absence of all-party agreement, however, this will be difficult to achieve in countries where political power depends on electoral success. The consequent failure is said to explain the ill-success in most underdeveloped areas of the world in starting self-sustained growth embracing the whole of the economy, and

---

* Reprinted from *Oxford Economic Papers*, February 1961.
[1] See, for example, the 'Introduction' of the Report, by Mr N. Kaldor, on Indian Tax Reform, p. 1.

not merely some small sector in which foreign capitalists are interested for the sake of supplying foreign markets.

The most important brake and limit on the potential expansion of productive activity in underdeveloped areas is represented by the defective operational framework of agriculture.[2] With few exceptions, represented by a few imaginative landlords in Spain and some of the French settlers in North Africa,[3] and a few, often foreign, enterprises in other countries, land, whether held in vast latifundia or broken smallholdings, is incapable of giving adequate returns.

The insufficiency of the agricultural framework may be due to a number of reasons and take various forms. Models of, or plans for, economic growth which do not take due account of the existence of these hindrances to economic development are likely to go awry even if, in Keynesian terms, 'savings' (including taxation) and investment seem to balance. *Institutional reforms* aimed at eliminating these hindrances, or at least modifying and improving the defective agricultural framework, and *direct controls* which can deal discriminatingly with certain acute bottlenecks, without having to cut income, would seem indispensable.

The great dormant potentialities of these improvements should be emphasized; they probably represent by far the most hopeful avenue of development, both in respect of the utilization of the vast idle manpower of all these countries and also as one of the most fruitful and productive ways of employing scarce capital resources.

In the case of the vast feudal or tribal landholdings, as exemplified from Spain and Morocco to Iraq, Persia or even farther east, landowners have no interest in improving the land. Their interest is to be able to derive an income with as little trouble from, and subject to as little fraud by, their tenants or farm workers as possible.

As Professor Dumont has conclusively demonstrated,[4] in such cases land reform, resulting in the breaking-up of

---

[2] See, for example, *Mediterranean Development Project, Interim Report*, FAO Rome, 1957, and chapter 1, above.

[3] These have since been expropriated; but see chapter 6, below, on the Green Revolution.

[4] See *Terres Vivantes*, Plon, Paris, 1961.

vast estates, far from being a mere welfare measure, is also necessary from a *purely economic point of view* in order to create the incentive by which to secure the improvement of the land and the more intensive cultivation of such small areas as remain to the estate owners, who will want to maintain their accustomed living standards. This is, however, prevented by the fact that the owner is content with his income, the magnitude of which depends not on efficiency but on inequality of ownership. In these cases again, the maintenance of the traditional system of land-tenure, and its very inequality, is the main obstacle to the full mobilization of resources.[5]

In those areas where the land is broken into small-holdings — among which India presents an especially difficult case — the problem is even harder to solve. The operational unit is unfit for much improvement in the technique of exploitation. The partitioning of ownership hinders improvements, as single owners are incapable of dealing with technical problems such as irrigation or drainage. The elimination of the larger feudal landlords left in being a vast agglomeration of smaller landlords, or even a hierarchy of landlords, often absentee. These 'landlords' or lease-owners, or even the owners of the 'superior' rights, might themselves be miserably poor.[6] Their ownership rights, together with social tradition (connected with religion), magnify the operational defects of the system. The existence of a large licensed and subsidized class of leisured poor, prevented by considerations of status or caste from working, renders economic mobilization difficult. The great number of these 'landlords-merchants-money-lenders' confers upon them an important voting power in a democratic system, magnified by their oppressive influence on the lower strata of the village

5 Traditionally, 'Western' economists seem to equate inequality and growth. See, for example, Professor Kindleberger's *Economic Development*, McGraw-Hill, New York, 1958, p. 225.
6 See V.M. Dandekar and G.J. Khundanpur, *Working of Bombay Tenancy Act, 1948*, Gokhale Institute, Poona, 1957. Their social superiority, however, has prevented effective land reform. Often they were able to get their tenants to renounce the new rights conferred on the cultivators. They frequently combine the function of landlord, merchant, and money-lender and exact an extortionate price for each.

society. It is this system of land-tenure and traditional behaviour which creates underemployment.

Finally, it should be added that in the absence of a large-scale reorganization, piecemeal attempts at improvement might not merely fail to be effective but might actually do more harm than good.[7]

The consequence of these deeply imbedded impediments, arising out of the traditional system of land tenure and social arrangements, is an immense amount of underemployment. It does not seem an exaggerated claim, therefore, that success in planning development for self-sustaining economic growth will depend mainly on the success achieved in mobilizing this reserve – practically the sole hidden asset of most under-developed areas. Given the overwhelming numerical pre-ponderance of that sector in the whole economy of such countries, a decisive increase in agricultural productivity could make all the difference. Failure in this sector would condemn the greatest success on the industrial front alone to relative ineffectiveness for long periods, as in Soviet Russia, in lifting average productivity and, hence, living standards. Foreign aid, invaluable as it may be, is no substitute for such effective mobilization. Indeed its value might consist mainly in per-mitting this mobilization to take effect over time, thus reducing the scope and severity of the compulsory measures needed for any given achievement.

The magnitude of the possible effect of a successful mobili-zation of idle manpower has been consistently under-estimated. This failure of appreciation has been mainly due to the assumptions about the shape which development pro-grammes ought to take. It has been implicitly assumed that development would, in the main, have to take the form of industrial growth aimed at absorbing the unemployed of the rural areas, of a removal of surplus labour from the land. Elaborate calculations were made, therefore, to determine how much 'true' underemployment existed. This was defined as that part of the labour force the removal of which would not affect output. Since primitive agriculture is highly

---

[7] This has been demonstrated by the indirect effects (salting) of irrigation systems and the social effects of the Green Revolution.

seasonal in character, this severely limits the availability of labour. In the context in which some of these calculations were made (e.g. by Professor Rosenstein-Rodan, for southern Italy), these assumptions were legitimate. Certainly, a reduction in the absolute numbers on the land, and not merely their proportion in total employment, is an essential part of the effort to increase national income. What is not justified is to assume that this is to be the main or sole means of rural improvement. Two considerations especially have been, I think, consistently neglected in shaping these programmes.[8]

The first point is that the demand for labour increases rapidly as agriculture becomes modernized on the basis of irrigation (unless large-scale mechanization is permitted[9]), while even after the removal of the 'true' underemployed the seasonal character of traditional agriculture would leave some one-third to one-half of the remaining labour force unemployed in time of slack. Thus productivity in agriculture would still remain so low and so inflexible as to render any development planning difficult, if not hopeless, because of the potential inflationary threat were a programme of expansion superimposed on this type of economic system.

The second consideration is that agriculture presents at one and the same time not merely an investment opportunity with exceedingly high marginal productivity, which is not utilized only because of the structural and institutional impediments to development, but one which could use manpower for labour-intensive methods of construction. Thus there is here a chance for the seasonal utilization of unemployed rural labour, the only reserve and, at the same time, the greatest curse of underemployed areas. In this way, fuller employment could be attained without incurring the extra cost of transportation and the necessary urban

---

[8] This neglect, however, has not been permitted to mar the programmes elaborated for the Mediterranean countries by FAO. See *Mediterranean Development Project, Interim Report*, FAO, Rome, 1957; *Final Report*, 1959.
[9] From this point of view some modern implements (e.g. tractors) facilitate a disproportionate increase in the extent or frequency of cultivation, and so do not necessarily result in the displacement of labour. Others (e.g. combine harvesters), on the contrary, do displace labour, thus strengthening the position of the large landowners and largish peasants. Even in India insufficient attention is being paid to these considerations.

rehousing investment which is so great an obstacle to national economic planning in these areas. At the same time, the capital investment in dams, irrigation canals, drainage, and roads would increase permanent employment opportunities and productivity.[10]

The problem was exhaustively discussed in the *Interim Report of the* FAO Mediterranean Development Project.[11] It was there concluded that development planning would have to be founded on the creation in strategic sectors of a 'creative imbalance', a new level of demand, while at the same time widening the basic bottleneck of agricultural production. In peasant and, even more, in tribal societies it is difficult to introduce far-reaching changes on a voluntary basis of popular participation, since the benefits of these are not apparent sufficiently soon to make their causal connection unmistakably evident. Yet it is obvious that the only way in which the large mass of idle manpower can effectively be used without scarce and costly implements (or other materials) is agricultural improvement.

In democratic countries, such direct mobilization of rural manpower, as has been practised for example in China, is hardly feasible. The only direct compulsion which could be contemplated is general service in the army, or in special labour corps for education, and the undertaking of investment. Even if no money were paid, such organization of labour would disrupt the connection between the individual and his rural base. This means that his maintenance would fall on the state, an appreciable burden which necessarily limits such direct methods outside the village or district framework.

An alternative would be to organize community development on the basis of a liability to contribute a number of days' service, from which individuals may free themselves by the payment of sufficient tax to maintain a worker in his

---

[10] The so-called Green Revolution has been successful in areas where the availability of water could be relied upon. Cf. K. Griffin, *The Green Revolution*, UNRISD, Geneva, 1972.

[11] *Op. cit.*, paras 111-2, 118-24. (As leader of the team which produced this Report, I must acknowledge my indebtedness, especially to Mr Ergas, Mr Holland and Professor Nagi.)

stead. In some countries the introduction of a poll tax might be easier, with the alternative of serving a number of days in work teams.[12]

Beyond such devices to utilize labour service, the mass of the population would have to be provided with appreciable immediate incentives, making them eager to try out new methods of rural organization and production. A drastic reform of obsolete land-tenure systems would also be necessary. As a minimum, the formation of productive co-operatives has to be envisaged.

The organization of co-operatives would facilitate the rational use of land and water, and the carrying through of infrastructure and agricultural investment. The story of the Ghezira scheme shows what can be accomplished through adequate organization, education, and leadership, in assimilating scientific methods and obtaining a substantial yield in an originally primitive environment within a relatively short period. The first requirement would be the training of inspectors to take charge of such co-operatives, since it is essential to give a new leadership in the villages, a leadership divorced from existing feudal or tribal restrictiveness. This has been shown to be far less time-consuming or educationally difficult than was thought even a short time ago.[13]

Resistance to innovation has been fierce. It might be overcome if the reorganization itself is made immediately attractive.

Two parallel lines of action would seem to be needed. The first is the organization of marketing boards so as to eliminate the usurious dealings of merchants. Land reform in a number of Asian countries (including some parts of India) came to naught because the landlord-merchant-money-lender remained in effective control of the peasant. As the West African marketing boards have shown, the most important function of a reform of marketing is to enable the peasant to receive something resembling the current consumer price for his

[12] See Introduction, above.
[13] There is little doubt that despite the shocking neglect of agricultural training colleges by the British and even the Indian government, there is more expertise at hand than is being made use of at present. Professional unemployment acts as a terrible deterrent to progress.

121

produce and not a price distorted by interest deductions or by deductions administered in view of possible seasonal fluctuations. The net effect on consumption of such an increase in peasant income would be slight since the landlord-merchant did not save much.

The second line of action is to assure the peasant some immediate increase in his income through the co-operative, but in such a way as to minimize inflationary dangers by increasing production. This could be achieved by *linking public works in infrastructure investment to rural reorganization schemes and by channelling paid employment through the new co-operative organization.* Thus membership of co-operatives could and would be made immediately profitable because peasants would only receive employment and income if they joined the co-operative.[14]

Most of the linked public works could, as in China, represent undertakings which require neither complicated implements nor materials. Wage rates need be no higher than the *average* income that peasants and landlords are deriving from their unreformed holdings. This, of course, would be far below the level of urban wage rates. This gap is one of the main reasons for the existing maldistribution of resources, causing an overconcentration on primary production by the creation of a wide divergence between social and private costs in industry to the detriment of the terms of trade and the average real productivity of the country.[15] Thus, the 'monetary' capital-output ratio in this type of public works would be even more favourable than it would be in 'real social' terms, because the money-wage costs would be far below those ruling in industry. Accordingly the threat of inflationary consequences would be less.

Another, hardly less important, argument strengthens this conclusion. There is in most of these countries a substantial unused productive capacity for handicraft or primitive industry, the products of which cannot compete qualitatively with

14 The organization of Egyptian co-operatives in the areas affected by land reform was compulsory. The grant of additional incentives might be wise.
15 See my article 'Welfare and Freer Trade', *Economic Journal*, March 1951, pp. 76-80, and, for an estimate of the degree of distortion, the two FAO *Country Reports on Iraq*, Rome, 1957 and 1959, for which I was responsible.

large-scale industry. Since public works could bring purchasing-power to the village population, which is not
accustomed to buying high-quality products, it would be
fairly simple to divert this purchasing-power towards these
products.[16] The argument that redistribution of purchasing-
power inevitably leads to an increase in demand and thus to a
worsening of the balance of payments is incorrect in a large
number of underdeveloped countries. Not only do the rich not
save much, if at all; their demand is concentrated on foreign
products and products with a high import-content. Redistribution towards the lower-income classes might actually
help rather than hinder the achievement of balance-of-
payments equilibrium.

Most of these public works can be suitably timed to coincide with the seasonal slack in rural areas. They can, therefore,
make use of workers who could not, without costly replacement in terms of machines, be utilized in industrial development. Moreover, the output created is a net gain in the
additional sense that it does not require large and costly
additions to urban capital, houses, water, and so on, for its
materialization.

A programme of public works could, moreover, help in
shifting the balance of development programmes in favour of
employment creation. This is the more essential, since it is
likely that, mainly for balance-of-payments reasons, the non-
rural part of the programme will have to be concentrated on
basic industries producing intermediate products and capital
goods which, for technical considerations, are likely to be
capital-intensive in the sense of providing relatively few
employment opportunities.

Rural reorganization, if linked with public works programmes, might be accepted with less resistance, since it
might help with the initial stages by assuring due compensation for old rights. Their being channelled through co-
operatives (together with the marginal increase in income)

16 Possibly in conjunction with the village-exchange scheme initiated by
Mr Sushil Dey. See S.K. Dey, *Industrial Development -- a New Approach*,
Calcutta, 1955; and *The Village Exchange – a Programme for Industrial Extension
in Western Bengal*, Development Department of the Government of West Bengal,
Calcutta, 1954.

might weaken the stranglehold of tribal or feudal relations which have in the past widely prevented – even in India – the effectiveness of community development schemes.[17] A new source of income placed in the hand of 'outsiders' might – as in the Ghezira and in some regions of Egypt – provide that loosening of the impediments to rural reform and progress which is essential if a new deal is to be introduced.

Linked public works programmes can thus fulfil an essential role in a plan for integrated development. They could be useful in helping to achieve social change without prior violence and subsequent compulsion. They might speed up development and reduce the danger of eventual failure when foreign aid is curtailed. Conversely, they probably represent one of the most effective uses of foreign aid. Together with technical assistance, they might become the main weapon in helping to eliminate the formidable food bottleneck which constricts expansion. They might provide the framework in which technical knowledge and administrative capacity can be infused into the countryside. Thus the development impulse given to the original industrial sector might receive an adequate and expansive response instead of either causing inflationary pressure and hoarding or slowly petering out. Given the inevitable acceleration in growth of population, they might make the difference between the success and failure of efforts to achieve reconstruction without revolution. A failure of rural reorganization, should Chinese reconstruction succeed, would spell an inevitable victory for the totalitarian approach.

It might be asked why such schemes have not been adopted when their advantages are so obvious. The answer to this question is not difficult. It lies partly in the resistance of vested interests, which feel menaced, and partly in the shortage of manpower to which leadership could be entrusted. These two factors, however important they may be, do not explain the extent of the failure. This cannot really be understood without recognizing that instead of *channelling foreign aid towards co-operatives, and insisting on their accelerated*

[17] See, for example, the *Report of the UN Committee on the Evaluation of Community Development Schemes*, FAO, New York, 1959, IND/31.

*organization, the administrators of foreign aid have resolutely
set their face against them.*

In some cases, the use of resources derived from foreign
(especially bilateral) aid in co-operatives has been prohibited,
instead of being made a condition of the grant. This discrimination is presumably due to the fact that the Soviet
Union also makes use of this form of agricultural organization. The difference of content is ignored because of the
similarity of form; and the resistance of vested interests,
instead of being combated by the foreign experts, is
strengthened.

Without a radical rethinking of the strategy and tactics of
international aid, it is difficult to avoid being pessimistic
about the chances of success in promoting self-sustained
growth in the non-Soviet world. The use of foreign resources
without reorganization will merely raise rural incomes temporarily but (as the case of Iraq prior to 1958 shows) will not
generate a multiple expansion in national income.[18] Once
disappointment sets in, and the flow of aid diminishes, little
permanent improvement will remain from the initial stimulus.
Change cannot be effected without the wholehearted co-
operation of the mass of the rural population.[19] Incidentally,
only co-operative organization and marketing can prevent an
increase in food production from generating an exactly
corresponding increase in income and, thus, from exerting an
increased demand on productive capacity.[20] There is an
urgent need for a reversal of the opposition by governments
in control of aid resources to the formation of co-operatives.

There can be no question whatever but that a decisive
increase in production would very much facilitate the extrac-

[18] This has been demonstrated in Iraq, despite the extremely favourable conditions for successful development: abundance of foreign income, water and land.
See the *Country Report for Iraq*, *op. cit.*
[19] It would be wrong, therefore, to think that a diversion from industrial towards
agricultural investment could bring about a radical improvement in production
without a basic reorganization. See, for example, the *Report on India's Food
Crisis and Steps to Meet It*, Ford Foundation Agricultural Team, 1959.
[20] But see above on the existence of unused capacity to meet an increase in
demand for simple goods.

tion of additional supplies.[21] The creation of sufficient collective (budgetary) saving must come as a by-product of the organization of increased production. It is one thing to restrict people's consumption, and quite a different one to prevent their consumption from rising exactly in proportion to their productivity. This goes for the urban as much as for the rural sector, for rich and poor alike.

In this connection, it should also be remembered that practically the only way in which rural supplies can be effectively mobilized is through co-operatives which can organize marketing and extract taxes simultaneously. Inasmuch as the cultivators at present are oppressed by extortionate marketing practices, the weight of the taxes might not be felt by them but by the displaced merchants whose activities benefit no one but themselves. Thus tax collection becomes a by-product of the drive for higher production, and skilled administrators are not wasted on purely negative tasks in this vital sector.

There is a large (and still growing) surplus in the West of practically all those products for which demand might be expected to rise in the intermediate period of reform and reconstruction, prior to the rise in production and the establishment of an effective organization to handle the increase in crops. This, providentially, facilitates the policy of linked works. Since rural reorganization would lead to a faster increase of output than could otherwise be contemplated, a more rapid use of foreign food supplies might be permissible. Thus a shock effect might be achieved, tempting rather than coercing peasants and 'landlords' to co-operate.

No illusions must be fostered as to the difficulties which would face any government in implementing a programme of organizing a co-operative increase in production through linked public works. Traditional behaviour patterns are stubborn. They are stiffened by the existence of vested interests desperately anxious to prevent a diminution of their privileges, however miserable the absolute level of existence

---

[21] Professor Galbraith's belief to the contrary (*The Affluent Society*, pp. 178-9 and 215) contradicts his own basic thesis, which I believe to be correct and important, that utility decreases as available supplies in general increase.

to which the system condemns even them. What might be claimed is that a 'linked' public works programme might sufficiently diminish resistance such as to enable the successful launching of rural reform. Without such reform it is very questionable whether the best efforts on the industrial front will not prove insufficient to bear the increasing burden of a fast-growing population. If persuasion and incentive do not work, compulsion, however repellent, will prove inevitable.

6

*Seed-Change in Development**

The sudden and extravagant swings in economic doctrinal fashion seem to take even the most hardened observers by surprise. In no field of economics has there been such a change as in that concerned with the development of the less privileged areas. We are now entering what has been proclaimed by the United Nations as the Second Development Decade, the very conception of which is a confession of failure. At the end of the 1950s all looked well on the way to success. Most experts at the time thought that the impulse given by the increased help of the fully industrialized countries would in the end solve the problem of poverty, much as Marshall Aid had dealt fully with a war-devastated and stricken Europe. Then, in the second half of the 1960s, an ever-deepening gloom spread. The population explosion was clearly overwhelming the expansion in harvests; and, as Mr Brown points out in the preface of his book, in 1966 the United States Department of Agriculture's Economic Service 'prepared its "1984 graph" which showed that the United States could continue to fill the widening gap [between food production and consumption] only until the end of 1984, after which the food needs in the hungry countries would

---

* Review of Gunnar Myrdal, *The Challenge of World Poverty*, Pantheon Books, New York and Allen Lane The Penguin Press, London, 1970; Report of the Commission on International Development, *Partners in Development*, Praeger Publishers, New York and Pall Mall Press, London, 1969; Lester B. Pearson, *The Crisis of Development*, Praeger Publishers, New York and Pall Mall Press, London, 1969; Lester R. Brown, *Seeds of Change*, Praeger Publishers, New York and Pall Mall Press, 1970. This chapter comprises an abridged version of a review article published in *The New York Times Book Review*, 19 July 1970, and a shortened version of an article entitled 'Pearson and Jackson', which appeared in *Venture*, January 1970. Lester Pearson died since this chapter was prepared.

exceed our capacity to respond. This doomsday date was arrived at by projecting historical trends under a series of conservative assumptions' (p. x).

The United States Department of Agriculture was not alone in making these dire predictions. The FAO projections were, if anything, more pessimistic and alarmist. The Development Decade, begun with such fanfares, was by 1966 said to be a failure. This judgement was mainly derived from the economic commentators' invariable custom of basing their analyses on (very uncertain) global figures, and their 'projections' on a few observations of the immediate past.[1] Naturally, in so far as India and south-east Asia figure very largely in the aggregates of development statistics, an unfavourable weather cycle in that area would have a very adverse (if totally spurious) effect on the measurement of global performance.

However premature, such views had serious repercussions. In that gloomy atmosphere the willingness to extend further aid was going sour. The governments of the donor countries were coming under severe pressure to cut back on aid, pressure that was not eased by Britain's balance-of-payments difficulties and the increasing weight of United States military expenditures. The donor governments, to ease their troubled consciences, pointed to the inefficiency and corruption in the recipient countries and to the inadequacies of the multilateral agencies. The defenders of aid, apart from falling back on general moral arguments, could only respond by showing that aid was well spent and that, in the end, we could hope for a better future. This, then, was the background to the appointment of numerous committees and commissions, both national and international, in most cases under the influence of the pro-aid lobbies. Especially the Pearson Commission, appointed by the World Bank, handled this essentially defen-

---

1 The most recent perpetrators of such mechanistic projection-mongering have been the latter-day prophets of environmental doom who, on the basis of allegedly dynamic computerized models, presume to predict complex global phenomena decades into the future without the slightest regard for social and political influences. See, for example, a recent study produced for the so-called Club of Rome by D.H. Meadows *et al.*, *The Limits of Growth*, Earth Island Ltd., London, 1972.

sive operation admirably.

In the last two or three years, however, a great change seems to have come over the Western international Establishment. The defensive tone has altered. Not only were there prospects of a complete turn-round in the production of food in the tropical and sub-tropical regions, but a potential check to the growth of population was also in the offing, and both in a way that appeared to be compatible with 'free enterprise' and individual initiative − or so it was thought. The contraceptive pill and coil were accepted in the best circles, and the new 'miracle' seeds seemed to be living up to their name. It was now thought that the less developed countries would be able to achieve self-sufficiency in food production, perhaps even becoming exporters, and that they were now on the way to common prosperity. Moreover, such prosperity, it could be argued, would ultimately repay the donor countries handsomely for their aid by providing their producers with new mass markets and, hence, all the benefits of increasing returns that this would entail. The optimists, one could say, were suddenly once more on the ascendant, although both on the Left and the Right − as so often happens *les extrêmes se touchent* − there is a school of thought which denies this possibility and decries the motives of deliberately helping the poor and weak on their way. Aid, they say, prevents the emergence of the new institutions needed for the effective transformation of primeval poverty and is therefore self-destructive. Let the market take over, say Chicago and the LSE. Let the underdeveloped governments plan, say the radicals of the Left, and lift themselves up by their own bootstraps. Fortunately such views have met with little success.[2]

The books under review taken together reflect the perplexity of the rich, mostly ex-colonial or economically dominant, countries as to how they should approach the complex problems of the poor, underdeveloped, Third World. On each is stamped the individuality of its author and, to some extent, the precise moment of writing. They give a

---

[2] Although the protagonists and propagandists of aid might find themselves ultimately stumped by the history of massacre, expulsion and cruelty, combined with incompetence and corruption which their opponents may bring to bear.

balanced commentary of the difficult problem of decision-
and policy-making at this vital juncture; but they are all
written in the belief that the fully-industrialized, privileged,
rich countries *should* help in fighting misery, disease,
ignorance and apathy.

Professor Myrdal's approach is breathlessly urgent, believing
as he does that, unless the social and economic institutions of
the Third World are changed, the introduction of modern
industrial techniques, with their promise of greater material
affluence and power, into the context of traditional societies
might result in vast convulsions and bloody revolution. On
the question of population, agriculture and education, he puts
forward an inter-linked, and certainly challenging, programme.
He realizes that without institutional reforms the new 'breakthroughs' will not help:

> Better seed grains can certainly not be a substitute for
> agrarian reform. . . . The spread of the use of new seed grains,
> as of other improved techniques, will not reach far without
> an agrarian reform. Indeed, without such reform, the
> availability of the new seed grains will join the other
> forces of reaction that are now tending to increase in-
> equality among the rural populations of the under-
> developed countries (p.125).

As to education, he demands sweeping reforms of the
school systems. Elitism, with its roots in colonial dominance,
must give way to a greater emphasis on adult education, and
to education that is fundamentally linked with the agrarian
programme. His approach to the population problem is convincing in its impatience and in the stress that he places on
the part which the poor countries themselves must play.

Much the most important aspect of his analysis, and his
greatest contribution, is in his treatment of what he calls 'the
Soft State', that is, the nepotism, the favouritism, the corruption, the unbridled self-seeking of the dominant class. He
ends this section with a passionate appeal to the Western
'donors' to support change, though he is as scathing in his
criticism of the way in which the developed countries have
discharged their responsibilities as he is of the failures
experienced for socio-political reasons in the recipient

countries. One wonders whether, on the basis of his analysis, any improvement is possible without a violent break.

I cannot share Professor Myrdal's disgust at the basically political (*raison d'état*) justification for aid. I do not think the Swedish record to be that good (0·5 per cent of GNP in 1968, as against 0·75 per cent in the (less affluent) UK and 0·66 per cent in the United States) even if the 'juggling' of aid statistics is taken into account, and certainly no grounds for adopting a holier-than-thou attitude. Nor do I believe tied loans to be 'bad'; if tied aid means more aid, why not tie? Should not the 'richer' among the poor in the end repay, so that aid to the poorest of the poor can grow faster? Withall, Professor Myrdal's is a great achievement; nonetheless I feel that he is being less than generous to those writers who shared his views, joined in his struggles and, ultimately, contributed substantially to his work.

The appointment of the Commission on International Development, under the chairmanship of the former prime minister of Canada, and winner of the Nobel Peace Prize, Mr Lester Pearson, came at a critical and pessimistic time in development politics. The mid-1960s were dominated by the spectre of famine, both as a result of the population explosion and of the ineffectiveness of aid, especially on the agricultural front; only with the help of American food supplies was this calamity averted. It was at this time that the President of the World Bank, Mr George Woods, thought of appointing a committee for the purpose of strengthening his hand. American aid was beginning to be affected by the Vietnam War. Germany, which had become the world's largest creditor nation, was hesitant about giving official aid; her contribution consisted mainly of private, mostly commercial, credits. And Britain's deepening economic difficulties added a further adverse element to the overall picture. The first important fact to appreciate, then, is that the Pearson Commission had to address themselves not merely to a hesitant, if not hostile, Congress, but also to a group of non-Anglo-Saxon contributors — Japan, Germany and France (herself under pressure), as well as the smaller, but intensely conservative, continentals, such as Holland and Belgium. Their purpose, manifestly, was to reassure the donor countries of the world that they did not participate in vain in the effort to reduce misery and poverty in the less developed countries by helping them along the road of development: a purpose, moreover, which they have triumphantly succeeded in achieving.

The Report of the Commission, *Partners in Development,* paints a rosy picture of the potentialities of aid. A neat analysis of the balance-of-payments implications of aid shows that an all-round, simultaneous, untying of aid would increase the value of aid to recipient countries, without burdening the balance of payments of any one contributor. The return on foreign aid is shown to be satisfactory. In particular, the food problem, which had been so acutely worrying in recent years, is, according to the Report, well on its way to solution as a result of the Green Revolution, whose continuance and widening scope are taken as read. If aid proper were increased to 0·7 per cent of the GNP of rich countries, and provided only that the population explosion can be controlled, a self-perpetuation of general world development, with beneficial consequences for rich and poor alike, could be taken for granted.

The origins of their appointment explain, at least partly, the Commission's unqualified enthusiasm for private investment. In their opinion it should be encouraged, because it brings to traditional societies the technical and managerial know-how so essential to structural change and the inculcation of new attitudes (in their turn an indispensable condition of progress). Yet, as I have demonstrated elsewhere,[3] the effect of private investment is often to distort the capital structure of the host country in such a way as artificially to favour the export of primary products and the import of manufactures. This follows from the fact that not only the transport system, but also the capital market, become mere channels for international trade rather than a means of fostering development by the integration and exploitation of the country's resources. On the contrary, the foreign-trade sector will face relatively low rates of interest in the capital market, while domestic entrepreneurial finance will be

3 See chapter 3, above.

expensive (20-25 per cent per annum), and peasant credit dearer still (50-120 per cent per annum).

They also explain their silence on the grave political problems — not least corruption — which have burgeoned in the recipient countries. The Commission rightly play down the waste of resources to which these will consequently give rise. But from the viewpoint of immediate politics they stress, quite rightly, the inefficiency and waste that arise from the deficiencies of the policies and institutions of the donor countries themselves; for example, the practice of tying aid; the refusal to shoulder local costs; the effect of annual budgeting without longer-term commitments; the absence of an international corps of technical assistance personnel with adequate career opportunities. (The problems of recruitment posed by the regulations in respect of national origin on UN-established staff are not discussed.) Finally, the Commission stress in their Report the hope that, on the basis of a further and larger effort, the problems of development can ultimately be solved. Multilateral aid, also, should take a more prominent part; and, in order to make it more effective, the Commission recommend that the United Nations call a conference of its 'family' of multilateral agencies with a view to securing a measure of co-ordination between their various activities.

In their desire to persuade conservative political opinion in the rich countries that the effort is all worthwhile, indeed that aid should be expanded (and if this is not possible, then at least liberalized), the Pearson Commission have taken on board a number of slender hopes. Much the most important of these is their faith in the so-called Green Revolution, the magic wand of investment in new seeds (and techniques) which, in their view, has completely transformed the outlook for the developing world.

Now there is no doubt that real advances have been made in a number of countries (the Philippines, Ceylon and Taiwan in rice; and parts of Pakistan, of India and the north of Mexico in wheat), but results so far have been extremely varied and patchy, both within and between countries. Additionally, it is likely to make for very awkward 'second generation' problems, as emphasized by President McNamara in his Address to the Governors of the World Bank in

Seed-Change in Development

September 1969; indeed, from the point of view of balance and strategic sense, this speech was far superior to the lengthy but 'discreet' disquisitions of the Pearson Commission.

In the best of circumstances it seems that the Green Revolution will mean progress for the technically advanced peasant with a large amount of land; also that there will be an incentive to maximize the *surplus* on the land, rather than the yield per acre, and with it total family consumption.[4] Should these developments result in a fall in rural employment, and if this were followed by a corresponding decline in the rate of expansion of industrial employment (because of parallel improvements in industrial efficiency), we should be faced with a revolutionary situation of the severest kind; and it would be the direct outcome of a failure to implement measures of social engineering and economic control.

The absence of social awareness is, perhaps, most patently demonstrated in the Commission's remarks on education and research. Like the responsible UN agencies, the Pearson Report calls, not for a reconsideration, but a broadening, of the conventional type of education. In this vital respect President McNamara has shown greater awareness. He wants to divert expenditure away from bricks and mortar; what is needed is a modification, not an uncritical transplantation, of modern agricultural (and industrial) knowledge into an environment of traditional primitive agriculture. A new strategy is needed, of which Pearson has no inkling.

It seems obvious that the Commission's sane recommendations in favour of more, and more liberalized, trade will not be heeded because they would impose burdens on the most sensitive and backward sections of the economies of the rich donor countries. Thus, here too, there would arise a conflict between those who wished to exert the maximum effort to change the present unsatisfactory position and those who, wishing to avert such conflict, wished to find a second-best solution. My feeling is that the Pearson Report's counsel of

4 This question is treated at greater length in two illuminating papers by Wolf Ladejinsky of the World Bank: 'The Green Revolution in Punjab – A Field Trip', *Economic and Political Weekly* (Review of Agriculture), June 1969, and 'Green Revolution in Bihar – The Kosi Area: A Field Trip', *ibid.*, September 1969.

perfection will be nugatory.

As countries become richer, it is right that new ones should enter the aid-giving process; but this procedure should take place gradually in an orderly fashion. This can only happen if countries below a certain level of *per capita* national income (say $400 per annum) are exempted from making contributions, while the rest are required to make contributions at a considerably higher rate (say 2 per cent of national income).

In his Leffingwell lectures, entitled *The Crisis of Development,* Pearson, coming 'hot-seated' from the chairmanship of the Commission, faithfully conveys the results and recommendations of the earlier Report. He emphasizes (p.80) that aid is a temporary phenomenon, but that the period for which it will be necessary depends on developments in international trade. He reaffirms the view of the Report that private investment in the less developed countries depends on the returns to it, but also on the encouragement that it receives, and that it could play an important, if not overwhelming, part in promoting development. Unlike Myrdal, Pearson has little to say about the serious problem of the rapid increase in technical progress, the agonizing effect of which is to reduce the value of the products of less developed countries. Also there is little mention of the problem of change in education and land tenure, except to acknowledge vaguely that some such problem really does exist. However, he reiterates what he regards as the Report's most important recommendation, that the President of the World Bank should organize a vast conference of the representatives of all the various multilateral and bilateral agencies and of the recipient countries in order to discuss the question of the co-ordination of aid through a Council. Obviously Pearson does not understand that, however charismatic its current president, the Bank, as it is presently constituted, i.e. as a bank, cannot possibly undertake this essentially political task. Moreover, he says nothing about the disturbing findings of the Jackson Report[5] as to the capacity of the United Nations agencies to

[5] Cf. *A Study of the Capacity of the United Nations Development System* (2 vols), United Nations, Geneva, 1969. See also chapter 12, below. (As somebody once said: 'The Bank is a bank is a bank.')

direct aid. The lecture mirrors the man, rich in honours and distinctions, a man who has contributed and is still contributing very greatly to the possibilities for development by showing that the really disturbing questions need not arise, if only we would all behave reasonably and show a little sensible goodwill.

As the Head of the International Development Service (the technical assistance arm of the United States Department of Agriculture), Mr Brown has been one of the pioneers of the Green Revolution. As such he must have shared in the gloom of his colleagues in the mid-1960s (see above). Now, however, he is an ardent believer in the Green Revolution, and in the market mechanism. The essence of his book is contained in the preface: 'This book tells the story of the turnaround on the food front. Its heroes are new high-yielding cereals and the men who developed them' (p. ix).

Mr Eugene Black, a former President of the World Bank and now Chairman of the Overseas Development Council, emphasizes in his well-balanced foreword to the book that there are 'alternatives open to us as a result of this historic breakthrough' (i.e. the development of new seed-strains). But he continues:

Skillfully handled in the seventies, the Green Revolution can become the vehicle for eliminating most of the malnutrition and hunger that now cripples half the people of this planet and for providing millions of new jobs in the countryside. Poorly managed, the new seeds and their associated technologies could displace millions in the countryside, forcing them into the already overcrowded cities (pp. vii-viii).

Mr Brown is less careful. Although he too discusses the social problems which poor countries face as a result of the introduction of alien technical advances, the multi-national giant 'agro-businesses', the large pastoral and agricultural companies using the newest methods, hold no terrors for him; nor does land reform. Indeed, he often slurs over some extremely difficult problems which are already worrying thoughtful people. His book abounds with curious and revealing contradictions. Interestingly enough, not a word is said about educational reform, nor on the establishment of co-operatives which, as in the case of the Ghezira scheme in Sudan, have achieved such breakthroughs. The disappointment of those exaggerated hopes for the First Development Decade may well be repeated in the Second if the powers-that-be fail to accept the need for more ruthless evaluation and thorough-going reform than has been the case hitherto.

Even if one tends to be depressed, and even exasperated, by Professor Myrdal's seminal work, one must yet hope that it is his, rather than Mr Brown's study, that will serve as a guide to politicians; for if they choose the easy road in the short run, the result will be more inequality and bitterness in the countryside and a fall in the absolute standard of living of the landless labourer and small peasant. And if this happens, the prospect must be faced of a Maoist-type of revolt in the rural areas — certainly in Asia and, possibly, also in Latin America — the force of which will moreover be overwhelming because of the widespread support that it will draw from the vast masses, despairing of a redemption that never came.

7

The Economics of Educational Planning
and Agrarian Progress in Developing
Countries: Sense and Nonsense*

THE DANGERS OF THE CONVENTIONAL
APPROACH

Creating self-sustaining growth

To a student of the development of ideas and policies, the
strange switch in the treatment of agriculture from neglect to
over-emphasis cannot come as a surprise. The only conscious
development planning that existed before the Second World
War had been of the Soviet Russian variety. The pattern of
Soviet planning had been predetermined by the political and
historical framework in which (so the leaders of the revolution thought) lay escape from general primitive poverty. Such
rudiments of industrialism as existed were foreign-owned and
-financed, foreign-managed, and foreign-inspired in technology. The spectacular Soviet success (to be emulated by
Japan, but following a different route) in emerging as a major
economic power, and in being able to increase the standard of
living of its population, contributed substantially to the
present conviction of the need for planning.

The implications of this were (and still are) momentous.
In the poor countries of the world, an overwhelming proportion of the population (as much as 85-90 per cent in Africa
and 78-80 per cent in Asia) depends for its livelihood on

* This chapter combines material first published under the title 'The Economics
of Education: Sense and Nonsense', *Comparative Education*, October 1964, and
evidence submitted to the Select Committee on Overseas Aid, March 1970.

agriculture. Any plan, therefore, which relies heavily on industrialization to solve the problem of poverty is, by this fact alone, doomed to failure. Rural misery will continue to increase without an urgent transformation in the basic strategy of development. The rigidity and lethargy of feudal agriculture, moreover, makes for a rapid exhaustion of food supplies as incomes increase, thus leading to inflation or to balance-of-payments crises, both of which vitiate any effort at improving living standards.

Unfortunately, from the point of view of conventional theory, the motivations and institutions of traditional agriculture necessarily appear 'perverse'. Agriculture will not fit into a model of marginal maximization, mobility and perfect competition, yet the basic attitudes of both feudal landlord and peasant nonetheless cannot be regarded as irrational within their given social framework. However, the 'creation of the atmosphere' required for 'individual initiative' to work its wonders would imply a complete revolution, not merely of property relations and other basic social institutions, but in attitudes (especially religious attitudes), and in technical knowledge: a change from classical to practical, adult education. The conventional approach, which would solve the problem of rural backwardness within a framework of market economics, begs the vital question: can the traditional primitive economies, in the midst of a population explosion, create (or be helped to create) the 'atmosphere conducive to self-sustained growth through individual initiative' before they are engulfed by political upheaval?

The technical and vocational approach

Development requires that the investment of resources and the application of new technical knowledge occur simultaneously. To be effective, technical knowledge must be introduced on a wide front; even a relatively small improvement can then be of decisive importance, while the highest standard of knowledge or training, if available only in a restricted area, will prove irrelevant from a global socio-economic viewpoint and be likely to create an exclusive and privileged class. Moreover, the cost of 'quality' *ipso facto* inhibits its widespread introduction into the educational system of poor countries. Successful development thus demands new socio-technical solutions in the field of agriculture, as in that of education.

The dangers of conventional education

Even ten years or so ago, the economic significance of education was almost completely neglected by conventional analysis. In recent years, however, an ever-swelling flood of orthodox economic literature has been devoted to just that theme. At the same time, though, a number of related misconceptions have become fashionable in the field of educational planning and policy which, while perhaps of little matter in fully developed countries where resources are abundant and some waste may be tolerated, may have pernicious consequences for less developed countries struggling with insufficient resources (including foreign aid), and under conditions of great difficulty, to achieve self-sustaining growth. Before setting out some of my own particular recommendations, it would be worthwhile perhaps to deal with some of these first.

THE MECHANISTIC FALLACY

Carefully directed social expenditure can have a much greater total effect (including all secondary effects) than types of expenditure which may result in some imposing visible structure, but whose effects on output in other sectors of the economy are zero or negative. Expenditures on the health, education and feeding of workers, on the provision of information, the creation of skills, etc. can raise output considerably, if properly directed and linked with improved equipment and appropriate institutional reforms. But these expenditures have for long been recalcitrant to theoretical treatment because:

(1) they are permissive, creating opportunities for output growth without being its sufficient condition;

(2) their direct output is often not easily measurable;

(3) their effects are widely diffused;

(4) their effects are spread over a long time;

(5) there exists no determinate functional relationship between inputs and outputs, partly because success is contingent on complementary measures;

(6) independent value, as well as instrumental value, is attached to both the initial expenditure and the resultant flow of satisfactions;

(7) considerations of 'deserved social rewards' enter into the determination of costs (e.g. teachers' salaries);

(8) they cut across the traditional distinction between investment and consumption (on which many growth theories are built), according to which a sacrifice in current consumption can make future consumption greater than it would otherwise have been;

(9) they are frequently correlated with other causes of higher productivity from which they are not easily separated.

Although many of these considerations apply, perhaps, to a lesser extent, also to expenditure on physical capital, they are more glaring when social expenditure is considered and, therefore, social expenditures have been, until recently, unpopular with model-builders. But the bias which emphasizes allegedly measurable, separable and determinate relationships to the neglect of other types is unwarranted. Actions about whose results it is possible to make only the vaguest guesses may be much more important than actions whose trivial effects are supposed to be precisely foreseeable. The challenge of estimating the returns on certain types of social expenditure has been accepted, but in the process of analysing them the same mistakes have been made which have vitiated the use of more traditional concepts and relations, both in analysis and in their application to development planning.

First, there is the belief that the contribution of 'investment in the human factor' can somehow or other be isolated in the process of historical growth, and that it can be assigned numerical magnitudes which can then be used for extrapolation for policy purposes. Such calculations of the impact of education on economic progress turn out, on closer inspection, to suffer from all the fallacies of which it is possible to be guilty in enquiries of this kind.

For one, they derive from a model of the economic system which is completely static in character. But worse than that, they assume a production function — of the Cobb-Douglas formula — which, even among all the inapplicable static models, is the least plausible. In this, national income is expressed as the product of capital, labour, and a 'residual', which stands for the 'human factor', including improved knowledge, improved health and skills; for better organization and management; for economies of scale; for external economies; for changes in the composition of output; and for whatever else is not explained by the increase in capital and labour. In this way, what is not caught under the head of 'capital' or 'labour' is attributed to the 'residual' element. The formula which they use thus *assumes* and does not empirically *ascertain* or *measure* the impact of the increase in capital or labour inputs (if one can measure the latter at all in a developing country) on output, that is, proportionality.

Some authors, such as Mr E.F. Denison,[1] for instance, assume in their calculations the existence of perfect competition, and then attribute a substantial proportion of the residual, 'unexplained', element in growth to the advantages of mass production: yet they must know that perfect competition can only prevail under conditions of increasing cost (as in the case of traditional agriculture with unchanging techniques), while mass production is so advantageous precisely because of economies of scale and the monopolistic or oligopolistic practices to which they conduce. Thus there is complete inconsistency in this treatment. And historically the assumption that the productivity of a factor of production, such as labour or capital, declines as its volume increases is just rubbish. The possibility that the relationship is different (and, of course, those authors who afterwards try to correct their results by assuming the impact of increasing returns to scale implicitly acknowledge this fact), or that it might be less easy mathematically to work with because of changes through time, is disposed of by dismissing or dis-

---

[1] Cf. E.F. Denison, *The Sources of Economic Growth in the United States and the Alternatives Before Us*, Committee for Economic Development, New York, 1962.

regarding it.

Yet, despite these objections, a systematic relationship between the volume of productive factors and output, implicit in the statistics, is then relentlessly calculated and, *from the assumptions it follows* that, if there is no fall in productivity or returns as the quantity of the respective factors of production is increased, this failure must be accounted for by some other 'residual' factor. This extraneous factor is once more dissected, in the same illicit fashion, into a systematic trend-like movement which is called technical progress, or increased knowledge, or what have you. The rest of the historically observed increase in output, the residual of the residuals that remains after all these operations, has lately been attributed to education.

The pitfalls and fallacies of this type of reasoning would be too obvious to need consideration, except that all over the world a whole school has grown up doing this exercise, and that policy recommendations have been based on it.

In the first place, as we have already said, the basic relationship between capital and labour and output has not been *demonstrated* on the basis of technological enquiries: it has been *postulated*. Therefore, the conclusion that a divergence from it must be accounted for by an improvement in knowledge or education amounts to no more than question-begging. Yet it should have been clear that the answer to the question 'What has been the contribution of factor X?' can only be found by answering the different question 'What would have been the case in the absence of factor X in the past?', or even '... had it been present in different amounts?', or, *horrible dictu* '... had it been of a different quality?' This last and most disturbing criticism is dismissed by assuming that *education is a homogeneous input.*[2]

In truth, we do not know exactly how education is related to technical progress, nor do we know how technical progress and investment are related. Nor, again, do we know why the relationship between the volume of capital and its yield varies so much from one country to another, and at different times within the same country. What we do know is that the

2 We shall return to that question below, pp. 150-5.

relationship has hardly ever been constant, and that only the least plausible explanations have as yet been offered.

It must be said, in all fairness, that most authors are rather coy when dealing with this problem, though not when putting forward vast schemes for research which, *a priori,* do not seem to have much sense. In their opening chapters, and again in their conclusions, they will not say outright that educational or technical progress *was* the cause of increasing production: they merely say that it was associated with that increase, or contributed to it.[3] When it comes to policy recommendations, however, or to demands for funds for further research projects, this scientific modesty is discarded and the qualifications disappear.

But even the more detailed and less assertive efforts seem to be obnoxious. It is quite illegitimate to claim that an educational system which, in the general cultural, political and economic framework of (say) the United States, was accompanied by a certain growth rate, will be accompanied by a similar growth rate elsewhere under totally different conditions. It is equally illegitimate to assume that, on the basis of these data alone, a *different growth rate* can be calculated for other countries by assuming constant parameters and substituting different variables for the educational effort. Such an education in the feudal aristocratic countries of South America, the ex-colonial aristocratic areas of British Africa, or the *littérateur* ex-colonial areas of French Africa, might not produce any growth at all. (This, again, is a question to which we will return in a later section.)

In short, then, the approach by which it is attempted to estimate the historical contribution of education to national prosperity, and hence to predict its possible future contribution by extrapolation, has no value at all — and this for the following reasons:

(1) It attributes a *residual element in the growth of output* to education by wholly illegitimate methods, simply because it cannot be explained by the increase in the other factors of

---

3 This is very much the same sort of quasi-cheating as that employed by monetarist economists, those who believe in the Quantity Theory, when they state that 'inflation is caused by *or at least associated with* increases in the volume of money', and then recommend the use of monetary policy as a panacea.

production. The very procedure begs the question: and the conclusions arrived at are both unproven and unprovable.

(2) It assumes, equally unwarrantably, that investment in education is not merely a cause, but the sole sufficient and necessary cause, responsible for the whole, or certain artificially selected portions, of the residual growth element experienced in certain historical cases.

(3) Finally, it assumes that this causal connection (which has been postulated and not proven) would not merely hold in a completely different context and historical setting, but would remain valid in an operational sense, i.e. is reversible.

It is an interesting fact that, in addition to all this, these models must assume throughout the existence of complete factor mobility, perfect competition and full employment. But in none of the various historical examples treated have these conditions in fact obtained: the economies analysed, indeed, have suffered from violent cyclical fluctuations. Thus, even if the approach did not suffer from its fatal logical flaws, the quantitative relationship which is the object of the exercise would obviously vary widely if estimated under conditions of differing degrees of imperfection or monetary disequilibrium in factor and product markets.

THE MYTH OF THE MARKET

Secondly, and perhaps even more misconceived, is the attempt to calculate the rate of return to the individual on capital invested in education. This has evolved, I suspect, for political motives, in order to substantiate a plea for *laissez-faire,* that is to say, to make education 'pay for itself', to abolish free education and to institute a system of loans to prospective students, to be paid back from the increase in their earnings as a result of their being educated.

There is in this plea a specious appeal to equity, specious because the sons of the rich would not be burdened by such obligations. These proposals are usually accompanied by suggestions that personal taxation be cut in order to sharpen incentives. Besides fallaciously mixing up necessary and sufficient conditions, and confusing causes and effects, these calculations seem also to assume that the *social and political framework* is a strictly *neutral* influence on the fate of the individuals which comprise it. Yet surely it must be suspected, at least *a priori,* that it might contribute to, if not wholly condition, the differentials between professional, skilled and unskilled remuneration.

Accordingly, differential remuneration is attributed purely to the difference in the cost of education (including earnings forgone), on the one hand, and the loss of experience due to not being in a job while receiving education, on the other. A sort of perfectly competitive educational opportunity system is imagined in which relative prices genuinely reflect relative social costs. The authors seem to forget that while differential education might be correlated with differentials in income it need not be their cause; they forget in this respect also the tremendous force of monopolistic factors.

This view of the world is fantastically misleading, even in a country like the United States, although there individual effort, if backed up by exceptional ability, might get people up the educational and professional ladder. It would be absurd to maintain, however, that equal opportunity is accorded to equal talent even there. In fact, from this point of view, the concentration of economic power has in recent times reduced, rather than increased, mobility. In the first instance, it can be shown that there are groups in America which are increasingly falling behind on the educational and social ladder, and that their falling behind can be attributed to the initial inequality in their own and their parents' incomes and that of the community in which they live. It has also been shown that equal education by no means provides equality of opportunity in getting jobs. In fact, even in the United States, it is the initial class situation of an individual that in the typical case decisively determines his career opportunity.[4]

Far worse, such calculations ignore both the indirect returns accruing to others besides the educated individual, and the direct non-financial returns to the individual. On the

4 These observations seem trite now that they have been fully borne out by the unrest in the Negro ghettoes and in the universities; they were, however, completely ignored by the Chicagoesque school of economics.

other hand, they pay a good deal of attention to income forgone during study, which constitutes a large proportion of the investment, presumably because it is calculable. But neither the income forgone by other groups in society (such as housewives, voluntary workers, people on some favoured occupations, e.g. in universities, accepting a lower income than they could get in other occupations), nor the nonfinancial benefits enjoyed during education are estimated.

Finally, since the returns have to be calculated over a lifetime, the *present* income differential between educated and less educated, if it can be attributed to differences in education, reflects the educational situation in the 1920s. It is, to say the least, doubtful, and ought to be doubtful even to the economists of the Chicago School, that the expansion of education advocated by them would have the same economic results in the future as can be observed for the past, in terms of increases in output accruing to the individual and the community. Especially in less developed countries, to which these calculations are being applied, the present pernicious income differentials should surely be attributed to the feudal or tribal ruling-class status of the educated, which is derived from exploitation and is incompatible with economic development, rather than to educational advantages supposedly conducive to such development. In those countries literates refuse to undertake, not merely manual labour, but also productive work of a technical nature.

But even in the United States it would be rash (apart from these objections) to try to establish a rate of return on the cost of education; and elsewhere all these problems are exaggerated by defects in the sociological framework, such as feudal-aristocratic, cultural or tribal restrictions on class mobility. Expenditure on education by families is highly correlated with the income and wealth of the parents, with ability and motivation, with educational opportunity vouchsafed by urban residence and proximity to educational centres. On the other hand, access to well-paid jobs is reserved for those with family connections. Much less could one maintain that professional differentials in England are dictated by free competition between individuals. They are determined by monopolistic restraints deeply embedded in society. The situation in ex-colonial territories, whether in Africa, Asia or Latin America, is far worse, and even in some Mediterranean countries there exists an almost impenetrable barrier between rural misery and the life of the capital cities. There the differential between urban and rural incomes might be as high as 1 to 4, or 1 to 5.

All that this shows, however, is not that there is a high return to education, but that the upper class have succeeded in clinging to an income scale which evolved during the colonial period and which is out of scale with the national average. In the civil services and universities, income levels, governed by the traditional standards of the feudal or expatriate colonial oligarchy, provide no clue as to the relative rates of investment in 'people': they reflect, not differences in actual productivity, usefulness, experience or knowledge between individuals, but the injustice of the system.

Under a colonial regime, moreover, the service administration had to recruit people from the metropolitan country. As a result they were forced to pay salaries commensurate with (but much higher than) income levels at home. This was tolerable so long as the function of the administration was merely to preserve law and order. In a 'night-watchman' state the numbers thus required were low and the burden of high salaries could be borne. However, it would be impossible to sustain an administration needed by a modern state on such an extravagant basis. Thus, all calculations as to the 'profitability of education' are not merely devoid of meaning or fallacious, they have a deeply immoral political implication.

But if this seems self-evident, why has it not had a deterrent effect on all these arithmetical manipulations? Partly it can be explained by their appeal to snobbery and to the self-esteem of the educated; also it appears to provide an economic justification for existing income differentials, thus buttressing vested interests and deterring reform. The creation of agricultural extension services or credit systems, the reorganization of the civil service, and the establishment of state corporations, all these are complex and difficult matters involving a change in attitudes and a reform of existing institutions. It would mean the erosion of privilege. How reassuring, then, and how simple that the econometricians should come along with their elegant mathematical models, isolating in their 'residual' variable all the complex conditions of progress, in this case 'the vast heavy investment which all countries undertake at all times in the development of their human resources'.

This (with heavy irony) is contrasted with my 'reactionary' designs for fobbing off the newly independent areas with a second-rate (or worse) system:

> Poor nations should not waste their resources on education; they should have only as much education as they could afford. At best, quantitatively they should not have more primary, secondary or higher education than was needed to run their public services. Qualitatively that system should be so devised, so cut, reduced, economized on and made into a multi-purpose hodge-podge seeming to serve all kinds of mutually contradictory purposes at the same time, that it cost the country and its resources the minimum possible, preferably nothing at all.[5]

PITFALLS IN EDUCATIONAL PLANNING

This brings us directly to the third fashionable fallacy in the treatment of the economic aspects of education, that is, the assumption that there exists some direct relationship between global expenditure on education and its total overall effects: that is to say, the assumption that education is homogeneous, a characteristic of mathematical approaches to educational planning which is especially pernicious in the context of poor, primitive, agricultural countries to which it has recently been applied.

Education is not a homogeneous input. This has been recognized in a rough and ready way by dividing it into consumption-educational and investment-educational expenditure. Unfortunately the division between these two classes is exceedingly difficult to draw and has often been done so in a manner which, to my mind, is entirely inconsistent with the true situation. In particular it has been assumed that

---

[5] Quoted from Dr M.S. Adiseshia, then Assistant (later Deputy) Director-General of UNESCO, at a UNA Conference in Cambridge, 1962.

certain types of education, the introduction or generalization of which has coincided with greatly accelerated development in Western Europe and North America, would do the same in other, differently situated countries, with different economic, social and political frameworks and institutions. There can be little doubt, however, that 'education', in the sense in which it is now propagated by 'educationists', would hardly lead to the kind of agricultural or industrial revolution which took place in Britain in the eighteenth or early nineteenth century. The vast industrial expansion in the United States at the end of the last century was based on illiterate European immigrants. In France and Germany, on the other hand, educational advance clearly preceded economic expansion. Yet mass education in these countries was the direct result of military preparedness, and not the consequence of deliberate economic expansion. In the contemporary world, Germany and Japan enjoy economic buoyancy. In neither country has expenditure on higher education — even in technical fields — been particularly striking. Moreover, the wide variations in the rate of growth of some countries when the 'educational input' was constant, and its decline, in Britain, for example, even when there was a considerable improvement in 'education', should have warned the black magicians of econometrics against basing their exercises on simple, hence mathematically attractive, assumptions.

This feature of the educational debate is the more pernicious, since there has been in all continents a tendency to imitate the educational institutions that have won a high reputation in Europe. The wave of European imperial domination which overwhelmed most of the world (including the Portuguese and Spanish domination of Latin America) carried its tradition with it. In the British sphere of influence it was the Oxbridge dilettante; in the French, the Sorbonne *littérateur* and the lawyer nurtured on Roman and classical law, who took pride of place in society and the administrative system. The Dutch and Luso-Iberian-dominated world followed a similar course, in which administrative careers were the only way to fame and wealth, unless one belonged to one of the great feudal land-owning or merchant-prince families.

Interestingly enough, it was the United States (followed to some extent by Australia) which consciously broke with this tradition. They not only smashed the feudal dominance of the colonial aristocracy, but by organizing intensive, practical education from the elementary level to the Land Grant College (which was non-classical in orientation), they created the basic agricultural excellence which eventually made possible their explosive industrial development. In contrast to this real revolution in land-tenure system and educational attitudes in the United States, the effect of postwar liberation from colonial rule (at least in those areas outside the Soviet orbit) has been largely to maintain the rural *status quo ante*, to create a new elite dominated by the classical humanitarian-liberal precepts of European culture and education, if, indeed, it has not actually confirmed or strengthened an existing elite in its position. Even those countries which managed to shake off colonial domination before the advent of the industrial revolution, such as the independent countries of Latin America, have nevertheless been influenced by, and have since faithfully assimilated, the legal and literary cultural traditions of their former mother country. There is the same disdain for technical education, the same neglect of agriculture, the same exaltation of what used to be called a liberal education.

The very assumption that education can be a homogeneous input is absurd. Teaching of a certain classical type might not only fail to produce positive results, it might even impede growth. Teaching *per se* can have no influence in the abstract unless those taught are given jobs and are not despised for their knowledge as tradesmen or technical experts. The isolation of education from other measures, and the aggregation of all types of education, obscures the kind of education needed for, or conducive to, development. Such an approach, in other words, as Mr Streeten has pointed out,[6] suffers from both illegitimate isolation and misplaced aggregation. What it

6   In a paper entitled 'The Use and Abuse of Models in Development Planning', delivered at a conference at Manchester University in April 1964 on the Teaching of Economic Development. See also a paper written in collaboration with Mr Streeten, 'The Coefficient of Ignorance', *Bulletin of the Oxford University Institute of Economics and Statistics*, May 1963.

amounts to, in effect, is that, by singling out some notional causative factor, assumed to be either the necessary and sufficient condition, or else a principal strategic ingredient, of development, policy-makers (or, strictly, their advisers) are absolved from having to specify precisely what type of education, combined with which other measures, is required. *But the wrong kind of education, unaccompanied by the proper complementary measures, can check or reverse the process of development.* An unemployable but educated class can be a cause of uncertainty and risk which is prejudicial to economic activity; young people brought up to despise manual work can reinforce any existing resistance to development. The same 'educational input', though it might have brought prosperity to the United States, if applied in a different framework, may lead not only to increased urban unemployment as a result of a refusal to work on farms or otherwise take on some kind of manual labour, but also, as we have seen, to the emergence of a ruling elite which gives the wrong advice and whose 'ideals' stand in the way of development. It can encourage ignorance of, and contempt for, the professional and technical qualifications which are a condition of economic development.

So insistent has been this emphasis on 'quality', however, and so meagre the attention given to quantity, that the closely restricted circles of 'culture' are quite irrelevant so far as the problems of the mass of population in these countries are concerned. Worse still, in the process of naturalizing the civil servants and the higher echelons of foreign private enterprises colonial nationalist movements, eager in their striving after equality, have poisoned the social structure in their own newly emergent nations, by extending to the new elites the very privileges that had been accorded to erstwhile expatriate colonial officials. This development is obviously quite incompatible with the legitimate aspiration of these countries for accelerated and balanced growth.

As a result of this insistence, however, it has been proposed that educational systems akin to those in Western Europe and North America should be established in Asia and Africa (although, oddly enough, the North American model would be less dangerous than that of Western Europe, for reasons which will be made clear later). Education is to be concentrated on literacy, and a full complement of secondary and higher education and research facilities is to be provided within an exceedingly short period of less than a score of years. This is to be accomplished in ways which are familiar to us in Europe.[7]

The building programme implied by these educational dreams would absorb a large part of current investment capacity, even if foreign aid were to increase sharply. Salaries, as they are contemplated, are obviously more akin to professional salaries in high-income countries than anything which could be accommodated in Africa or elsewhere on the basis of a primitive agricultural sector. If, for instance, we in Britain were to pay our school-teachers in the same relation to the average level of income as is suggested in some of the proposals for Africa, their salaries would be between £5,000 and £6,000 a year (1957 values). On the same basis, the capital cost of a place in an English university would be £50,000 compared with the actual figure of £2,500 to £3,000. The nonsense of this approach is obvious as soon as the comparison is made.[8]

The crucial point in this type of approach is that it does not pay the slightest attention to the need for balanced development. It will prove impossible to increase educational expenditures in this way (even if it were desirable, which is far from proven) and yet still have sufficient resources left over to devote to directly productive investment for the acceleration of economic growth. Yet without this growth, educational progress will produce a discontented, unemployable class of young desperadoes just waiting to be led into violence. Welfare and administrative services must not pre-

[7] In fact plans such as have been put forward for these countries have been implemented by the French under the Constantine Plan in Algeria, including lovely prefabricated school buildings, institutions for nuclear research, etc. The result has been the rise of a prosperous new elite, combined with horrendous open unemployment, and an even more horrendous degree of rural underemployment.
[8] Cf. T. Balogh, 'Britain and the Dependent Commonwealth', in A.C. Jones (ed.), *New Fabian Colonial Essays*, The Hogarth Press, London, 1959, and 'Misconceived Educational Programmes in Africa', *Universities Quarterly*, June 1962.

empt resources potentially available for development; indeed, it will be self-defeating if they do, for the consequent failure of economic development will push everybody towards complete totalitarian mobilization.

THE CONSEQUENCES OF PREMATURE INDUSTRIALIZATION

A second important feature of many development programmes which it would be well to mention at this point, since it has direct implications for agricultural and educational reform, is their reliance on industrialization. Bearing in mind the unspeakable wretchedness of rural conditions, and the enormously higher incomes available in the towns, it is inevitable that there will be a flight from the countryside. Faced with the resulting problems of urbanization and urban squalor and misery, it is understandable that governments should try to relieve the situation by planning for accelerated industrialization at any cost.

Two points may be raised here. First, even if such industrialization were as successful as that in England and America in the nineteenth, or in Russia and China in the twentieth century, which, because of the greater handicaps and the relative scarcity of natural resources, is not at all likely, it would not be possible to absorb even the increase in population into industry. It seems, then, that we must expect the rural population in these countries to expand indefinitely in the foreseeable future. Secondly, premature industrialization on the basis of small productive units, such as have already been established, would permanently cripple any effort to raise living standards towards European levels. It follows, then, that any hope of an alleviation of rural misery must rest with a revitalization of the countryside, especially with an evolutionary improvement in food production and nutritional habits. The old Africa of the jungle and of wild life, for instance, so prized by some well-meaning do-gooders, cannot possibly provide a decent life for men and women. The exciting and hopeful thing is that the physical possibilities for such a transformation are stupendous. Agricultural backwardness, however, can only be overcome by creating the conditions with which to facilitate the transmission and application of technical knowledge. In the planning of educational progress, therefore, and to re-emphasize the point, it is of paramount importance to overcome the immense prejudice in favour of formal, classical education and to replace it with a system which is in conformity with modern requirements. To this problem we now turn.

PLANNING A NEW APPROACH

What, then, should be the new approach to education in the less developed countries? First, it must transform the primitive agricultural sector; secondly, it must be integrated into community life and thus avert the serious danger of creating an artificial and power-hungry elite apeing an expatriate way of life which it is beyond the country's means to sustain; thirdly, and consequently, education must supply the technical and administrative cadres needed to develop the country; and, perhaps most important, fourthly, the cost of education must not be so crushing as to preclude its harmonious integration into a viable plan for general development. In what follows I shall restrict myself to the problem of rural education, partly because of the importance of agriculture for the welfare of the population, and partly because it is least understood.[9]

A balanced programme must give the highest priority to general education and to training for rural advancement. The provision of technical knowledge, both in the rural areas and for a programme of urban industrialization, must be orientated from this basic standpoint. Fortunately the possibilities in this respect are immense.

Education must be made part and parcel of a general campaign for rural renascence, and as such must be integrated with a purposeful mobilization of the one great asset that

9 A brilliant exception to this is M. René Dumont, to whose intrepid work in this field I owe much. See R. Dumont, *False Start in Africa*, André Deutsch, London, 1966 (first published in French as *L'Afrique Noire est Mal Partie*, Editions du Seuil, Paris, 1962).

these countries possess, their enormous reserve of available manpower during the slack seasons on the land. If the people themselves, under expert guidance, build their own educational system, and 'pay for it' — but in a very different sense from what is traditionally meant — this will enhance the esteem in which the new facilities will be held, and a large step will have been taken in the general social and economic development of the country.

However, the problem of the attitude of teachers and educationists to technical and vocational training does not end here. The connection which grew up between the universities and research institutions in Africa, for instance, and their metropolitan counterparts, together with the understandable ambition of research workers and teachers eventually to obtain employment in their own country, further strengthen this anti-technical and anti-vocational bias in the social and educational system. A person doing practical work aimed at solving some of his country's particular problems will have found that, by so doing, he had not necessarily improved his prospects of promotion in his profession: in order to gain recognition, he will first have had to apply himself to the task of proving his excellence as a pure scientist. As a result of this, in Africa, *academic* research work, such as it was, and much of the research done in the metropolitan countries (in sharp contrast to the example of nineteenth-century America and twentieth-century Australia) became largely irrelevant from the point of view of the African territories. So far as the numerous research institutes were concerned (especially those in the British African territories), their work was concentrated mainly on cash crops, according to their importance for the mother country, to the startling neglect of food crops which were of primary importance to the indigenous population. Yet, even so, in many cases, the results of all this research work were not made available to the local people, but rather regarded as the fruits of academic endeavour *per se*. Consequently, a great deal of knowledge has been stored up waiting to be used; as such a reorientation of research might help in gathering it together into a more appropriate relationship to the present needs of the new emergent states.

Elementary education

At the elementary level, it must be the aim of education to impart to the youth of the countryside directly, available technical knowledge which will enable them to increase production. Quite simple agricultural improvements could double output in vast areas within five years — such as weeding, the elimination of so-called shelter trees, sowing at the right time, the application of fertilizers, the use of improved seeds and their better handling — while nutrition, convincingly demonstrated rather than discussed in the abstract, could give a palpable incentive for increasing output and raising living standards.

Above all, the aid of elementary education must be directed at increasing the prestige attaching to agricultural work so ceasing to alienate pupils from their environment and rendering them fit for the purpose for which education ought to be dedicated, namely the enhancement of rural welfare. Such education, therefore, must go hand in hand with the adaptation of the rural framework and pattern of life toward greater productivity. Since, at the same time, it is essential that too large a proportion of the country's available scarce resources should not be diverted from their other needs, these requirements should be met to as great an extent as possible by making use of its single most plentiful resource, the immense reserve of underemployed rural workers.

The rural elementary school must thus become the centre of this renascence in the countryside. As such it should be integrated with agricultural extension services and model farms. Rural sciences, such as elementary biology, soil chemistry and soil technology, the use of implements and crop management must be given an increasingly important place in the curriculum. Teaching, moreover, should be followed up by doing. It is not only essential that schools should have some land attached to them, so that children may be trained in more effective methods of production without being for one moment divorced from their original milieu, but that, in view of the overall economic problems facing such countries, the schools should become more or less self-supporting, hence diminishing the drain of general resources.

At present, elementary education follows closely the European pattern. It starts at the age of six or seven and continues, in principle, for four to five years. There is no reason whatever why this obsolete pattern should be perpetuated. Education should begin when the pupil is likely to be at his most receptive age from the viewpoint of learning and when he can contribute positively to the work of the model school farms. At the same time, however, facilities should be provided so that talented children may be able to continue their education at a higher and formal level with the help of scholarships.

At the physical level, the school buildings and the teachers' residences should be constructed by the villagers themselves, with some assistance from the central government in the shape of modern building materials.[10] This ought to enhance their value in local eyes, and at the same time save on national resources. It should be emphasized, however, that these buildings should conform to the new *national* character of the teaching service, which will be in sharp contrast to the metropolitan standards of the pre-independence educational system. But if teachers' salaries are to be attractive to the large number of able and ambitious young men that will be required, capable of giving effective, even revolutionary, leadership to the rural communities, and yet not be out of all proportion with the average national income, then other non-material incentives will have to be provided, for instance the possibility of promotion within the regular civil service.[11]

Extension work and co-operatives

The accent on a self-sustaining form of elementary education directed at raising productivity on the land must be paralleled by the training of adolescents and adults above traditional school age, the success of which will ultimately determine whether or not the developing countries can raise their standard of living towards a level comparable to that of the

[10] But to be used in a technically suitable manner, e.g. pressed cement-mud bricks.
[11] Many of these concepts have been evolved and to some extent put into practice by President Nyerere of Tanzania.

highly developed areas. The institutional framework envisaged here is that of the co-operative, for without co-operatives, which make possible the application of modern techniques and the servicing of individual members both with implements and economic (e.g. marketing and credit) facilities, the necessary increases in productivity and income will not be forthcoming. Yet, if co-operative endeavour is to succeed within the old framework of the extended family, or village, ownership (as in Africa), or minifundia (as in Latin America), a new spirit and new incentives will have to be inculcated. This will call for self-discipline and a capacity for sacrifice; fortunately this can be shown to be to everyone's benefit, and within a measurable time.

As at the elementary level, the rural school must be at the centre of this effort to improve agricultural productivity among the older people. The manpower required for this rejuvenation of the countryside is in gravely short supply and if it is to be fully utilized the schools' activities should incorporate also adult education and especially extension work. If, as we have mentioned, the basic operational unit of an improved and more efficient agricultural sector is to be the extended family or village holding, thus harnessing traditional authority and the old legal framework to a new purpose, the extension service must be brought into every village.

It is a question of organizational convenience, not principle, whether monitors or extension officers at the village level should be trained as teachers, or the other way round. At present (and for some time to come), even the application of very simple improvements in productive techniques would produce considerable results. There is no need to teach complicated things, hence it is unnecessary to establish elaborate training schemes for extension workers or to demand a very high standard of technical proficiency. This is a matter for the more distant future: what matters now is enthusiasm and leadership. Agricultural extension services should be reorganized and staffed not by 'technicians' afraid of using their hands, but by educators working side by side with the peasants. The extension workers should first concentrate on the extension farm and on the holdings of the most enterprising farmers. As soon as incomes have been seen to increase there, the peasants' instinctive distrust will be attenuated.[12]

Adult education should also be organized around the task of improving the general welfare of the villages, preferably in conjunction with community development schemes such as rural public works; part of the work on such schemes could be paid for in wages, the rest being construed as offered in lieu of a cash payment of a rural improvement tax. Personal interest should be engaged by giving people good opportunities to partake in the execution of public works and by offering them the incentive of training for better (and possibly paid) positions.

There should be the closest consultation with each rural community in deciding on local improvement schemes, which should, if possible, be weighted in favour of quick-yielding projects such as access roads, small dams, etc. and not merely amenities. Once the local decision has been taken, however, its execution would have to be ensured through the taxation system of the state or local authority. Every member of the local community, moreover, would be required to make some contribution, either in terms of money or labour. But the money-value of labour should be set high, so as to encourage contributions in that form and, again, to help in reducing prejudice against manual labour. Twenty or thirty days' annual contribution to the rebuilding of one's country is a small price to pay (provided the plans are well-conceived) when the work-year is less than two hundred (and often less than 150) days. Unfortunately, past experiences in this field are a terrible psychological hindrance. All such schemes based on direct contributions bear a fatal (if superficial) resemblance to the forced labour of the colonial past (especially in the Belgian and Portuguese, and some British, territories).

The more foreign help is available, the more can governments rely on incentives. But where traditional ways of life stand in the way of progress they must be weakened, if not altogether eliminated, if reconstruction is to be achieved. It

---

12 I tried to organize this in Algeria, but my efforts were in vain. In the end an agricultural university and colleges were set up at great expense. The impact on productivity was minimal.

would be unforgivable if all social forces were not used to promote progress because of an unjustifiable reluctance to use compulsion when necessary. This problem cannot be evaded by reciting unctious platitudes about democracy.

Failure in this field would retard rural renascence, and there is no time for delay; indeed, the increase in population, the exhaustion of natural resources, and the heightening of expectations make it all the more dangerous. Special care must be taken, however, to provide safeguards, such that the population at large may call to account those who exercise traditional or newly-created authority in rural life. In Africa, for instance, it is the irresponsibility of authority, and therefore the danger of abuse and self-perpetuating power, that is so objectionable in the present system of social compulsion.

Creating the technical cadres

The third important and necessary characteristic of this new educational programme is that it should be so conceived that both the new administrative, technical and teaching cadres and the general educational system should concentrate on producing a framework in which co-operative, communal work can flourish, and so increase productivity. This demands a basic reorientation of educational policy, since until recently training and education were undertaken on a selective basis which did not always favour the most efficient solution to the problem of advancing mass rural welfare. As a result, there have been started a number of very ambitious schemes which, though extremely costly, have had little, if any, impact on the life of the population as a whole. This is not merely so in the case of the existing organs of higher education, but also of rural settlement schemes, the cost of which has been so heavy as to preclude their general implementation.

This new orientation in educational policy must involve a close linking of general educational advance with rural change and with the modernization of agricultural production through a more intimate collaboration with agricultural extension, marketing and credit services. Such an approach in turn requires a reorganization of the administrative hierarchy and a modification of salary scales such as to favour technicians working in rural areas.

Not only this. This new concept of the role of education, as we have seen, implies a huge increase in the need for teachers-cum-agricultrual monitors. In Africa, the target should be at least one to every two thousand families with a monitor-teacher in each village. If a crash programme were to be planned, every district would require a camp-institute for the purpose, each one again operating largely on a self-supporting basis. Subsequently, as the supply of specialized teachers grew, it would be possible to entrust the extension work and elementary education to the higher echelons, though without weakening their close relationship with the field.

Centres for higher education and specialized research should be regionally based, bearing in mind that (as, for instance, in Africa) political boundaries cut across regions with similar natural conditions and problems in terms of climate, soil and water resources. The establishment of such common teaching and research institutions should promote the feeling of national and continental unity, so indispensable to future progress. But it is essential too that these services themselves maintain a certain unity. Also the need for a practical and technical bias in higher education must be stressed, and attention called to the ineffectualness to date of such reports as have emphasized this need in the past. Moreover, adequate attention has not been paid to the middle echelons who are, after all, the indispensable agents in the popularization and implementation of innovations in rural, and indeed urban, life.

EDUCATIONAL PLANNING

This brings me finally to the problem of educational planning. Does my criticism of the random methods hitherto adopted by over-eager, or perhaps just naive, econometricians and mathematical economists add up to a complete repudiation of all quantitative analysis? Nothing could be further from my mind. Qualitative meditation without the discipline of quantification would certainly not produce an acceptable alternative to the approach that I am criticizing. It is in fact this sort of humanistic-*littérateur* attitude which has resulted in the present dearth of technical talent in many European countries, but even more so in the (former) colonies which were in their charge. In view of the long gestation period in education we must try to plan ahead in some detail. The need for quantitative planning, over extended periods into the future, is inescapable.

In my opinion, educational long-term, perspective planning must proceed from the basis of a fairly detailed plan for socio-economic development; it cannot simply start from some arbitrary global hypothesis concerning the relationship between educational input and some ultimate product, with education assumed to be homogeneous within each stage of the educational structure, while each of these stages is taken to differ from another only in respect of its quantitative relation to global 'progress'.

(1) First, such a perspective plan must comprise a serious politico-sociological study of the problem as to how and to what extent traditional educational patterns have contributed to the failure of social and economic progress in the past. Such a study should form the essential basis of all educational planning. It must discover whether attitudes hostile to economic progress have resulted from a particular educational structure, and what modifications to the structure would be needed in order to foster a more positive approach to the technical requirements for such progress. I have already referred to the disdain for technical education. So long as the civil service and those appointments which it influences and controls are the preserve of the non-technically educated, the most able talents will continue to be diverted into non-technical kinds of education. The effect of this will be both to justify and reinforce the initial disdain and to make economic and social progress even more difficult, since the first-class technicians will just not be coming forward. Such real talent as is available will have a 'general' education and settle down in the capital city to a nice administrative job in the government — and mismanage the country.

The purpose of such a politico-sociological study will be to facilitate the planning of a new educational structure such as will accord adequate status to those qualities in the educated elite which are appropriate to the technical requirements of accelerated progress; at the same time such a reform in the choice of elite should attract the best talents by affording it sufficient scope to prove itself and for advancement.

(2) Secondly, educational long-term, perspective planning must be complemented by an idea of the desired pattern of economic development. On account of the great length of the period involved in educational preparation (and in this I fully agree with Professor Tinbergen), a perspective plan should have a horizon of at least twenty to twenty-five years.

I do not think that technical shortcuts such as, for example, the methods advocated by Professor Chenery[13] will be of much use in this respect, but they are certainly far better than Professor Tinbergen's approach of simply writing down an arbitrary equation. Professor Chenery proposes that planning should be based on the assumption that the distribution of manpower among different occupations at each stage of economic development is identical or closely similar as between different countries. However, such an approach neglects the fact that past experience can be drawn upon only in the case of those countries which have elicited *spontaneous* growth (or its failure). It is wrong, or at least illegitimate, to assume that this experience would be applicable to countries making *deliberate* efforts to *accelerate* growth. Moreover, can such efforts be successful if plans are not adapted to overcoming the *specific difficulties* responsible for the failure of growth in different countries? Such hindrances are likely to *differ* widely from country to country, while those which have shown progress in the past have shown success in a few sectors for broadly *similar* reasons. For these reasons I would be very sceptical as to the legitimacy of Professor Chenery's method.

Far more promising is the approach adopted by Mr Pitambar Pant of the Indian Planning Commission and by Mr Dhusis (in 1962-3) of the Greek Ministry of Co-ordination: that is, of drawing up a long-term perspective plan for industrial development and of then seeing (on the basis of

13 H.B. Chenery, 'Patterns of Industrial Growth', *American Economic Review*, September 1960.

current experience) what detailed categories of education and training, and in what quantities, are needed to meet the requirements of the expanding industrial and agricultural sectors. Even then, present trends may be misleading on account of the speed with which technical change occurs.

As we have stressed, however, the sociological barriers in the way of changing attitudes are very strong and will take a long time to overcome. Not only will this make for a detailed list of educational and training requirements; the educational effort will also involve a great deal of expense, in the sense that, at each stage of economic development the educational system required for the *following* stage, or even subsequent stages, will have to be supported out of current resources. For this reason, educational planning will have to be extremely conservative and cost-conscious, unless technical assistance can be expanded at a much faster rate than now seems likely. But such conservative advice is difficult both to accept and to implement, because politically very unpopular; indeed, in many parts of the world it would also be suspect for reasons of racial discrimination. It is, therefore, necessary that appropriate efforts be made to dispel such prejudice as there is against the adoption of a balanced educational programme within the context of a balanced overall plan for economic and social development, preferably on a regional, multi-country, basis (e.g. West Africa).

I do not underestimate the difficulties involved in such a new approach. The present state of affairs is geared to the entrenchment of privilege, and this, together with the whole historical framework, including current social and political trends, militates against its reconsideration.[14]

[14] The present organization of the multilateral specialized agencies is a further grave handicap (see chapter 12, below).

Part Three
International Aspects

8

Aid versus Trade[*]

THE RELATION OF TRADE TO AID

There is a general agreement on the need to reduce the gross inequality in the international distribution of income and also, I take it, about the undeniable fact that this inequality has been increasing, despite a growing volume of aid in terms of technical assistance and resources, not least because of the worsening of the terms of trade between primary goods and manufactures. It is this latter problem with which we are concerned here.

If trade is viewed from this angle, it cannot be treated independently of the whole complex problem of the relationship between rich fully developed and poor developing countries, i.e. separately from foreign aid. Fully developed areas cannot be expected to deal separately with questions which are closely interrelated and which affect jointly their international position and domestic situation.

Conversely, even if the proximate cause of the relative (and, in many cases, even absolute) worsening of the position of the poor countries has been the deterioration in their terms of trade, it does not follow that their improvement is the only or even the optimal way of reversing this misfortune. After all, development in the primary-producing areas has not been at all satisfactory when the terms of trade were more favourable, and it has to be shown both that their improvement would be better utilized *and* that the burden of

* Paper submitted to the United Nations Conference on Trade and Development, Geneva, 1964 under the heading 'Expansion of International Trade and its Significance for Economic Development', E/CONF 46/P/3 (contributed paper 3), 24 January 1964.

the improvement would be distributed in a satisfactory manner. I shall contend that in neither respect is the outlook favourable, and that the improvement of the terms of trade is not the best way of securing international economic equity.

Admittedly, within certain limits, trade questions can be divorced from the question of total redistribution from the rich to the poor areas; but we are not here talking about marginal variations in specific trade, either in volume or in value terms, but about *grosso modo* changes in the balance of payments big enough to affect the rate of development and economic health of the poorer developing countries. At this level, obviously, a sharp division between trade and aid can no longer be made, and I shall contend that an increase in aid, if well administered and justly distributed, is preferable to the same increase in purchasing power of poor countries brought about through a deliberate improvement in the terms of trade.

In order to secure the political acceptability of the greatest possible degree of redistribution of income from the rich to the poor, and thus reverse the present drift towards increased inequality in the international distribution of income, it would seem essential to ensure that the proposed instruments should operate in an equitable manner. Without that, a new approach to the relationship between nations is hardly likely to be achieved, except on the basis of immediate short-run political considerations (e.g. the Cold War), the persistence of which would be uncertain. In any case, such considerations can hardly be assumed to provide a strong enough moral basis for a sustained effort; and only a sustained effort is likely to achieve the aim, since the poorer areas are menaced by a torrential increase in population.

In the first place, the total amount of aid given to any one country would have to be closely related to need.

The importance of this can be stressed in the light of the unfortunate political effects of the aid generously given to Asiatic countries. In consequence of the openly political motivation in the distribution of this aid, the succour given to notorious dictators impaired the political impact of aid elsewhere, even when given in the most altruistic spirit.

It is equally essential that the burden should fall with

obvious equity on the contributing areas. Any attempt to lay the burden unfairly or arbitrarily on some countries, while others much more able to bear it escape its weight, would certainly create serious resentment in the unfairly hit countries and, in the end, undermine the spirit which is needed all round if this undertaking is to come to a successful fruition.

GENERAL CONSIDERATIONS ON THE TERMS OF TRADE: : THE SOCIOLOGY OF THE PREBISCH EFFECT

The relation of the terms of trade to aid

The worsening of the relationship between the prices of the exports and imports of the poor countries (the 'Prebisch Effect') has, to a very large extent, been responsible for the failure of international aid — which has become available in increasing quantities since 1952, both in terms of know-how and resources — to accelerate substantially the rate of increase in production in those areas. It has also been responsible for the increase in international inequality. It is not surprising, therefore, that people should conclude that this deterioration must be halted, indeed reversed, if the poor areas are to be helped. Opinions differ as to the most effective way of achieving this, but there has been very little dissent from the proposition that 'trade is better than aid'.

The deterioration in the terms of trade has no doubt played an important part in the growing international inequality in income distribution. It should be noted, however, that the rich primary-producing countries, notably Australia, have been able to offset, and in some respects more than offset, the deterioration in the price of primary produce by increases in productivity. This more-than-proportional increase in production, offsetting the fall in the relative attractiveness of exports as a result of the fall in their price, led to a greater equality in income distribution in the producing country[1]

[1] See *Survey of African Development Plans*, FAO, Rome, 1961. Even more evident is this in the case of Ghana, where new cocoa areas have been brought into full production. This phenomenon is closely related to the basic causes of the 'Prebisch Effect'.

than would have been attained if the price of exports had been higher and their production lower; since production for the outside market, even after the fall in price, was still much the most profitable use of land and other natural resources.

The terms of trade and the fully industrialized countries

Indeed, rational judgement on the relative merits of trade and aid will in the end depend on the diagnosis of the causes of the worsening of the terms of trade. If one believes that the unequal relationship is the outcome of the difference in the character of markets, the remedy is simple. The prices of manufactures, according to this view, increase absolutely and relatively to those of primary goods because entrepreneurs react to falls in demand by restricting output, and wage-earners in the rich countries are able to force up their wages *pari passu* with increasing productivity. Primary products, on the other hand, are sold in more or less 'perfect' world markets. The primary producer is unable to cut production because the alternative to his producing a cash crop is production for subsistence — a far less attractive proposition. In consequence, any increase in productivity or production is captured by the consumer.

It follows that the terms of trade could be improved by offsetting this difference in the character of markets for the respective products. An export tax on primary produce or a stabilization through currency reform of primary prices is proposed, to be followed by a devaluation of the currency of the (less dynamic) industrial countries. As the latter are less than fully employed and as the trade between industrial countries does not provide a 'net' stimulus to production in the latter, this procedure would involve no losses to those industrialized countries. A simpler alternative would be a uniform proportional export tax on all primary produce, or a more complicated scheme of variable export taxes supporting a system of restricting production.

I shall deal with the problem of export taxes and restriction of production below. In this context, I would just assert categorically that the former need not, and probably will not, lead to a restriction of production, while the latter, as we know, is difficult to organize directly, and is likely to break down.[2]

What needs to be discussed here, however, is the underlying sociological analysis of the problem. Politically, it would be far less difficult to obtain assent in the fully industrial countries to deficit finance or foreign aid than to measures involving international currency reform, a deliberate worsening of the terms of trade, and the like. It should be noted that the burden of the policy would fall inequitably on the shoulders of those countries which permitted imports from primary-producing countries. The more autarkic a country has been the less it would have to contribute. The benefits, moreover, would accrue to a number of very rich areas, notably the United States. This would not render acceptance by other countries easier.

The sociological framework of primary production in poor areas

So far as the primary producers are concerned, these proposals seem to be based on a superficial view of the complex sociological problems involved in the unequal relationship of primary to manufacturing production. The incapacity of the primary producer to 'capture' by price increases (or at least the maintenance of prices) a fair share of the fruits of an improvement in productive methods (or extension of production) is not due merely to the fact that manufacturing is monopolistic or oligopolistic while primary production is not. There are far greater differences, which could not be waved aside by an effortless use of a monetary gimmick.

In the first place, cash crops primarily for export are in a number of poor primary-producing countries, notably in Asia and Africa, *the main generators of money income.*

This means not only that, in the main, these commodities *must find an outlet abroad,* but also that no analogy can be drawn between them and the oligopolistic price-determination of manufactured goods. For the latter, the home market

2   Mr Kaldor has convincingly analysed the reasons for this (see 'Stabilizing the Terms of Trade of Under-Developed Countries', *Economic Bulletin for Latin America*, March 1963, pp. 4-5).

is the determinant one. In their case, therefore, increases in price due to cost-push pressures also increase income and *ipso facto provide markets.*[3]

Last but not least, the export cash crops, and they are the main — and often the sole — generators of money income, are usually also by far the most attractive crop. This is evidently so in poor areas of traditional subsistence farming, where the opportunity cost of growing cash crops is minimal. But it is also the case in areas of feudal tenure where certain cash crops (meat, wheat, and coffee in South America; wheat and olives in the Mediterranean) represent the easiest way of assuring a safe income from the sharecropping peasant or serf.[4] This has fatal consequences for the relative bargaining strength of primary producers. They have neither the technical know-how nor the sociological incentive to shift their productive activity, and thus obtain better prices for their exports.

Aid, trade and development

The 'Prebisch Effect' is thus deeply embedded in the sociological framework in which primary production occurs. Two important conclusions follow, which will be the basis of our discussion of certain facile and apparently plausible proposals. The first is that it is unrealistic to expect any reversal in the unfavourable trend for primary producers without a change in the sociological framework of the countries concerned and, secondly, that this change is much more likely to be stimulated under the impact of well-planned aid programmes offering alternative employment to rural labour than by commodity schemes or even by the liberalization of trade in manufactures. *Trade, and especially an induced improvement in the terms of trade, is no alternative to a well-conceived programme of aid combined with internal reform.* In the absence of such a change, its effects would probably be reaped by beneficiaries who would not contribute optimally to the final development of the poorer countries. 'Well-conceived aid is better than trade' would be

[3] See my paper 'Productivity and Inflation', *Oxford Economic Papers*, June 1958.
[4] See chapter 1, above.

a more truthful statement than the reverse, even if it would be foolish to press the point too far.

This conclusion is very much strengthened by the reflection that improvements in trade will not bring help to the most hard-pressed countries in proportion to their need, and that its burden will not fall equitably on the various potential contributing countries.

Developing countries with large exportable cash crops are *not necessarily the poorest*. They are, indeed, likely to be less poor. In addition, not all primary-producing countries are poor; some — such as the United States and the old dominions — are the richest in the world. If measures to improve the terms of trade for primary products are taken indiscriminately, it is very likely that it will be the less needy who will benefit most.[5]

In the same way, the main burden of any redistribution of purchasing power in favour of primary producers through an improvement in their terms of trade will fall upon those whose purchases already contribute to the maintenance of purchasing power in primary-producing countries, while those countries which, for geographical reasons, or because of purposive policies, exclude imports of primary produce, will either be burdened less or positively benefit. The United States and France have maintained an extreme protection for their primary produce and would probably benefit from such a scheme. Britain and, to a lesser extent, Germany and Japan would be losers, and the first is likely to be driven to greater autarky, either by way of increased restrictions and tariffs or by devaluation.

The stabilization of some commodity prices by means of export quotas and production controls should prove feasible. Moreover, certain creditor countries have imposed rather heavy taxes on the consumption of a number of tropical products. Their removal is obviously to be striven for, as is the relaxation of the deliberate import-saving practised by most socialist countries, which consume far less of these tropical products than the non-socialist areas with comparable

[5] It is interesting to note that the proposal to increase the value of gold has been opposed on precisely the ground that it would benefit the richest areas with large gold reserves.

national incomes, or even consumption levels. Thus, some stabilization or even improvement in primary-product prices should be possible, and any policy which prevented the implementation of such schemes should no doubt be reconsidered. Nevertheless, exclusive concentration on increasing primary-product prices is unlikely to prove as effective, either economically or sociologically, in improving living standards and in mitigating existing inequalities in the poor countries, as would an effort to stimulate their viable and balanced agricultural and industrial development with the help of aid.

The stimulation of trade as against aid has the further drawback in that it is not necessarily connected with the creation of conditions favourable to development. A large part of the gain on previous occasions, when primary-product prices were favourable, was dissipated in luxury spending. The poor benefited relatively little, and an increase in investment sufficient to start a cumulative improvement did not take place. No doubt aid has often been used, especially in Asia, for the propping up of tottering feudal elites, and has enriched people who did not contribute in any way to the development of their country. Nevertheless, it stands to reason that purposive aid planned for whole subcontinental regions rather than (small) individual countries, channelled into strategic projects well worked-out and administered partly through administrators and other experts from abroad, might be a better method of overcoming resistance to self-sustaining expansion.

SOME SPECIFIC PROPOSALS

Compensatory finance

The IMF has submitted a critical review[6] of the contention that there exists a shortage of international liquidity, in which it maintains that adequate institutional arrangements

[6] See *Compensatory Financing of Export Fluctuations*, Washington, DC, February 1963.

are available for the short-term compensation of fluctuations in the export earnings of primary-producing countries subject to specially high risks, both in respect of the quantity of the harvest and of prices.

I have dealt elsewhere[7] with the contention that no shortage of liquidity exists. Here I would simply assert that the presumption in favour of such a shortage is overwhelming in a situation where the United States has a very large current balance-of-payments surplus and considerable unemployment, but is nevertheless constrained to pursue a policy of monetary restriction. Even in the Common Market countries, with the exception of France, there has been a considerable deceleration in rates of growth. International monetary reform aimed at increasing the capacity to create liquid resources and to lend to underdeveloped countries through the World Bank or the IDA is overdue.[8]

So far as the IMF proposals on compensatory finance are concerned, they are ill-considered and insufficient: and this for two reasons.

The first reason is that the poor countries' quotas in the Fund are low in relation to the fluctuation in their export earnings to which they are at risk. In as much as poor countries cannot afford payment of the gold *tranche,* and since member countries' quotas are allocated in proportion to their respective contributions to the Fund, rather than according to their need to use the Fund, its machinery is severely deficient from the point of view of solving this problem. The second reason is that compensatory finance can only be a satisfactory device, either if it can be confidently expected that export proceeds would recover and, hence, that it were merely a question of bridging a known tempory shortfall, or if the provision of liquid resources were not subject to an

[7] Cf. T. Balogh, *Unequal Partners*, Blackwell, Oxford, 1963, vol II, chapter 23, and *Planning for Progress*, Fabian Society, London, 1963, pp. 23-5.
[8] See Mr H. Wilson's speech to the Anglo-American Chamber of Commerce, May 1963. In the following years, not only did international monetary reform get under way, but the rapid worsening of the United States' balance of payments wholly altered the situation. This is discussed in my essay, 'Fact and Fancy in International Economic Relations', *World Development*, vol 1, February and March 1973.

obligation of short-term repayment.[9]

Unless such conditions were fulfilled, it will be necessary for the deficit countries to replenish their reserves automatically by the imposition of deflationary domestic policies.

If, however, the constitution of the IMF were to permit it to engage in open-market operations in favour of the deficit areas — without obligation to repay — this might have the desired effect. As it is, the obligation to repay within three to five years will obviously put very severe pressure on debtor countries unless purposive action were taken at the same time to eliminate a deficit on their balance of payments from becoming a permanent risk. In fact, the IMF has always insisted on monetary 'disipline' even when only the first *tranche* of a country's quota (which, in fact, belongs to the member-countries) was drawn on, especially in those cases — mostly poor primary-producers — where this first *tranche* had not been fully paid in gold. In this way, a deflationary bias has been imparted to the international economy outside the Soviet orbit, since surplus countries are in no way stimulated to expand incomes. Even the timid safeguards embodied in the scarce-currency clause have not been utilized to restore greater balance to the new gold-standard mechanism.

The IMF report does not touch on the problem of compensating for the long-term trend of deterioration. The IMF would not, of course, accept that such a trend is inevitable.[10]

Export tax

It has been suggested that a system of export taxes might provide a solution for the deterioration in the terms of trade of the poor countries.

One alternative proposed was a combination of variable export quotas and export taxes to maintain supply at a level which would yield remunerative prices, without freezing the pattern of trade and the geographical distribution of production. This scheme would seem administratively impossible to sustain. Both it and the general export tax are subject to

9 Even a long-term obligation might prove onerous from this point of view.
10 And it is quite conceivable that a change in the foreign-trade policy of the Soviet orbit would radically change the trend.

the further objection that primary production is not confined
to poor countries but is carried on by a number of highly
developed countries which process part of their primary
production. Unless, therefore, extremely complicated police
measures are taken and these countries enforce the tax, both
internally and externally, the scheme might result, in a
number of cases, in a shift of production towards some highly
developed areas, and in an actual worsening of the position in
the poor countries.

But even if this objection could be overcome, such a
scheme seems ill-conceived. Most primary products, especially
raw materials, are under severe pressure from substitutes. The
systematic maintenance of high prices will itself stimulate
new research, and in a number of cases (e.g. oils and fats),
the substitution might take forms which cannot be reversed,
either for political reasons (e.g. the increase in dairy production), or because of a technical revolution (e.g. cocoa-butter
or rubber). It would obviously be foolish to assert that a
small increase in prices will lead to dramatic changes.
Unfortunately, the basic technological tendency is in that
direction, and any security which the potential producers
would get from a stabilization of competing 'natural' products
is bound to accentuate it.

Nor are objections to such a scheme confined to its effects
on substitution. A general export-tax scheme is not unlikely
to stimulate production because of the anticipation that
henceforth prices to the producer would be maintained.
Production is restricted not so much by the interaction of low
prices with a 'normal', fixed schedule of production costs, as
by lack of knowledge concerning modern technical advances
on the basis of which production could easily be expanded,[11]
and by uncertainty as to future markets. Not only would
stabilization schemes involving export taxes dispel such uncertainty; in so doing they would afford a sharp incentive to
producers to overcome their lack of technical knowledge. The
schemes put forward vastly overestimate the price-elasticity
of supply of primary products. If, on the other hand, prices
do not rise upon imposition of the export tax, and the producer

[11] In cocoa, for instance, yields of 2,000 lbs per hectare are known to be possible
in commercial quantities, as against a national average of less than 200 lbs.

has to pay part of the tax, this may not symmetrically result in a fall but in an increase in production. As we have seen, cash crops represent the best alternative both for serf-peasants and for tribal or feudal landlords. The 'normal' Protestant — North Atlantic — reaction to price changes is hardly likely under these circumstances. 'Backward-rising' supply curves have been found to be much more usual. In any case, production is not carried on in 'static' conditions with unchanged recources, including technical knowledge. Technical knowledge is available to multiply production. I would certainly not dare to put forward any definite views of what the impact of a general export tax on production would be, and I do not know how anyone can be sure of it.[12]

It is highly likely that the poor governments who obtained revenue from an export tax would, if production controls and export quotas were not imposed, try to stimulate production in indirect ways, such as supplying cheap fertilizers and spraying materials, providing education and extension services, and so on. Inasmuch as a revolutionary change in production possibilities is taking place in most of the areas concerned, this may lead to a completely unacceptable explosion in production. On the other hand, a policy of direct restriction would perpetuate internal privilege, since the production of cash crops is in any event more lucrative than any alternative activity; such a policy would only make it more lucrative. Moreover, a policy of restricting production would militate against the more dynamic countries, which would be increasingly driven to trying to break out of the scheme, hence undermining its efficacy. A restrictive scheme, based on export taxes, is, therefore, unlikely to work, although one based on physical controls is just as unlikely to work in a socially and internationally tolerable fashion.

There is a further and grave objection. If the benefits and burdens derived from the export tax and resulting from the increase in price of the commodities are respectively counted into total aid given and received, this is likely to represent a rather clumsy and unjust way of redistributing aid.

---

[12] When, in Ghana, a tax on turnover was imposed in the hope that prices had already been fixed at the optimum monopoly level and would not rise further, this hope was promptly (and predictably) disappointed.

A unilateral move of this type, moreover, might well arouse hostility; and if this led to a cut in other forms of aid, and if the poorest areas — which are precisely those which do not export much — did not receive any compensation, the proposal would be positively mischievous.

Liberalization

It has been suggested that a general liberalization of trade might help the poorer countries, especially if it is done unilaterally, i.e. if the poor primary producers are not required to make any counter-concessions. This proposal leaves out of account the extremely variegated situation in the so-called rich countries. If it were to be accompanied by a series of devaluations, liberalization would lose its effectiveness on imports, though it might still be of advantage to the poor areas — at least temporarily — if it reduces the price of manufactures in terms of primary produce.[13]

No rich country can be expected to tolerate unemployment caused by a general measure of liberalization. This has been shown by the escape clauses in the commercial treaties negotiated by the United States of America, which permit emergency restriction on imports detrimental to American industry, and also in the efforts on the part of Britain to limit imports, even from politically favoured countries. It would seem foolish to expect that unemployment will be tolerated, especially if liberalization is general and if there are no specific sentimental reasons (e.g. the ideal of Commonwealth solidarity) for sustaining the sacrifice incurred by the richer countries.

On the other hand, if liberalization combined with devaluation leads to severe currency crises, it is probable that the ultimate effect will be deflationary as each country tries to readjust its balance of payments by retrenchment. It is not altogether surprising that the change in the Western world towards liberalization and reliance on monetary control was contemporaneous with the worsening of the terms of

---

[13] Though if this analysis is correct, the relief is likely to be short-lived; devaluation in industrial countries is likely to lead to wage increases; while the (temporary) fall in demand will affect the price of primary products disproportionately.

trade of the poor countries. The effect of liberalization, in fact, was to restrict demand to slow down growth. This led to a worsening of the position of the poor primary exporters.

Non-discrimination

It has been suggested that bilateral agreements would not be compatible with real national independence, and it is argued that they would be liable to perpetuate neo-colonial relationships.

In point of fact, all effective concessions in favour of underdeveloped areas, especially in the field of manufactures, have been made bilaterally. This is true of all industrialization projects by the Soviet Union, which are based on credit plus repayment by bilateral purchase agreements. In the same way, British concessions to Hong Kong and India were strictly limited and on a bilateral basis. The Americans have given concessions to Japan on certain manufactures on the same basis.

It is not possible to sustain the contention that general multilateral free trade or a drastic all-round lowering of tariffs are more feasible or likely than limited, reciprocal, and co-ordinated commercial concessions.

Especially sharp have been objections to the Agreement of Association between the Common Market and certain African countries, under which the latter are to receive large-scale aid in the context of a customs-union relationship with the Common Market, while according them the right unilaterally to impose protective measures for the purpose of stimulating industrial or other development. Such an arrangement would be favourable to the African countries concerned, except insofar as it is doubtful whether or not they have the right to accord to each other greater preferential concessions than to the fully developed members of the Common Market.

It is probable that the Common Market treaties would not rule out the association of a complete customs union of African countries to the EEC as a unit. Unfortunately, the countries of Africa are characterized by great differences in income and productive capacity as between each other. A complete customs union between them would not be a viable or practicable proposition until the opportunities for development of the various prospective member countries had first been equalized by purposive regional planning of investment and partial tariff concessions, as well by migration, ranging over a long period of years. Such preferential arrangements, however, would bring them up against GATT and IMF rules. If, as a result of the failure to grant them the right to such discriminatory concessions all round, they will probably be forced to resort to a narrow national protectionism, in which case the Association Agreement will represent a deadly danger. With no scope for the creation of economically effective markets, on the basis of which industrialization could proceed, there is little hope of being able to sustain higher living standards.

THE ELEMENTS OF A SOLUTION

It would seem foolish to expect the advanced countries to permit an increase in the exports of primary producers, especially of commodities and manufactures in competition with their own industry, as long as they continue to suffer appreciably from unemployment. This means that the problem of inflation, especially cost-inflation, will have to be tackled. As long as wage and price increases continue to terrify the authorities of the developed world, it will be impossible to adopt a balanced approach to the problem of helping the poorer countries through increased trade; and the latter will be unable to achieve either a reasonable rate or the proper kind of development. All this entails the need for a fundamental change in the domestic policies of the countries of the developed world.[14]

The problem of avoiding sharp fluctuations in economic activity in the developed world implies the need for a radical reform of the international monetary system. The recognition of this need has prompted numerous contributions to the subject of monetary reform and, although this is not the place to deal fully with these,[15] one such scheme which

[14] I have discussed the problems involved in my pamphlet *Planning for Progress*, and again in *Labour and Inflation* Fabian Society, London, 1963 and 1970.
[15] I have dealt at length with this problem in *Fact and Fancy In International Economic Relations* (1973).

appears to be most clearly related to the issues raised in this chapter may be noted here.

There can be no doubt now, however, that, in the sphere of international monetary reform, one of the most important requirements is the establishment of an effective international central-banking mechanism; and the first step in that direction must be towards the creation of increased liquidity. *And one of the most important elements in such a design would be a provision for the penalization of persistent creditor countries.* This idea had originally been contemplated by Keynes, but had dropped out of sight by the time of the Bretton Woods Conference, and the practice after 1956 was to become quite openly discriminatory against debtor countries. One possible solution would be to provide for the compulsory lending of a country's reserves to the World Bank on a long-term basis, once they had increased beyond a certain point or had persisted at an excessive level for longer than a certain time. Another possibility would be to revive the dead letter of the IMF's ill-fated scarce-currency clause.[16]

The supply side

The Prebisch thesis on the unequal distribution of the yields from increases in productivity between manufacturing and primary-producing countries rests, as we have seen, on the sociological framework in primary-producing countries. Both under feudal latifundial and minifundial peasant communities, the opportunity cost of producing cash crops is very small. In other words, there is no profitable alternative crop. Hence production does not adjust itself to falls in price in the same way as in manufacturing. Even in rather rich primary-producing areas, we find that falls in price are answered by increases in productivity and effort.

If this analysis is correct, only far-reaching industrialization will enable countries to free themselves from the grip of poverty.

One of the most essential further tasks is the elimination

[16] See ibid.

of unnecessary middlemen and the restoration of the direct relationship between the peasant and the market. The first requirement here is to establish marketing boards which cut out seasonal fluctuations. This will also enable rural credit to be organized, and the peasant to be freed from usury.

Given the technical revolution going on in applied biology, it would seem rash to give subsidies through guaranteed prices rather than through the reorganization of production and technical aid.

Planning for progress

Much the most important task is to *maximize* the aid given to the poorer areas and to take measures to ensure, as much as possible, its optimal use. It is to be hoped that a portion, growing with national income per head, of the resources of the rich will be devoted to aid.

Tied loans, or even loans in kind, must not be ruled out, since obviously they increase the total amount of resources which can be put at the disposal of poor countries, given the precarious balance-of-payments position in which the 'rich' countries often find themselves. The alternative to a tied load or a loan in kind is not an untied, freely convertible loan or grant, but a *reduction in the total,* so as to provide for the possible repercussions of the grant on the balance of payments of the donor country. The present drift towards the commercialization of aid, which is very reminiscent of the bankers' orgy of 1923-9, is already beginning to produce a situation of over-borrowing. *It would seem to be essential that aid, as much as possible, should take the form of grants or soft loans;* the latter might perhaps be preferable, because it would appear to be easier to attach conditions to loans than to grants, thus, ultimately, increasing the effectiveness of aid.

In order to achieve this greater effectiveness, however, it will be necessary to establish machinery for regional planning, and to ensure that both bilateral and multilateral aid are channelled on the basis of sound regional plans.[17]

[17] This question is discussed at some length in later chapters in this section, especially chapter 12.

International monetary reform, as we have said, should concentrate of solving the liquidity problem of the developed world, so permitting the industrialized countries to maintain high rates of growth. This is more likely to contribute to the solution of the problems facing the underdeveloped world than any other measure.

It has to be appreciated, however, that a number of industrialized countries, for instance Germany and Italy, *will find it difficult to achieve full employment without running export surpluses.* From this point of view, therefore, it would seem to be essential to obtain some resources for underdeveloped countries by enabling these countries to maintain their export surpluses. This could be achieved by the IMF purchasing World Bank obligations and re-lending them to the developing countries, or by the surplus countries directly lending to the World Bank for the same purpose. *But it must be remembered that international loans will remain solvent only so long as a sufficient amount of grant aid flows to the underdeveloped countries.*

The GATT rules imply equality of opportunity between countries. In the absence of such equality they discriminate against the weak. It has been suggested that there should be a general waiving of the reciprocity rules on the part of the developed countries in their liberalization drive so far as underdeveloped countries are concerned.

However, general non-discriminatory liberalization, even if unilateral, is insufficient so long as the underdeveloped areas are not grouped into units which can potentially support optimal industrial units. The problem can only be dealt with by providing a waiver of the non-discrimination rules, provided that the exceptions are notified to GATT or an international trade organization, and provided that the discriminatory arrangements permit an increase in the trade of an underdeveloped country. It would be especially important to plan the establishment of new industries so as to be able to make sure of the feasibility of adopting modern productive techniques (adapted to the needs of the combined area) through mass production. This means that so far as these new industries are concerned, free or almost free trade should be permitted. The extension of old industries might be undertaken in a balanced way on the basis of tariff preferences so as to compensate the relatively weak areas in the underdeveloped region for the advantage they grant to the relatively strong.

In the end, the establishment of a common market with sufficiently strong organs of control, capable of purposive planning, would seem to be the logical solution. The same waiver should apply to the relationship of underdeveloped countries to one another. If this were done, the present hindrances to the common planning of economic development by underdeveloped countries would be mitigated. It might be provided that, when development had reached a certain predetermined level, somewhat stricter rules would be applied, and that, at any rate, aggrieved parties outside the area should have the right to demand compensation or alternative concessions.

TENTATIVE CONCLUSIONS

So long as the rules of international trade and international payments are based on a theory which itself is derived from the fiction of equal partnership between small and large, poor and rich, sluggish and dynamic, any endeavour to overcome the inequality in income distribution will be frustrated. No magic formula or economic gadget or policy trick exists which can deal with the worsening of the relation between the rich and the poor countries without fundamental long-term aid and development planning.

9

*The Impact of Aid**

Suggestions for an enquiry

The substantial increase in aid which is foreshadowed by Mr Kennedy's message on Food for Aid and his programme for Latin American reconstruction suggests an urgent need for reconsidering the impact which aid has (a) on the recipient country's political situation; (b) on the character and methods of its economic planning and outlook; and (c) on its relationship with the aid-giving country.

This timeliness is increased by suggestions in some of the aid-giving countries that the relative ineffectualness of the aid hitherto given should lead to a thorough reconsideration of the aid-giving process and, more especially, that aid should be made in some senses conditional on the recipient country agreeing to collaborate with the aid-giving country in elaborating a programme into a set plan for economic development. This plan is then to be put into effect by a commission consisting of nationals not merely for the aid-receiving but also of the aid-giving country. The foreign planners would thus no longer be in the position of advisers working with and through the government of the country concerned, but would have executive powers. Before any such suggestions are put into effect an enquiry shedding light on their probable impact in the recipient country and their relations to the contributing countries seems timely.

The background

An enquiry on the psychological impact of foreign aid in a

ᵏ UNESCO, *Case Study*, Geneva, 1961.

188

given country must necessarily start with a historical analysis
of the relations of that country with the outside world. It is
this historical background which will shape the predispositions
of government and public opinion to renewed foreign influence which foreign aid inevitably brings in its train. In this
respect we must distinguish between countries according to
their historical experience. There will be those who experienced actual political domination and those where the impact
of the metropolitan dominating country was merely economic.
No doubt very often dominance in a political sense brought
about penetration in an economic sense. It is obvious that
foreign administrators of a certain nationality would rely on
suppliers whom they knew and trusted, who would be their
own nationals, even if (as in the case of the British African
colonies) there were no protective tariffs to shut out the
foreigner in order to reserve the right of trade to the metropolitan area. *But there is a definite and important distinction
between political and economic penetration or dominance:*
and the after-effects in terms of suspicion or hostility are
very different.

We must therefore first of all distinguish between the impact
of current government and other non-profit activities in
providing resources and technical knowledge and those of
the great private corporations of metropolitan areas in
analysing the probable reaction in recipient countries.
Attempts have been made (especially in the United States) to
distinguish between government and private aid, including
in the latter universities and other non-profit bodies such as
Foundations.[1] The ideological bias in this classification is
blatant and seems unacceptable in recipient countries. The
sharp distinction which must be drawn is between profit-and
non-profit-motivated activity.[2]

Even so far as the historical process of economic penetration unaccompanied by political dominance is concerned, we
should have to consider two rather different types. The first
one we could call *general penetration*. The second is represen-

1 This was written, of course, before the nexus between government (especially
intelligence agencies) and non-government organizations became known.
2 Politically, however, non-profit activity might be more dangerous than private
activity.

ted by the establishment in an underdeveloped area of some *specific enclave of foreign activity* for the exploitation of some specific natural resource which the country may have had.

In both cases this economic penetration (including of course a financial one) might be backed, even if no colonial dependence is established, by some form of *specific legal privileges and exemptions* from local jurisdiction or legislation including tax legislation. This backing of economic penetration by political force might be openly expressed in such instruments as the capitulations in the Osman Empire, including Egypt, or in China and in parts of the Arabian peninsula. In these countries consular courts were accepted having a concurrent sovereignty over foreign civilians; this might be latent, based ultimately on either economic sanctions or military force itself. The military force might again either be overt or consist of a clandestine capacity to organize revolutions against any government which did not obey and respect the interests of the foreign companies or of the government.[3]

This preliminary survey already shows that the psychological attitude which is likely to be encountered in the present by governments in giving foreign aid will differ significantly from country to country depending on the historical experience of the country concerned. It should be noted that it is by no means self-evident that the difficulty of a colonialist metropolitan government in the erstwhile colony will necessarily be worse than that of a government which has had no political domination of a country in which its vested interests had penetrated.

Nor is this so unjust as it sounds. Overt colonial rule by a domestically democratic country (however autocratic its regime was in the colonial territory) would still come under scrutiny in Parliament or Congressional investigating committees. The fear of open scandal might well set much closer limits to the activities of metropolitan vested interests in

---

[3] There have been several instances of overt intervention, beginning with the Suez adventure of France and Britain, and in the Caribbean by the United States; the Russians, meanwhile, have openly intervened in Hungary and Czechoslovakia. Several apparently internal coups are said to have been originated by foreign powers, e.g. in Indonesia, Brazil, Iran, etc.

colonies than in economically and indirectly dominated areas. Indian sentiment towards Britain for instance often contrasted favourably in this respect with that towards the United States in Latin America.

Nor is it at all self-evident that the inhabitants of a given country will be favourably inclined to foreign governments or companies because it could be shown by a complicated economic analysis that without the penetration of metropolitan governments or private corporations, the country would in all probability have been even worse off than it was as a result of the penetration. Indeed the opposite is perhaps more likely, because the memory of the situation before penetration will have faded, and the contrast between the high efficiency and considerably higher salaries paid by foreign interests to a privileged few will contrast rather sharply with the average income of the country as a whole, and people will not be conscious that income would be even less if penetration had not taken place, because a basis for such comparisons would not exist.[4]

One more problem must be raised. This is the difference between what I call *purposive* and what may be termed *automatic* or built-in *exploitation*. The purposive exploitation of a territory by its metropolitan area was the basis of all colonialism before the nineteenth century. The Townshend system, the protectionism of Colbert in France, and the Spanish and Portuguese exclusiveness in the spice and bullion trade are typical examples. The colonial power reaped a monopoly profit between selling and buying and, in some cases, metropolitan companies had a monopoly of providing manufacturing goods. In some cases tribute payments were levied either by way of direct taxes on the inhabitants, for instance as in the case of America and also in the Spanish possessions, or by way of indirect exploitation, as in the case of the first rapacious period of the East India Company. In the latter case, illegally protected private rapacity was added

---

4 In a number of countries (of which Algeria is an extreme example) political independence resulted in a sharp fall in output; since, however, this coincided with a proportionately equal (or sometimes greater) amount of emigration on the part of the former privileged section of the population, those that remained were not involved in any hardship.

to the general exploitation of the country by way of levying taxes. This phase of exploitation by England ended by the middle of the last century. In other countries it lasted much longer. Some lingering remains still exist. Colonial governments granted monopoly privileges to certain private interests, e.g. wireless and communications or electricity companies, etc. before self-government was introduced. (Land grants to white settlers in such countries as Kenya, Morocco and Algeria are also remains of this phase of colonialism.) But by and large this phase of colonialism can now be regarded as almost totally extinct as an active policy.[5]

In the main, the automatic exploitation, which has come more to the fore, represents an unequal sharing of the gains and burdens of the impact of modern economic activity in the poor or underdeveloped territory. This inequality consists in the transmutation of the normal social or class tension within a country into an international and often inter-racial struggle. The problem is, of course, much more acute in the case when two unequal partners meet on the territory of the weaker one because the countervailing forces which have been liberated by the rise of political democracy and of trade unions in highly developed areas do not exist in the poor territories. Thus the 'free' operation of the market mechanism in an area in which there is, in practice, a large supply of labour results in most of the gains of the activity being appropriated by the stronger partner providing the capital. In principle, this was the case everywhere before the war when royalty or direct tax payments were of minor importance and represented no more than a fraction of the total gain. But the pressure of competition between poor countries trying to attract capital has, even since the war, kept royalties and tax payments on a relatively low level, especially in the case of manufactures in order to help in the industrialization of the primitive area. In certain cases (e.g. Argentinian oil) this may result in such favourable profits for the foreign capitalist as positively to burden the balance of payments.

Another aspect of this inequality arises from what might be termed the disparate determination of prices as between

5 See chapter 3, above.

primary produce and manufactures, a problem which has come to the fore, especially since the war. This is the result of the fact that a large number of primary commodities are produced by small and weak cultivators for sale in organized world markets. As a result, prices are disproportionately affected by changes in demand, exacerbated by speculation. This has been so even in the case of some commodities which are produced by large oligopolistic companies. Indeed, even where there has been government intervention in the form of export quotas (e.g. for sugar and wheat), or where there has been a policy of oligopolistic restriction (e.g. in copper, lead, zinc and, to some extent, rubber), a very marked price instability has been experienced even during the postwar period, which has been characterized by a relatively high average level of employment in the advanced economies. This price instability has been especially embarrassing in times of general deflationary pressure, which found most of these prices very vulnerable. In contrast, the prices of manufactures which primary-producing countries have to import have risen steadily as a result of the prevalence of cost-push-originated inflation in manufacturing countries. The inevitable consequence has been a heavy pressure on the terms of trade of the poor primary-producing countries, aggravated by:

(1) the fact that demand for primary products rises more slowly than national income in fully developed countries, while the demand for manufactures rises more quickly than national income in the less developed countries,

(2) the disproportionately fast increase in productivity in the production of food and other primary products in the developed countries,

(3) the displacement of 'natural' primary commodities by the development of synthetic substitutes and new products.

In consequence, and apart from during the war and the immediate postwar period, the terms of trade of the poor areas have deteriorated and are now some 30 per cent worse than in 1913 or in 1950.[6]

---

[6] Department of Economic and Social Affairs, *World Economic Survey 1962*, I: *The Developing Countries in World Trade*, New York, 1963.

Inasmuch as the stunted development of colonial or economically dominated areas has favoured the production of primary products,[7] this evolution objectively means an improverishment (or at least the limitation of the development) of those areas, which is nonetheless resented because it is economic and not political in its origin. This complex phenomenon of clandestine and automatic exploitation in fact shows up in the growing inequality of economic status and therefore, in the end, of human dignity between foreigners and the average inhabitant in underdeveloped areas.

The fact that the end of colonial domination has left large tracts of Asia, Africa and Latin America broken into non-viable units with completely artificial boundaries again increases the difficulty of establishing a greater equality. Only some sort of common market would allow the establishment of industries of a sufficiently large scale to be internationally competitive. This has been prevented by the erstwhile empires whose design of ruling by division resulted in this fractioning and balkanization of continents. The insistence of fully developed countries on the most-favoured-nation clause, which precludes the remedy of establishing partial common markets, is a potent source of dissatisfaction.[8]

The impact of aid

I have analysed the background questions which will determine the psychological setting in which the aid-giving process takes place. I shall now turn to the problems which arise as a result of the aid-giving process itself. It is, of course, difficult to differentiate in any given case between these two factors because the aid-giving process is likely to revive or be strongly associated with the previous experiences in the receiving countries. The matter is further complicated by the fact that in a great number of cases the need for aid, and more especially the need for technical assistance, arises because of the real or imaginary failures of the contributing government,

[7] See again chapter 3 above.
[8] To date, efforts in this direction have been of little avail.

or its private corporations, or a mixture of the two, in a previous phase of the history of their relation to one another. It is also obvious that there is an objective ground for suspicion on the part of the receiving country that the contributing country and its nationals have a feeling of superiority, even if it is not openly expressed. In any case the need to obtain assistance in knowledge arises out of a failure of the recipient – in not being able to produce experts in the various fields which are required for an acceleration of growth. This alone might create a feeling of resentment.

In a number of cases the lack of preparation of experts for the difference in social and cultural environment within which the government system and private enterprise must function in the receiving countries might itself have given the impression of a calculated bias in the policy of the government which is hostile to the prosperity of the recipient country even when there is no policy behind it at all.[9] It is obvious, for instance, that experts who have been nurtured in the North Atlantic Protestant atmosphere will, without thorough re-training, have certain notions about human motivations which are wholly inapplicable in most other parts of the world. As this misreading of economic motivations and psychological possibilities would inevitably result in the advocacy of measures whose success would depend on private initiative and the existence of entrepreneurial ability and willingness, they would give this impression of bias.

The psychological relationship in the field is in any case bound to be difficult. Even if there is no conscious government policy directed at influencing the recipient countries' domestic political struggles or foreign policy orientations, the executing experts can hardly fail to express the ideology of the contributing country. In the past decade this risk was very much increased by the relentless ideological struggle between the two main contributors to international foreign aid and the consequent intolerance of suspected deviations from strict ideological orthodoxy on the part of the executants of those governments unless positively instructed. This

9 This is an additional and subconscious factor beyond the conscious fear of experts of appearing unorthodox at home, which will be discussed below.

meant that many good technicians and civil servants were to recommend policies which ran counter to the orthodoxy of the day, even though they must have perceived its futility.

For the same reason the planning techniques and administrative customs, as well as, and due to, the different social environment in which the aid programme has got to work, might under certain conditions arouse hostility. Cases have occurred in which foreign technical experts and controllers of foreign aid programmes have insisted upon routines which were completely alien to and must have aroused the suspicion of the recipient governments and countries. Moreover, the very fact that they were put forward has in certain cases led to friction and could easily have been misrepresented as an attempt to impose ways of living alien to the country concerned and inimical to its national interests.

Only the most thorough and well-prepared indoctrination of experts handling contributions, or helping the receiving government in working out and administering development programmes, can possibly avoid real grievances. This has not been altogether successfully performed in the past, and I am sure that a reappraisal of the methods of choosing and preparing the personnel of the contributing countries for this task is essential, if for no other reason than to avoid giving wrong, i.e. sociologically irrelevant, advice — quite apart from the danger of giving offence.[10]

It is obvious that those who profess the need for a radical change in social and governmental institutions in order to achieve a decisive acceleration of economic development have a very considerable advantage over those who wish to preserve the basis of the existing order while modifying those aspects which result in social inequality and economic stagnation.

Nor can there by any doubt that the resources necessary to achieve a given progress are much larger in the latter than in the former case, at any rate after an interim period of political and social struggle and uncertainty associated with violent revolution.

There are two connected reasons for this disproportionate need for resources to achieve the same aim. In the first place,

[10] This problem remains as acute today as it was when this paper was written in 1960.

the absence of violence and revolution will mean that at any rate part of the inequality in income distribution which is prevalent in these countries will have to be maintained although it does not serve any incentive purpose.[11] The second is that the combination of the maintenance of the high and possibly conspicuous consumption standards of the upper classes and the principle of refraining from violent compulsion will make it imperative to give material incentives for the various poor producing classes to adopt new ways.

These incentives might have to be rather large if the force of tradition is very strong. In particular, rural reorganization might take a great deal of additional material resources. Yet if these material resources are not furnished; while a strong bias is exerted against revolutionary reorganization of the institutional framework of underdeveloped economies, a feeling of frustration might ensue which is bound to exacerbate feeling against the aid-giver.

It would be interesting to investigate whether some of the failure of aid to induce a better relationship between the contributing and the recipient countries has not been due to the fact that the feeling became prevalent in the latter that the contributing country, by insisting on maintaining the *status quo,* has actually exerted a net negative influence on the development of the country concerned. (This applies especially in Latin America, but it is also prevalent in some Asian countries.)

Disappointment with the failure of increasing international bilateral and multilateral aid might lead to despondency and thus to a relaxation of effort on the part of the contributing rich countries. This would be almost as dangerous as impatience with existing national and international organs responsible for the utilization of aid. It is of the utmost importance to recognize, both on the recipient and on the contributing side, that the mere provision of aid in terms of resources or technical knowledge is not sufficient by itself to start a cumulative process of economic growth. Social conditions must be created which are favourable to development.

The ideological bias inherent in the policy of contributing

---

[11] Indeed it might act as a disincentive (see chapter 1, above).

countries has been twofold in its effect on aid donations. In some cases, either explicitly or implicitly, it was made clear that aid would be given to private enterprise, and to governments solely if they respected private enterprise and gave it sufficient scope. (This has even been the case with the provision of multilateral aid by the World Bank, as has been demonstrated by Mr Black's admonition to India.) This happened in some cases in which private enterprise could not or would not meet the objective needs of development, e.g. because it thought the risk to have been excessive, or on account of the lack of resources. Another line of ideological influence has been the insistence on abolishing direct controls or severely limiting their scope, despite the fact that under those conditions the price mechanism might not work as it is supposed to, in such a way as to bring about an optimal allocation of factors.[12]

The irritation caused by the inappropriateness of attaching such conditions to aid would not have been less if they were not connected with the material interests of the aid-giving country. The fact that they might have condemned the recipient country to stagnation despite all aid, and thus might have increased the dependence of the recipient on aid, would induce a feeling of national frustration and irritation.

In other cases, however, the ideological bias in the policy of aid-giving countries towards *laissez-faire* was obviously to some extent 'rational' in the limited sense that it promoted vested interests. These might have been direct, inasmuch as the contributing country's nationals might have had concessions in the area or might strive for new ones. In this case the frustration of general development might serve these vested interests, for it would promote conditions in which primary production might be more profitable because of the greater availability of labour at low wage levels.

But the rationality of this bias would also be obvious if it was merely to protect or promote markets for the export industries of the aid-giving country. Planning would have displaced previous exports of consumer goods and this might not have been offset by an increase in the exports of producer

[12] See again chapter 1, above

goods. Should such a bias, rational or irrational, be suspected the contributing country's influence through its diplomatic agents and experts would obviously come under very close scrutiny.

One particular problem, which has become especially important in the Middle and Far East as well as in Latin America, has been the use of aid programmed in a sort of negative intervention in the countries concerned. Under the guise of preserving indigenous institutions' in the recipient countries, and not 'interfering in domestic affairs', contributions were made dependent, at least implicitly, or were thought in the recipient countries to be dependent, on the preservation of *existing* institutions. In a great many instances these institutions were really incompatible with an orderly evolutionary development of the country.[13] Formally, the intervention took place under the guise of non-intervention, of being natural. In fact, the contribution was used, or was thought to be used, in aid of existing vested interests. Thus, and this is especially noticeable in South America, the fiction grew up that the aid was purposely channelled in favour of the *status quo,* which from a political point of view was incompatible with the professed principles of the aid-contributing country, In some cases such intervention took place on the basis of assuring the safety of foreign investors in order to help the flow of capital investment towards the country, which capital import was deemed to be necessary for its orderly development.[14]

It would not be altogether unfair to say that this attitude has to some extent been responsible for the failure of aid and foreign investment to contribute in a commensurate manner to the acceleration of growth in recipient countries. It is also, in my opinion, one of the reasons why the magnitude of the aid available to individual countries had very little to do with the ideological or political success of the aid or with its material results.

---

[13] And were hotly opposed by people who alone in those countries wanted to achieve development.
[14] Even in India at an earlier stage the World Bank pressed for greater scope for private enterprise.

The fact that in most contributing countries public finances are organized on an annual basis has increased the *psychological* difficulties and made for greater ineffectualness both from the *objective* economic and technical viewpoint and also *politically.*

It had an unfortunate psychological effect because the conditional character of loans was underlined. In the political struggle in the contributing countries, moreover, the debate about aid assumed forms which were necessarily slighting to the self-respect or dignity of the recipient country, quite apart from suggesting that the political and economic-administrative compliance of the receiving country would be a condition of the continuation of the aid. Here then is a potent psychological reason for accusations that the dependent position of the receiving countries is to be re-instituted or perpetuated.

Objectively the annual exercise of voting and appropriating moneys in the contributing countries introduced a measure of uncertainty in the planning of the recipient countries which was often fatal to the efficiency of the aid programme, because the risk of discontinuation had to be taken into account, and thus large-scale economic plans were ruled out in favour of short-term stop-gap projects. The tendency of both the World Bank and contributing countries to tie grants to certain specific projects further rigidified and limited the effectiveness of planning. It has given rise, even in countries where the planning procedure is well worked out and which possess effective administrative and planning staffs, to a great waste of resources, as capacities were built up when existing ones could not be fully employed on account of shortages of raw materials for which credits could not be obtained.

A somewhat similar factor on a slightly different plane is presented by the method of determining aid. Is its volume fixed on the basis of some objective test? Is the allocation of the programme to receiving countries, and the nature of the programmes which are to be fostered by the contributing countries, determined unilaterally or by consultation and mutual agreement? The sole instance in which some objective test was in fact being used to determine the magnitude of the aid, and in which negotiations took place as between equals, is Marshall Aid. Even in this instance there were complaints in the smaller and less developed countries, whose civil services were not altogether up to the new task, of interference both in scaling down their programmes and determining their character, i.e. in choosing the individual projects to be included.

It seems essential, therefore, if aid is to succeed objectively in improving conditions in the recipient country, and if it is to be successful from the point of view of the contributing country in the sense of improving relations between itself and the recipient, that a thorough enquiry should be made to discover how those parts of the population which would be willing and capable of elaborating and carrying through aid programmes could be encouraged, without the contributing country giving the impression of trying to dictate the work and planning, or even its execution, either of which would prejudice the success of any plan, however well-conceived from a technical and economic viewpoint.

This means, therefore, that the pace cannot be forced from the outside. What can be done is an educative programme which makes it clear what policies in the recipient country might encourage a quickening of aid by the contributing countries beyond government grants and loans.

While the imposition of conditions for aid might well prejudice the success of the endeavour of the contributing country to secure the full confidence of public opinion in the recipient country, a well-managed educative campaign will be less exposed to this risk. On the other hand, support must not be given to groups of institutional arrangements likely to prejudice economic or social progress in the recipient country. This might seem obvious. It will not in practice always be easy to carry it out. The historical involvement of aid-giving countries (e.g. the United States in Latin America or Britain in the Middle East) has created a strong sense of loyalty on both sides and these loyalties involve exactly those vested interests which have to some extent been responsible for the failure of faster development in prospective recipient countries and have created the need for aid.

On the other hand, it will often be found that the contributing country — especially if it operates through multilateral agencies – will be able more freely to discuss and explain the needs of the situation in terms of economic policy and institutional reforms than would be possible for hard-pressed political leaders in newly emerging (and even in old-established) countries. Provided, therefore, that the confidence of public opinion has been won, that such advice has no ulterior motive, explanations by foreign governments and their representatives might well play a most important role in ensuring a greater efficiency in planning than would be possible without their intervention and without arousing hostility. It must be said that such intervention is likely to be more acceptable if it emanates from *multilateral* rather than *bilateral* sources (though the history of the United Nations in the Congo shows that even multilateral agencies are capable of arousing hostility if they exceed the passive role of offering advice on points on which they were asked for it by the recipient government). But there is no doubt that a passive role will not create the conditions of success. A *positive attitude in planning is required* from the contributing agencies.[15]

This will not be easy. One of the important failings of aid has been the multiplicity of agencies concerned, and their competitiveness. It is essential, therefore, to investigate how far advice has suffered in objective value from the desire to avoid awkwardness which would throw 'aid business' towards other agencies and thus lead to a loss of control over aid by any particular agency. This is especially important in the case of multilateral agencies, but there are cases where it has affected the policy and advice of bilateral agencies. In the long run the frustration of advice would again give rise to unfavourable reactions by the recipients to the aid-contributing country or agency.[16]

One of the most urgent tasks is therefore to inquire what sort of co-ordination might be built up at field level. It might be necessary to try to obtain the services of high-level

[15] But see chapter 10 on the shortcomings of multilateral aid.
[16] The Jackson Report shows that these obvious desiderata had not been met even by the end of the 1960s; if there has been any progress at all since then, it has not been very notable (see below, chapter 12).

economic diplomats to represent the UN family of agencies at country and regional level, who could organize the planning of aid programmes and, through persuasion, could get bilateral support for such co-ordinated plans.[17] As it is, the administrative procedures of individual (both multilateral and bilateral) agencies favour the individual project which is manageable, while a 'global' approach seems theoretical and unmanageable. Procedure, moreover, often favours haphazard choice. The consequence is the illogicality and ineffectiveness of many aid programmes. Paradoxically such failures redound psychologically to the discredit of the agency in the recipient country — even though its fault was one of complaisance rather than commission.

The execution of any plan can be fully effective only with the participation, indeed enthusiasm, not merely of the policy-makers in the governmental executive organs but also of those broad masses which it affects personally. This is partly a task of education, but the process of education can be aided and speeded up if proper incentives are given. I have already pointed to the need for much greater economic resources if a break with the past is to be achieved without violence or a degree of compulsion which should be regarded as intolerable in democratic countries. Perhaps one of the most important tasks of foreign aid is that with its help large sections of the people might be given immediate benefit for their willingness to adopt new ways of living and new methods of production which are indispensable for the quickening of economic progress. It can also provide the means with which to bear the immediate social cost of broadening education, including the loss of children's earnings bitterly needed by parents. All such changes are difficult to achieve because of the weight of tradition, apart from the objective resistance of vested interests which will be hurt. The provision of immediate and substantial incentives on the one hand, and of adequate compensation on the other, might be a way by which the obstacles in their progress can be overcome.

[17] The nearest thing to such co-ordinated plans are the World Bank Reports and the FAO Mediterranean Report (and since then a Preliminary Report on Africa, published in 1962).

It should be one of the most important endeavours of the enquiry to ascertain whether and under what conditions the handling of aid under multilateral auspices is preferable (even from the point of view of the political objectives of the controlling country) to bilateral negotiations.

The elaboration of comprehensive development plans demands primarily political leadership of the highest order, combined with a clear yet realistic vision of the future. All that can be done by investigations such as are proposed is to establish in concrete terms the direction in which that leadership must be focused, in order to achieve the maximum results at the least cost.

10

Multilateral versus Bilateral Aid [*]

A sensible appreciation of the role, implications and future of bilateral aid necessitates a brief review of the problems encountered in the mutual relations between the less and the more fully developed countries. Only in the light of these problems, some psychological, can we make sensible decisions about the way in which aid should be channelled, distributed and composed.

Opinions on matters of political economy usually move in violent swings, much like fashions in the length of ladies' dresses. The problem of foreign aid is not exempt from this fluctuation in conventional wisdom. Just at the moment (and for reasons that are quite comprehensible) bilateral aid has come under obloquy and attack, having reached its apogee at the time of Marshall Aid — an apogee perhaps better justified than the present disfavour.

THE ATTACK ON BILATERAL AID

The fear that bilateral aid might lead or contribute to eventual military involvement or undue political influence has been used by high-minded people of great goodwill as an argument for its root-and-branch condemnation, without due enquiry into its political advantages. Nor have the potential, or even actual, drawbacks of its alternative, the use of multilateral channels, been explored, and suggestions made for their improvement. This failure is the stranger, since an improvement of the organizations responsible for the direc-

* First published in *Oxford Economic Papers*, November 1967.

tion of multilateral aid would considerably strengthen the case for the internationalization of bilateral aid. However, in my view, even an improvement in multilateral aid would not weaken the political argument in favour of bilateral action, i.e. as between nation and nation.

The political and economic arguments in favour of a multilateral approach to the problem of world inequality are powerful. It is true that bilateral aid has often been based on irrelevant criteria, aimed at political ends, subject to changes and interruptions from budget to budget, and has thus been an unsatisfactory basis from which to maintain a steady and unrelenting pressure towards eliminating, or at least mitigating, inequality in the world. Moreover, there has always been an element of what we might call, perhaps somewhat unjustly, ostentation (or, more euphemistically, the domestic political need of 'donors' to show the extent of their generosity) in bilateral aid. This has resulted in a tendency for bilateral aid to be tied to grandiose projects when there existed an equal or greater need for general aid to overall programmes of development. Even from the donors' point of view, bilateral aid very often misfired. It created more tensions, more hostility, more impatience, and was more liable to associate, or even identify, donor countries with a *status quo* which was often abhorrent to a majority, or at least a very large minority, of the population concerned, hence often obstructing rather than aiding 'development'.[1] The forceful maintenance of such a *status quo,* moreover, was often facilitated by the aid given.

Whatever the disadvantages of bilateral aid, however, I feel that this fashion of denigrating it has gone too far. Some important advantages of bilateral aid are beginning to be overlooked and the balance of judgement is thus being distorted. As Senator Fulbright said:[2]

> Extended in the wrong way, generosity can be perceived by its intended beneficiary as insulting and contemptuous . . . .
> The problem of bilateralism is psychological and political

---

[1] See chapters 1 and 3.
[2] United States Senate, Congressional Record, Proceedings and Debates of the 89th Congress, 2nd Session, vol. 112, no. 120, Tuesday, 26 July 1966.

rather than managerial. It is a problem of pride, self-respect and independence, which have everything to do with a country's will and capacity to foster its own development. There is an inescapable element of charity and paternalism in bilateral aid — even when it is aid in the form of loans at high rates of interest — and charity, over a long period of time, has a debilitating effect on both its intended beneficiary and its provider; it fosters attitudes of cranky dependence or simple anger on the part of the recipient and of self-righteous frustration on the part of the donor, attitudes which, once formed, feed destructively upon each other.

I can see Senator Fulbright's reasons for so uncompromising a stand, even if I differ from him perhaps in causal analysis. I am more sceptical, however, when I come to some of his positive proposals. He says:

Foreign aid . . . can indeed be a powerful means toward the renewal of strained partnerships, toward the reconciliation of national animosities, and above all toward the economic growth of the world's poor countries under conditions that foster dignity as well as development. To accomplish these ends we will have greatly to increase our aid program and to transform it from an instrument of national policy to a community program for international development.

And how is this miraculous transformation to be accomplished? He continues:

I propose, therefore, the internationalization and expansion of foreign aid. I propose its conversion from an instrument of national foreign policy to an international program for the limited transfer of wealth from rich countries to poor countries in accordance with the same principle of community responsibility that in our own country underlies progressive taxation, social welfare programs, and the effective transfer of wealth from the rich states to the poor states through programs of federal aid. The time has come to start thinking of foreign aid as part of a limited international fiscal system through which the wealthy members of a world community would act sensibly and in their own interests to meet an obligation towards the poor members of the community.

So great a transformation in the character and conduct of aid cannot be achieved all at once. At present, however, virtually no progress is being made towards the internationalization of aid. The implementation of the Foreign Relations Committee's amendment to the foreign economic aid bill requiring the channeling of 15 percent of the Development Loan Fund through the World Bank and its affiliated agencies would be an encouraging but, in itself, inadequate step forward. A more significant advance would be a favorable American response to the request of Mr George Woods, the President of the World Bank, for greatly increased contributions to the International Development Association, the Bank's soft-loan affiliate.

What steps can be taken toward the development of an international system for the limited redistribution of income between rich countries and poor countries? First the aid-providing countries of the world should terminate bilateral programs and channel their development lending through the World Bank and its affiliated agencies, especially the International Development Association. Second, the Bank and its affiliates should be authorized to dispense the increased development funds that would be at their disposal as they now dispense limited amounts — that is, according to social needs and strict economic principles. Third, the Bank and its affiliates should execute aid programs through an expanded corps of highly trained international civil servants, encouraging objectivity by the assignments of field personnel, so far as possible, to countries and regions other than their own. Fourth, the Bank and its affiliates should be authorized to recommend amounts to be contributed each year by member countries to an international development pool; contributions should be progressive, with the main burden falling on the rich countries, but, in keeping with the principle of a community responsibility, with even the poorest countries making token contributions.

Multilateral versus Bilateral Aid

It sounds simple. I fear it is not. It is merely the yearning of a man of goodwill for a good solution, but unsupported by an adequate analysis of its future implications. If embarked upon without due inquiry and reform, it can only lead to further disillusionment and reaction. It contrasts strangely with the violent criticism of the policy of the very institutions which the senator favours which has been voiced and is being voiced in the most articulate of the countries receiving aid through this channel.

NEW CAUSES OF FAILURE

A new approach is more than overdue. It must rest on a ruthless re-examination of past policies in order to lay bare the mistakes committed both in the contributing industrial, and in the recipient underdeveloped, countries, both by the bilateral and multilateral agencies. A mere condemnation of bilateral aid, such as we have quoted, however comprehensible it is, does not really meet the point. We must realize that there are good grounds for believing that a *concentration on multilateral aid would tend to diminish the total amount of aid*, not so much for balance-of-payments reasons – though this objection is not unimportant – as for political reasons. There are, moreover, some grounds for believing that *bilateral aid, if duly reformed, could make a specific contribution to increasing the effectiveness of aid,* which multilateral agencies, as they are at present, cannot achieve.

THE OBJECTIONS RECONSIDERED

First, there is the obvious objection against bilateral aid being continued by the erstwhile colonial powers in the newly independent territories. It is said that this represents neo-colonialism and the continuation by other means, as it were, of the previous domination. This is hardly less objectionable in the eyes of the critics in Latin America, which has been under the (mainly economic) domination of the United States (in the Caribbean area, of course, her political domination was the rule in the early part of this century), than of those in the dissolved empires of the European powers. From a slightly different angle, this type of objection is extended to the Cold-War aspect of bilateral political aid. It is said that politically motivated aid is both less effective and more objectionable, that a number of recipient countries would in fact be unwilling to accept it, and that, if accepted, it would create resentment rather than gratitude. Experience in a number of aid-receiving countries bears this out.

I have no doubt that this line of attack on bilateral aid, and the consequent favouring of multilateral aid, is perhaps the strongest yet made; far stronger, as we shall see, than the attack on the ground of its ineffectiveness or excessive emphasis on technical excellence. In a number of areas there is an ambivalence towards, if not distrust and hatred of, the erstwhile colonial administration. The replacement of the citizens of the former colonial power by local men with indifferent qualifications cannot altogether be attributed to the comprehensible haste of the indigenous population to occupy positions of high status and income, nor to the justifiable criticism of these colonial administrators as being hardly fitted to creating a new positive welfare state. It has also been due to the understandable desire to rid the country of the tangible remains and reminders of past domination.

Nor can there be any doubt that the Cold-War rivalry has in numerous cases backfired on the contributing countries, especially where it has resulted in the propping up of corrupt, and administratively bankrupt, regimes which have wasted, or worse, the resources so provided. It is equally obvious that no international organization will distribute aid in the *ad hoc* political fashion as both East and West have done until now. Thus one might go far in accepting this line of criticism of the aid-giving process and its motivation in the bilateral field. What is more questionable, however, is: (1) whether a switch from bilateral to multilateral aid would necessarily mitigate these shortcomings; (2) whether the total amount of aid could be expected to remain unaltered; and (3) whether the switch towards multilateral channels would increase the effectiveness of aid.

The total amount of aid can hardly be expected to remain on the same scale if it were switched from bilateral to multilateral channels. Thus its effectiveness would have to increase more than in proportion to the decrease in volume if the switch is to be favourable to the mitigation of international inequality. As we shall see this is, as yet, doubtful. The volume of aid, therefore, becomes a decisive factor — at any rate in the short run.

Even political motivations in giving aid must, therefore, not be condemned out of hand. If Britain, for example, devoted her efforts almost exclusively in the support of Commonwealth countries, this is perfectly understandable, and morally admirable. Britain has exerted a decisive influence on the development of some (as in the case of India), and has even been responsible for the creation of other, Commonwealth countries. In some cases, e.g. the Caribbean, this responsibility has even gone as far as to embrace the basic composition of their population.[3] Britain, therefore, has a moral responsibility for setting such countries on to the path of self-sustained growth, a responsibility which, because it is consciously felt, created also the political will without which the necessary sacrifice would not be made. *Thus, bilateral aid in many circumstances represents an addition to what would otherwise be forthcoming* on a multilateral basis, where much vaguer and looser moral considerations apply, however important and admirable such general aims or feelings are. A reduction in the magnitude of aid at the present juncture would be inimical to the interests of the poor countries. It is significant that the contribution of those countries which are actuated by past political responsibilities and current political aims, e.g. France, has been higher relative to their income per head than those which are making their contribution in a spirit of altruistic disinterestedness.

Now it is unquestionable that in some respects the power which attaches to the giving of bilateral aid to influence the pattern of development plans has been put to mischievous use, and has not been in the interests of the recipient developing countries. Insofar as this has happened, the effectiveness of bilateral aid will have been reduced. Ideological aims, the

---

[3] It is for this reason that the questionable nature of the assurance given on the Commonwealth Sugar Agreement at the Lancaster House Conference in 1971, preparatory to Britain's entry into the Common Market, is so shocking.

hostility to what were termed 'socialist' institutions such as co-operatives (despite the fact that they flourish in the United States), the dogmatic push towards commercial liberalization and monetary manipulation, protests against even a mild direct taxation of foreign and, therefore also, domestic investors: such are the economic counterparts of the political mischief caused by the propping up of regimes incompatible with accelerated growth and greater social justice. In addition the tying of aid to certain conspicuous projects or to domestic supplies from the contributing countries reduces the effective, as compared with the nominal, value of the aid. Thus it is argued that even a cut would be preferable if the reduced amount were channelled multilaterally.

There are, however, a number of powerful arguments which support the contention that it is a *reform of bilateral aid* rather than an *unconditional switch towards multilateral aid* that is required.

The first argument is that the effective decision-making in the international agencies – as against formal responsibility or national distribution of recruited personnel – is to a very large extent concentrated in the hands of the same nationals at whom the protest against bilateral aid was in fact directed. This is not surprising. The large, highly developed countries, most of which have had an imperial past, are the main reservoir of skilled manpower and, more particularly, of the skilled manpower familiar with the technical and administrative problems of the areas which were formerly dependent on them. The only important exception to this picture is the United States; and one of the impact-effects of the Cold War, and associated hot sub-conflicts such as Vietnam and Cuba, has been to make the impartiality and disinterestedness of American experts seem even less credible (however unjust this may be in a great – indeed overwhelming – number of cases) than of those of the former colonial powers. The fact that members of the international agencies are often subject to security clearance and liable to be exposed to general, if not organized and specifically official, pressure by their national governments has at least tended to heighten this problem. If bilateral aid is largely replaced by multilateral aid, is this tendency not bound to increase sharply?

Then, in the second place, it is not to be supposed that the mere fact that an international agency is not national will *ipso facto* endow its principles and modes of operation with efficiency, wisdom and charity.

The financial and monetary criteria underlying the operations and influence of the multilateral financial agencies in particular do not seem to have given satisfaction or proven invariably successful, especially in the vast underdeveloped areas of the world. These agencies, and not only the World Bank, are in close contact with precisely those governmental and semi-governmental organs, like Treasuries and central banks, which are not going to be the most expansionist in their attitude to economic policy. Moreover, these agencies have to rely for their funds on the capital markets of the highly industrialized countries which, however progressive the government in office, remain most closely under the domination of the banking institutions. Hence, they are constrained to take into account reactions in those circles to the criteria by which they judge requests for resource aid. No such limitation is imposed on bilateral governmental contributions.

This objection does not apply to the same extent in respect of those multilateral agencies, such as the Technical Assistance Board and the Special Fund (subsequently combined under the UN Development Programme), which rely on the outright contributions of member governments. Yet technical assistance and the limited activities in the field of pre-investment exploration are frustrating unless they can be carried forward to full fruition through investment.[4] There is thus a grave danger, which has not altogether been eliminated by the successive liberalization of the international financial institutions, e.g. by the creation of the International Development Association, that very narrow and largely irrelevant principles will be applied by them in judging and in influencing economic development plans.

It is yet to be seen whether an increase in the specifically

[4] The limitation of UN activity to 'pre-investment projects' has been a grave mistake and was probably the result of international political pressures.

public, member-government contributions to their resources would alter the *esprit de corps* of these institutions. While it should be emphasized that under the new management both international financial institutions have made surprisingly rapid progress towards truly progressive international attitudes, Senator Fulbright's vision seems to be too much influenced by his revulsion from certain aspects of American policy, which obscures the important and difficult problems in the planning and stimulation of development, and which are liable to produce unfortunate effects even in multi-laterally channelled aid.

Hardly less important from the viewpoint of the progress of less developed areas is the efficiency of, and co-ordination between, multilateral agencies in helping to establish sensible development plans and assisting in organizing their execution.

Here again the objections against the present bilateral regime are more justified than the confidence that all its criticized aspects will automatically disappear with the change in the methods of channelling aid. The yearly budget-ary struggle to secure allocations for bilateral aid, the tendency to favour individual spectacular projects in affirma-tion of their 'donor's' prowess or might, while general aid is starved and existing capacity kept idle, have all come in for just criticism.

What has been less discussed is the problem posed by the very multiplicity of multilateral agencies, and their tendency to overlap, if not conflict, with one another in their efforts at empire-building and in their comprehensible, but one-sided and unfortunate technocratic approach to the problems of development, dominated as it is by the mostly misleading experiences and traditions of the fully developed countries, whose wealth has long been established. In the new inter-national agencies created since the Second World War, as well as those surviving from the interwar period, therefore, we have powerful sources of imbalance and hindrance to development.

Multilateral agencies − beginning with the International Labour Organization − were established before there had been any general recognition of the organic interrelationship between the development of the various sectors and institutions of a community and its social and economic structure. Indeed, it had not occurred to most people that the activities of the multilateral agencies should be governed by the absolute priority of reducing international inequality by accelerating the development of the poor areas of the world. The ILO had been created to enhance and promote social equality through the acceptance of trade-union rights which, until Roosevelt, had been flatly denied in the United States, the most advanced industrial community in the world. It served as a model for those agitating for the recognition of the rights of farmers and peasants, down-trodden as they were by the Great Depression. It was not realized — oddly enough — that it was not easy to reconcile cheap food for the consumer with high agricultural incomes, nor that the enforcement of high wages in activities in which under-developed countries possessed an exceptional international advantage might easily prevent industrial expansion from occurring on a broad front. So it came about that a growing number of multilateral agencies were created — each responsible for some vital aspect of economic or social life, each with its own independent governing body consisting of the representatives of member countries. These representatives — with the unique exception of Britain[5] — are chosen by the Ministries responsible for that particular activity: the Ministry of Agriculture in the case of FAO, the Ministry of Education in that of UNESCO, and so forth. But it is obvious that these Ministries — in the developed countries, that is — have little, if any, knowledge of the problems of traditionally poor countries and of the sociological preconditions of change. Thus, there is no possibility of generating effective pressure towards co-ordinating the activity of these agencies. Unfortunately, their multiplicity has led inevitably to the overlapping of their duties, and to conflict.

[5] With the establishment of the Ministry of Overseas Development, Britain became the first country to recognize that the problems of development are organically related and must be dealt with through a co-ordinated and planned attack on the social and economic obstacles in the way of progress. (But see note 8, below.)

THE REFORM OF MULTILATERAL AGENCIES AS A CONDITION OF SUCCESS

This overlapping of duties in turn has objectionable results, especially when combined with the inevitable restriction on the degree of positive initiative which they can take. All this seems to reduce the effectiveness of multilateral agencies, because it makes them liable to *compete for projects* rather than *plan development programmes* in the most effective way.

The dearth of co-ordinating planning staff in this framework is a further important cause of much of this failure. If the best way for a representative of any one country at one of the specialized agencies to achieve success is for him to try to increase his own agency's programmes within the total amount of technical assistance available to that country, and if he is not versed in economics and absolutely convinced that success depends solely on the co-ordinated planning of all aspects of development, then he will hardly resist the temptation; especially if the political leaders of the country he represents are pressing hard for large, if not altogether well-thought-out projects. His expert critical faculties, even if he had had any, are liable to get blunted. As a diplomat he will know on which side his bread is buttered, irrespective of the long-run interests of the recipient country in terms of real national income and social integration.

Since aid cannot be given, strictly speaking, before a request has been made by a prospective recipient country, the marginal importance and expansion of the specialized agency will to a considerable extent depend on the compliance of the head of the local mission with such requests, whether sensible or not. This must influence the quality of the advice tendered. If, in addition, there is no strong co-ordinating and evaluating team at headquarters (in contrast with the technical experts) then the tendency will only be strengthened. These factors are not present to the same degree in bilateral relationships, where increases in aid are watched with a hostile eye by powerful financial departments. Only a powerful overall controlling body, capable of overriding the autonomy of individual agencies and having organs which can gather detailed knowledge of requirements, could provide a hopeful framework. This does not exist: the linking of the Special Fund with the Technical Assistance Board into the United Nations Development Programme has provided no more than the nucleus of such an organ.[6]

In the second place, there is a greater possibility of influencing the use of resources in the case of bilateral relationships than if aid is channelled through multilateral agencies. This is because the directors of multilateral agencies are subject to political pressures (through their desire to get re-elected) from the very governments they are supposed to advise, from which officials in donor countries administering bilateral aid are relatively free. The fact that this capacity for bilateral pressure is liable to be abused — and has been abused in the past — is not a justifiable argument against it. After all, it is possible to imagine bilateral relationships being animated by an unswerving desire to increase aid as much as possible, and to make it as productive as possible, irrespective of political considerations. Even from the viewpoint of recipient governments, influence from abroad might be welcome, since it permits the blame for unpopular measures to be shifted on to others. Nor can we assume that all developing countries can adequately judge the most effective way of using aid irrespective of local, or even personal, considerations.[7] considerations.[7]

In the interests of effectiveness and efficiency, it is essential that the decision-making as to the allocation of aid between the various agencies and the control of operations at country level be centralized; only then will it be possible to replace competitive bidding with rational development planning. On the other hand, the process of establishing plans should preferably be decentralized to the regions and sub-regions.

One of the most vexed problems created by multilateral aid is that of choosing and training personnel. Recruitment policy is bedevilled by the strong (and comprehensible)

6 It is to be hoped that under the new management the UNDP will develop into an effective economic co-ordinating organ: but we must not anticipate such a happy conclusion (see Introduction).
7 These considerations assume increasing importance as the less developed countries increasingly resort to barbarism as a political expedient.

pressure of national delegations to secure an 'equitable' distribution of what in most cases represents employment of unparalleled affluence. In many cases technical assistance amounts to nothing more than a reciprocal recruitment of nationals to be exchanged with one another at high salaries. Some developing countries have actually lost more trained personnel than they have gained. In the absence of a competitive examination system, this pressure tends to result in the acceptance of unsuited personnel.

There is a further problem arising from the desire of national administrations to move people into international agencies who have proven to be failures or 'awkward' in their own country. While on occasion the latter prove excellent acquisitions, this is not always the case with the more numerous first category. A qualifying examination and the organization of a staff college seem the essential preconditions of success. The distribution of employment among member countries on the basis of a quota system must be qualified by proof of suitability. The awkward problem of maintaining balance between the various nationalities is perhaps not as acute in the case of 'field experts', as in the case of permanent appointments at headquarters, but it is troublesome even there. Recruitment, moreover, seems to be even more haphazard.

The representative of a specialized agency in a recipient country is usually the most senior expert in that country of the agency concerned. There is, of course, no reason why such an expert should be able to represent his agency adequately and possess the diplomatic skill, political sense or general economic knowledge that are necessary if his advice on general programming questions is to be valuable. On the other hand, it is difficult to find experts capable of seriously scrutinizing from a general developmental viewpoint the proposals of − not to say of evolving and submitting coherent plans to − recipient governments, who at the same time understand the problems dealt with by the specialized agency which they represent and who are capable of persuasive diplomatic action. Yet no effective effort has been devoted to the organizing of such training. It would be quite impossible to fill the requirements of a multiplicity of agencies

satisfactorily if they all wanted to have their own representatives. Planning staffs and United Nations representation
in member countries must be combined.

One of the gravest defects of international aid is the lack
of knowledge of the manpower requirements of the plans and
lack of co-ordination in the planning of training and recruitment. Three interrelated problems are involved:

(1) The training and briefing of experts from advanced
countries who are to give advice and/or man the training and
educational establishments created in underdeveloped areas.
Without adequate training, there is a considerable danger
that these experts will impart technocratic advice and
education that will be sociologically or politically irrelevant,
and which might be totally wrong from an economic point of
view. Much harm has been done in the past because of the
hostility and contempt that such unsuitable advice has
aroused. The results of a large amount of work then get
merely pigeon-holed and are wasted.

(2) The training of experts from underdeveloped areas in
the institutions of developed countries. The problems created
by the influx of large numbers of students into foreign
countries are difficult and often result in hostility rather
than in gratitude being engendered.

(3) The establishment of large-scale training and educational institutions in underdeveloped areas. Unfortunately,
very little attention has been given in highly developed
countries to discovering the best way of meeting this need.

Apart from the all-important questions of choice of
personnel and of the organization of the planning staff in the
multilateral agencies, there is the even more important
problem of securing democratic accountability by means of
an adequate chain of responsibility, something which is
conspicuously lacking at present.

The heads of international agencies, once they are elected,
are autocrats, provided they can obtain majority support,
i.e. in fact the approval of the governments of recipient
countries. Hence, effective democratic or expert control over
the technical administration is not feasible. Indeed, it has
happened in some agencies that criticism has led to the
blacklisting of the authors responsible. This is a severe

deterrent to criticism in the specialized field in which they operate. In this respect, there might be distinct advantages to be gained from a corporate form of management.

The control over these agencies by the General Assembly and other superior bodies of the United Nations does not correspond to parliamentary control; there is no opposition party to criticize programmes (including those of the national governments) from the point of view of the ultimate recipients. The international bureaucracy is only controlled by the national ones and the political element is superimposed and mostly dominated by high international policy rather than technical considerations. Control over the Special Fund and the Bretton Woods institutions is still more tenuous. Before the United Nations, and even more the World Bank, could be entrusted with a monopoly, or even a considerable share, in the direction of foreign aid resources, as Senator Fulbright suggests, far more direct representation of a democratic character would have to be secured, perhaps akin to the parliamentary organs of the various Western European institutions.

All this does not mean that one should be in favour of switching aid from multilateral to bilateral channels. Bilateral aid is still far bigger than multilateral aid, and I am thoroughly convinced that this discrepancy should be decreased, not increased.

My feeling is that bilateral aid has been excessively, often unjustifiedly, abused, and that before multilateral aid is lavished on the basis of general political or moral considerations, however well meant, there needs to be much closer and critical scrutiny of the way in which it is channelled than has hitherto been the case. What it does mean is that we should try to strengthen the sub-regional planning of multilateral agencies, with a view to their mutual co-operation in a reformed and co-ordinated system of bilateral aid, while continuously shifting the emphasis towards multilateral channels as these themselves improve in quality.

REFORM OF BILATERAL AID

I think that in dealing with bilateral programmes Britain

can claim to have made three extremely important innovations since Mr Wilson formed his administration. These should commend themselves generally, but have not as yet attracted attention.

The creation of a Ministry of Overseas Development

The first of these was the creation of a separate department for the administration of aid for overseas development, with a minister of cabinet rank.[8] This separation, on an equal footing, of the administration of aid from other departments charged with foreign policy gave recognition to aid as an end in itself, in contrast to aid for political ends or in conjunction with considerations of defence policy. This was a momentous decision and, in my opinion, will in future play an important, indeed decisive, part in transforming 'aid' into a true international social service given as of 'right'.

The fact that in creating this department the government endowed it with a powerful planning unit is an overdue, but nonetheless path-breaking and welcome, development. The organization of staff whose attention is devoted entirely to making aid effective – i.e. viewing it from the standpoint of the recipient country – is the first step towards the international reorganization of the aid-giving process and towards the fitting of national administrations in the contributing industrial countries for their future duties in an effort at multilateral sub-regional planning. The change from the classical, quasi-diplomat, towards the expert in development planning is a decisive break with the misguided traditions of the past.[9] We have yet to see its full consequences, especially in terms of policies affecting population control, agriculture

8   The downgrading of the Ministry of Overseas Development, which began with the demotion of its minister from cabinet rank, and culminated in its incorporation as a subordinate department in the Foreign and Commonwealth Office, is a regrettable development. It will serve to strengthen the suspicion that aid is merely a means of foreign policy and, hence, reduce the influence of the advice that attends it.
9   The root-and-branch condemnation by the former director-general of the Economic Planning Staff of the Ministry of Overseas Development is not altogether justified.

and education, as well as the evolution of new techniques in industrial development.

The organization of training

The second, and hardly less important (but closely related) reform, was the establishment of the Institute of Development Studies. In this country, too little attention had been given to making administrators (or even technical experts) fit for the vital jobs with which they were entrusted. In the foreign service (especially as far as economic intelligence and technical assistance were concerned) this question has been (if possible) even more neglected than in the home departments. Indeed, the need for such training and preparation would have been repudiated by the wrongly 'superior' approach of the dilettante. Our academic organizations were not much better in this particular field, which explains the lamentable failures experienced, especially in Africa. In most other countries, it must be said, the position was no better, and the United Nations agencies, as we have mentioned, never filled the gap.

Thus, there is now the prospect of Britain being able to: (1) train experts — for her own overseas services, for the United Nations and its agencies, and for overseas governments; and (2) help to develop new techniques (both of policy and production, including new implements) for use in the less developed countries. This is a most satisfactory development.

Interest-free loans

The last important innovation in our system of bilateral aid was the provision of interest-free loans. On balance, the provision of aid in terms of loans rather than grants is preferable, and this for several reasons. In the first place, loans call attention to the need for more careful planning and husbanding of investment. On the other hand the contemporary trend towards high rates of interest (mainly due to the fact that domestic interest payments in fully developed countries can be offset against direct taxation) has produced calamitous conditions for commercial debtors who are unable to do this, among which the less developed countries are prominent. Unless a halt can be called to this race towards economically unjustifiable levels of interest, defaults (equivalent to an increase in outright aid) will be inevitable. The British initiative therefore is doubly welcome.

SOME PSEUDO-PROBLEMS

In contrast, I have never been over-excited about the tying of aid to the supplies of the contributing country. If satisfactory international monetary arrangements could be arrived at, with some of the increase in international liquidity being channelled towards aid, there would be no justification for tying aid. There is little hope of reaching this situation just now. Until we reach it, the alternative to tying aid is cutting it. I prefer tying. On the other hand the tying of aid to specific projects can be exceedingly wasteful and should be avoided, except if the aid is additional, and a result of unemployment in the contributing country.

Far too much has been made also of the differences and conflicts between so-called programme and project aid. The real difference is between the sensible and foolish allocation of aid. It is not really possible to pick sensible projects without having some idea of the overall, economic and social aims, without a 'plan'. Over-elaborate plans based on econometric models (derived mainly from static neo-classical assumptions), on the other hand, are mostly nonsense. This is the result partly of the lack of data, and partly of the simplification of extremely complex social phenomena in order to make them determinate and quantifiable. They do not even give as much guidance as common sense, however fallible that may be.

THE URGENT NEED FOR CO-ORDINATION AND TRAINING

The partitioning of Africa, South America, the Middle East

and South-East Asia effectively prevents sensible large-scale industrialization and development in the areas most in need and defeats the end of aid. The most urgent task is to secure an effective co-ordination of multilateral and bilateral aid. Pressure should be applied to secure the compliance of both types of agencies in an overall sub-regionally elaborated plan. Equally necessary is it for the training of personnel to be extended and for there to be a sensible and sociologically-orientated planning of national and international contributions.

After the first phase of high-minded optimism, we seem to be in a slough of despond. There is little more justification for the latter than for the former. What is required is hard-headed, socially conscious and morally animated professional planning and skilful education. We need also a strict co-ordination of bilateral and multilateral aid on the basis of sub-regional plans in which the political and moral impulses in both contributing and receiving countries are fully mobilized. In fact, we must have both bilateral and multilateral channels because we need far greater and far more effective action.

Part Four
Planning

11

*Planning for the Second Development Decade**

An analysis of the aims and means, shape and pattern, of the Second Development Decade, as evolved by the United Nations, must be based firstly on the principal Report to the United Nations by Professor Tinbergen and his planning staff.[1] In addition there is to be considered the Report of the (Pearson) Commission on International Development,[2] appointed by former President of the World Bank, Mr George Woods, and which reported to his successor, Mr Robert McNamara. Then there is Mr McNamara's own speech on the population explosion to the Governors of the World Bank in September 1969 and to the Notre-Dame University in Illinois, which, I must say, required considerable courage; Mr McNamara has been the first of the great chiefs of the United Nations 'family' to have spoken out firmly and clearly on this important subject.

In a way, the very conception of, and need for, a Second Development Decade is, in itself, a confession of failure. The 'First' Development Decade was actually established to enable the countries of the Third World what was very unscien-

* A lecture delivered at the International Institute of Educational Planning in 1970 and reprinted from *Revue Européenne des Sciences Sociales* (Cahiers Vilfredo Pareto), Librarie DROZ Geneva, Tome X, No. 26, 1972.
1 Committee for Development Planning, *Report on the Fourth and Fifth Sessions*, Economic and Social Council, Official Records: 47th Session, United Nations, New York, 1969 (E/4682); and *Report on the Sixth Session*, Economic and Social Council, Official Records: 49th Session, Supplement No. 7, United Nations, New York, 1970 (E/4776).
2 Cf. *Partners in Development*, Praeger Publishers, New York, and Pall Mall Press, London, 1969.

tifically called to 'take off': that is to put them on to a self-sustaining path of development which in the end would diminish, and finally altogether eliminate, the grave and increasing international differences in material standards of life (I deliberately do not use the word 'satisfaction' or 'welfare'). The people who coined the phrase did not for a moment contemplate that, given aid and goodwill, this aim could not be reached or sustained. They – good Americans as they mostly were – could not imagine that an American aeroplane might not take off at all or, having taken off, might crash. They conceived, therefore, of the sort of continuous process of development which the United States had achieved, reaching a common or social goal through individual effort. They ignored the fact that in the nineteenth century the United States was in a very special position, the only parallel cases being Canada and Australia.

Equally, they ignored the fact that the rise of the fully industrialized communities, and their former dominance over the rest of the world, had created a new situation, not comparable with the position of the United States after the Civil War. This had far-reaching consequences for the social and economic structure of the less fortunate areas and, hence, for their ability to undertake the sort of development contemplated. In addition, the clash of cultures had destroyed, or damaged by weakening, the old traditional framework, without in many cases imparting an impetus for sustained community development.

This neglect shows itself in the tendency to apply experience gained in developed countries (including even quantitative relationships between certain factors and forces) to the problem of development in totally different societies, often differing equally widely among themselves. Capital-output ratios, the distribution of manpower and the like, derived from the historical experience of one country, cannot be applied to others without searching sociological analysis. This approach puts the main emphasis on economic factors because, superficially, they are quantifiable. The availability or scarcity of productive agents is investigated, as is their relation to one another, and so on. Yet, as the Latin American scene shows, starting with similar endowments often produces very different results. The much neglected social and political framework is by far the most important determinant of development.

The example of the United States was not paralleled, even in Latin America. The politico-economic structure in Latin America, its development (and capacity to develop), were weakened as a result of the sub-continent's peculiar history. Unlike the United States, the countries of Latin America, with the exception of Mexico for a few decades, and of Bolivia for a shorter period, had never benefited from a thoroughgoing anti-feudal revolution. That revolution in the United States broke the power of the landowning aristocracy by confiscating their immense possessions and led on to the Homestead Acts. It was this which enabled the United States to settle down to a balanced development, including the pioneering of mass education even in the rural areas. The Latin American revolution, under Bolivar, was in appearance much like the American revolution against European auto-cratic domination. In fact it represented the counter-revolution of the feudal classes against the crown which, increasingly, had tried to protect the peasant, who happened to be, mainly, Indian. Maybe not in its intent, but in its effect, the Latin American 'liberation' was much more like the Rhodesian affair. If Bolivar was unlike Mr Ian Smith, his followers at any rate were not very unlike Mr Smith's followers. There was also, of course, in the United States, a most interesting and intuitively simple, yet effective, approach to the problem of education. The Americans of the nineteenth century knew that their main occupation was agriculture; they did not neglect education in rural areas and agricultural research. This is a far cry from the European-dominated areas which, faced with relatively similar problems, con-centrated on a classical education for the elite, despising (and exploiting) the ignorant peasant masses. In the long run it was this educational effort, combined with the free frontier, which made all the difference and also determined the shape and pattern of American industrial development.

The problems which face the Second Development Decade arise from the fact that the First Development Decade did not solve them. I had always been very doubtful whether it could, because the process of development does not consist merely in increasing investment and hoping that foreign aid will close the 'investment gap' or 'savings gap'[3] ; nor does it consist in foreign aid closing the theoretically identical 'foreign-exchange gap'. Development is a much more complex problem and not primarily a technical-economic problem. It cannot be achieved quickly, because the causes of stunted growth lie in the historical development, and are deeply embedded in the social structure and political power relations.

Independence from foreign rule itself has often tended (as in Latin America, but also in a number of African and Asian countries) to increase, rather than free the body politic from, these integuments. Even where (as in Algeria and Vietnam, and to some extent in Burma) there have been violent revolutions and a displacement of the former elites, the old traditions have often reasserted themselves after a surprisingly short time. Very often the process of liberation has resulted in newly liberated local elites imitating the ways of the former expatriate administrators, which in itself had not been an influence favourable to the process of development. A further obstacle has been the 'softness' of the state, that is the prevalence of corruption and nepotism.

At the same time, independence from colonial rule has had the effect of raising expectations at all levels. It has led to the creation of vast social- and consumption-capital superstructures in the effort to emulate far richer countries enjoying much higher standards of living; but in the absence of adequate productive-capital substructures, the introduction of costly educational and administrative systems, instead of promoting, has constituted a potent obstacle to the propagation of self-sustained development.

I had always been critical of plans (such as in India) which aimed at ending reliance on foreign aid. I regarded foreign aid as a modified form of international income redistribution.

---

[3] Both calculated on the basis of simple 'Keynesian' aggregative relations which are assumed to be stable and (in the case of some authors) valid for all countries. In actual fact, most of these have turned out to be highly unstable and operationally worthless even in fully developed countries with relatively high mobility of, and substitutability between, productive factors. For the traditional rural sector they are wholly worthless.

I thought that ending it before a substantial equality of opportunity had been achieved was morally and politically unjustifiable. On the other hand, I believed projections, based on experience in the economically successful countries, with their radically different institutional structures and functioning, to be methodologically unsound and misleading, because far too optimistic. Such exercises were nothing but the indulgence of a snobbish desire for scientism and exact-looking quantification. When these projections were proved blatantly wrong by events, I was neither disappointed nor dismayed. Indeed, I must say that I think that the developing countries in the 1960s, on the whole, did not do so badly at all. If one looks at the figures, it is astonishing, for instance, to see how high a rate of growth they attained – between 4.8 and 5 per cent. It is, of course, very difficult, if not impossible, to know what to make of such figures. The measurement and, indeed, the meaningfulness of national real income figures, and even more of per capita real income figures in the case of most traditional areas, are of doubtful significance and in any case subject to wide errors. On the whole, however, the statistics on the rate of change are perhaps less futile than absolute figures. I remember very well that, when Mr E. F. Jackson set out to measure the Nigerian national income, one of the problems which had to be resolved was how to value the cassava in the ground. If the increase in cassava in the ground were taken into account, then the national income would be appreciably higher than if it were disregarded. Which is it to be? Should one regard the mammy's work as equivalent to retail output or not? These are very difficult problems conceptually and statistically.

In fact, a rate of growth of GNP of 5 per cent per annum is quite high: a rate of growth, indeed, such as England has not achieved since the 1840s and 1850s. It is altogether encouraging. Now it is true that the increase in population has wiped out a large part of the advance in per capita terms. The greater numbers absorbed what could have been a very sizable improvement for the individual if their numbers had not increased quite as fast. That was a problem which in the early 1960s only began to be dimly realized and the discussion

of which was, for religious and related reasons, fiercely
resisted. With the population explosion becoming manifestly
unmanageable and its consequences beginning to stare into
everybody's face, discussion, even rational and dispassionate
discussion, now seems tardily and tentatively to be possible.
We might hope therefore that in due time – let us hope
before some appalling catastrophe has befallen the least
fortunate – something effective will be done about it.

My first conclusion, then, is that while the First Development Decade has not solved the basic problem, it was not
unsuccessful. In fact, it enabled the maintenance of a respectable rate of overall expansion in the poor areas. No doubt
most developed countries (though not Britain) made faster
per capita progress; consequently international inequality
increased. This is no doubt unfortunate mainly because it
tends to exacerbate racial ill-feelings. The poor are, on the
whole, non-white; the rich are, on the whole, white. But
deploring the increase in inequality should not lead us to think
that a *de*celeration of the progress in the rich countries
(except if consciously willed – say to increase equality at
home or to deal with pollution) would help the world by
increasing equality. It might make the rich less able and in
all probability even less willing to contribute to the development of the poor. Thus, if increased inequality is, at the
same time, accompanied by intensified measures of redistribution, therefore giving hope to the Third World for
an eventual emergence from primeval absolute poverty, this
would be preferable to universal stagnation, even if stagnation
were to promote greater equality.

The disappointment of exaggerated claims gives rise to
pessimism. In no field of economics (and economics is a field
subject to violent changes in sentiment) has there been such a
sharp variation in sentiment in the last few years (monetary
policy not excepted) as in this field. The optimism of the
early 1950s (the result mainly of a favourable turn in the
weather cycle, especially in Turkey and India) had by the
1960s been followed by a deep pessimism (again partly
induced by a deterioration in climatic conditions, but also by
the realization of the impact of the population explosion).
Now, more recently, yet another complete turnaround has

been produced by the discovery of the wonder pill and the miracle seed.

The Establishment has faithfully mirrored these movements in sentiment, which are duly repeated by the Reports, on the basis of which the United Nations and the World Bank are invited to formulate policies. The Tinbergen and Pearson Reports and the whole philosophy of the Second Development Decade have been, in a way, conceived in disappointment. They represent an effort to console the main donor countries and to prove to them that their efforts and 'sacrifices' have not been in vain. I have no doubt that this was politically essential. Foreign aid was going sour; its violently nationalistic enemies, especially in the United States and Great Britain, but also in other countries, were becoming increasingly active.[4] The partisans of foreign aid were on the defensive. They had hoped for much better results in the First Development Decade and wanted to find some explanation as to why such results had not been achieved without at the time time damaging their cause.[5] I am not saying that I believe that the results that they had in mind 'ought' to have been achieved; I cannot emphasize enough that the actual results were surprisingly good.[6] On the other hand, I do believe that it is a good thing that the Establishment has been forced to re-assess the problems of development. My disappointment has been caused by the regrettable fact that, with one exception, the Reports which have come out of this great heart-searching have not accomplished this urgent, indeed vital, task.[7] The distinctive feature of the Reports that I have seen is that the one great

---

[4]   They had also found some reputable-sounding academics to support their case.
[5]   Hence their hostility to Gunnar Myrdal's seminal work on Asia, which brings out – as it should – the sociological factors (the 'soft state') in the social or political structure of the recipient countries which contributed to the disappointment (a view which I do not share).
[6]   Certainly after independence most 'new' countries have shown a much 'better' performance, as measured conventionally, than they did under colonial rule. Since they lost a number of 'experienced experts' in the process, this is simply a confirmation of the inadequacy of the policy-making of the metropolitan powers – or, perhaps, of their stupidity: I myself believe it to be the latter.
[7]   The documents prepared for the Copenhagen Conference on Rural Education have, in fact, completely accepted the case of the critics of 'classical' education.

advance that I had hoped for from the conventional disappointment with the First Development Decade – that is that people would think out the problems involved in development anew and re-assess their policies – has not happened. The one exception instanced is that of the Report by Sir Robert Jackson and his staff.[8] That Report has aroused a great deal of hostile comment; it has even incensed the heads of UNDP, although if it were implemented, it would, rightly, give them much greater powers of co-ordination over the various and very numerous United Nations specialized agencies, each of which is dominated by its own specialized technocracy. This violent reaction was due I think to the perhaps unnecessarily controversial tone of the document: but how could I, of all people, complain about Sir Robert's controversial style? It was due also to the fact that it did not pay sufficient tribute to the immense accomplishment of the United Nations Special Fund and Technical Assistance Programme in lifting multilateral aid to an altogether new level, both quantitatively and qualitatively. On this point even I would sharply dissent from the Report. Yet it is one of the most courageous, one of the most revealing, and one of the most valuable papers ever to have been produced in the United Nations 'family'.

Professor Tinbergen's Report is addressed to the United Nations Economic and Social Committee, Mr Pearson's to the World Bank. They share the same approach. They are – and I hope I am not being unfair – based on the belief that there is really nothing fundamentally wrong in the way aid has been managed. What we really need is much more of the same thing. That is the justification of this fundamentally optimistic approach to the problem of development. In the case of Professor Tinbergen and his colleagues it was professional pride which boasts of being able to plan on the basis of a mechanical econometric model and thus to determine the future of a country, a continent and the whole world. Its rationale has been clearly spelt out by Professor Tinbergen:

[8] *A Study of the Capacity of the United Nations Development System* (2 vols.), United Nations, Geneva, 1969.

In emphasizing the importance of capital formation, it is by no means implied that the stock of capital is the only factor, the only limiting factor affecting the rate of output. But, at the same time, it needs to be recognized that, given the serious limitation of data in developing countries, particularly such variables of employment and skills, the investment-output approach provides perhaps the only feasible means for assessing the implications of alternative targets of economic growth.

I would have said, with due respect, that this is probably the inverse of the truth. In the first place, measuring investment is by no means easy, especially in rural areas; and, after all, up to 80 per cent of the population of African countries, up to 70 or 75 per cent of Asian countries and up to 50 per cent in Latin America, live in rural areas and depend on agriculture. From a welfare point of view, from a political point of view, development planning which is not based on, or which at least does not pay paramount attention to, the primary-producing sector is likely to lead to discontent or worse. The type of choice which the Tinbergen approach offers to political leaders is misleading and disastrous. The econometrician grinds out his impressive, highly quantified and meaningless formulae, on the basis of mechanical, simple, pseudo-Keynesian relationships. They are meaningless even from his own untenable viewpoint. Not only is rural-sector investment an elusive concept; not only are the relationships generated between rural investment and income of a fundamentally different character from those in highly industrialized, integrated, and monetized countries on the basis of which these relations have been formulated[9] (and, even in these countries, policies based on Tinbergenesque predictions have gone very sour indeed); but the unique relationship between investment and the consequential increase in income is so loose as to be useless, indeed worse, misleading.[10] The

[9] See above, chapter 1, and D. Seers, 'The Limitations of the Special Case', *Bulletin of the Oxford University Institute of Statistics*, May 1963, pp. 77-98.
[10] In a Report on 'Quantitative Models as an Aid Development Assistance Policy' (OECD, Paris, 1967), plainly written by the econometric enthusiasts dominant on the committee (including Profs. Tinbergen and Chenery), Jordan is

incremental capital-output ratio, for instance, varied between 1.36 and 10.67 in the case of twenty-nine developing countries investigated. The variation within any single country was also exceedingly high. Indeed, the whole development process aims at changing these relationships. To choose a 'model' in which coefficients are stable and relations linear, and then to produce 'alternative' schemes to policy-makers, is a procedure which is bound to give wrong answers.

Moreover, there is in practice the problem of measurement itself. How does Professor Tinbergen succeed in measuring the investment rate of peasants? I have some experience of this matter in Hungary and elsewhere. It is unlikely that a peasant would report any increase in his investment or improvement on his land to the nearest statistical officer. He would be afraid that his taxes might increase. On the other hand, the rural officers would hardly be able to recognize or value the work. There are, moreover, conceptual problems; does one value the investment at the rate of the peasants' money income or their subsistence income (and how is that to be valued?); or at the wage and price levels appropriate to the urban sector which might be seven to ten times the cash proceeds in the traditional sector? Which is to be chosen? The answer is: you don't really know and therefore you reject it. All one does, then, is to value investments, in roads, housing, electricity and other infrastructure projects, and in factories, in the urban, i.e. monetized, sector: and so plans are formulated which neglect the rural sector entirely.

Our difficulties do not end there. Even in urban investment there are immense complexities. Is investment in luxury apartments in Beirut to be called investment or should it more properly be classified as a kind of hoarding? That is the question. What do these new luxury flats produce? Are they not a hedge against a depreciation of the currency? Are they

solemnly, or should one say humourlessly, mentioned as having a 1.36 incremental capital-output ratio and winning the 'Oscar' of growth for it. Instead of printing this nonsense, it would have been better to question the data on which such an 'evaluation' is based. But, then, one cannot in earnest say (p. 240): 'While availability of material creates problems[!] the greater defects appear to be on the side of inadequate use of the economic studies which are in fact available.' Inscrutable are the ways of econometricians.

not a hedge against revolution in one or other of the sheikdoms? Can they be treated as investment in the sense in which we know it? What of investment, again, in the form of monetary hoards? Take savings which are deposited in Swiss banks vaults. How do we count them? We know very well that over half of Peru's capital formation before the last coup took place outside the country. How do you deal with it statistically in your models?

Beyond statistics, can one neglect the policy implications of foreign aid? Will the export of capital not increase under certain circumstances with the increase in foreign aid?[11] Can foreign aid, by supporting the dominance of classes and interests inimical to development, not lessen the chances of its success? All this is painful and I quite understand that Professor Tinbergen, instead of talking of the need for far-reaching institutional change, such as exchange control, tax- or land-reform, prefers to talk about capital-output ratios as solidly existing between certain quantified limits. This would suggest that these problems have been solved or are implicitly taken into account, when in fact they are not.

The most interesting new factor which has not been taken into account by the Tinbergen Report is the reported 'breakthrough' in agriculture as a result of the development of new seed strains which under favourable circumstances can multiply agricultural output. I do not believe that it is as persuasive a breakthrough as the Pearson Report believes it to be.[12] Yet, there has been a Green Revolution. There is no doubt that the Rockefeller and the Ford Foundations have on the basis of a very small investment — less than 20 million dollars — helped scientific institutes to produce seed strains, both of rice and of wheat, which yield a multiple harvest. It

---

[11] For instance, if the IMF insists on convertibility as the first goal of policy. Even the mandatory exchange control over capital exports while a country is borrowing from the Fund has been relaxed (see my paper 'Old Fallacies and New Remedies: the SDRs in Perspective', *Bulletin of the Oxford University Institute of Economics and Statics*, May 1970).

[12] The Pearson Commission, feeling compelled to persuade conservative and sceptical Dutchmen and Germans, had to make the most of the new seed strains if consent was to be obtained for further aid to developing countries. They were visibly intent on minimizing the problems of the developing countries, and on maximizing the opportunities opening up for them (see chapters 6 and 12).

should be said that at the moment they are restricted to certain regions where there is at least a minimum control over water supply and where, consequently, fertilizers and pesticides can be used without undue risk. We have seen similar developments before. The introduction of irrigation into the arid areas of India also produced sensational results. So did the great dams on the Nile for over a hundred years.

The Ghezira scheme got off the ground in the Sudan, and the semi-bedouin peasant also produced cotton where none had grown before. Sugar cane was never produced there either, nor animal feeding stuff. The revolution wrought in certain limited parts of the Sudan was immense. This does not mean, of course, that the revolution happened all over the Sudan. If you travel two miles either side of the Nile, away from the Ghezira scheme, the age-old problems of the nomads and semi-nomads still exist but they can be coped with much more easily, much more readily now that the Ghezira scheme is there, yielding foreign exchange as it does, with profitable participation for the government.

Still, the present advance is, perhaps, of greater importance quantitatively. There is no doubt that in certain regions, as for instance in the Philippines, Ceylon and Taiwan in the case of rice, and in Pakistan, Mexico and India in the case of wheat, there has been an astonishing increase in output.[13] The Pearson commission think that this is the solution to the agricultural problem and also take it as the final solution to the problem of getting development under way. While Professor Tinbergen still tries to calculate investment (or rather saving) and foreign-exchange 'gaps' in a misleadingly simplistic manner in order to show the 'need' for aid and also its 'effects', the Pearson Commission, with no more sophistication, extend the results so far obtained in limited areas all over the Third World and come to the conclusion that aid will not need to continue after the end of this century.

Now it is quite evident that the constraint of traditional agriculture has been one of the main obstacles to balanced expansion. Its rigidity represents the bottleneck which only

---

[13] Fascinatingly enough, this has also been almost wholly neglected, and brought only as an afterthought into the FAO indicative World Food Plan.

too often produces inflation and prevents a self-sustaining process of expansion. Industrial or urban expansion increases demand; agriculture cannot meet it. Growth is interrupted. In the absence of the agricultural bottleneck, the whole process would then take a very different pattern. With greater security of markets, greater production would then ensue. Decisive advances could be made in industrial production, which would in turn assure an expanding market for agriculture. This would turn the terms of trade in favour of agriculture, which would again stimulate a further intensification of agriculture, and the whole process would be transformed from a vicious into a virtuous circle.

The problem is, however, first of all, that, except at the cost of vast investment, a further extension of the irrigated agricultural area is difficult in many regions: but it is not impossible. A different type of approach might produce further important advances; large dams will perhaps no longer play the most important role. Success in the main might depend on small hydrological works. These can be cost-effective and, though they are capital-intensive in operation, they can be labour-intensive in construction. This represents an immense advantage from the viewpoint of the Third World where the only reserve resource is unskilled, underemployed manpower.

Alas, small hydrological works are unglamorous. Their construction is difficult to organize. They need real zeal and leadership qualities of a very high order. Anybody who has been through the process of trying to persuade people, to persuade peasants, to collaborate in small hydrological works must know how difficult it is to get action. Moreover, their construction implies the consolidation of holdings, because some peasants will have to give up some of their most fertile land for the purpose of the irrigation canals and, possibly, for storage. Although the assured increase in the crop permits compensation, the assurance of security to the highly suspicious peasants is an immensely complex problem. Little progress has been made in this respect. In some parts of India, for instance, some of these small water-works (they are called tanks) are in a worse condition now than they were at the time of independence. There are very good reasons for this. Before independence it was the zamindar who kept up the tanks, in return for a compulsory contribution from the village. With the zamindar gone, there is no means of ensuring that they are maintained. The peasants themselves have often not been able to replace them by their own co-operation.

These considerations suggest that the Green Revolution, the development of new seeds, the technological achievement, magnificent as it is, does not automatically provide a 'solution'. It could provide a solution if, and only if, the framework of traditional agriculture were to be transformed on a large enough scale to allow the new techniques to be applied by the mass of the population. Otherwise, a tremendous social and political upheaval is almost unavoidable. If the large landowners and the rich peasants alone can apply these seeds, their income will rise despite a fall in price resulting from the more than proportionate increase in the size of harvests (which, in a country with a vast urban poor, will be a desirable consequence). The income of the small peasant will, however, actually fall, and, if the prosperity of the large-scale producers enables them to mechanize production, the misery of the landless workers (already living near the bare subsistence minimum) will be intensified. A more certain formula for stimulating a rural revolutionary movement on the Chinese Maoist model can hardly be imagined.

If Pearson has hardly begun to visualize these urgent problems, Tinbergen completely ignores them. This is a point which I want to emphasize. The most peculiar feature of the Tinbergen Report is that the annual rate of increase in agriculture has been put at too low a figure. Although it is slightly higher than all non-agricultural sectors taken together, it is, on the whole, lower than the growth of manufactures. This, in my opinion, means that the problems now facing the world have not been properly digested. The models completely ignored the question of what sort of problems the Green Revolution poses and what should be our response to them. As we have seen, it will exacerbate inequality both within the rural regions and between different rural regions; some regions will be able to make use of the Green Revolution, while others will not. Consequently, both inter-regional and the intra-regional class differences will very rapidly increase. The rich will become considerably richer, but without being able to provide increased employment opportunities for the poor. This is one of the gravest problems now facing us, as we are now witnessing in India, where the violence of the small peasants and the landless workers is already increasing.

Models such as Professor Tinbergen produces are irrelevant and unrelated to reality. Projections based on fixed capital-output ratios used as operational decision-making devices are useless. Yet these indefatigable econometricians continue to churn out their misleading stuff and appear to take in administrative innocents who ought to know better.

What are we to do, confronted with these desperate problems, yet in a better potential position to cope with and eventually banish hunger, destitution, illness and misery? It seems obvious that only intelligently drawn-up plans, taking the individual problems of continents, sub-continents, countries and their regions into account, and backed by the formidable economic strength of the multilateral and bilateral aid agencies will be able to help us to cope with the population explosion, the paramount of all our problems; to transform traditional agriculture without causing a revolutionary storm in the countryside; and to set the Third World on the way to industrial development.

In particular, national plans must take into account regional complexities and (sub-) continental requirements, whose importance has been vastly increased as a result first of colonization, which, especially in Africa, led to the tearing apart of tribal, geographic and economic units, in the breathless race for territorial aggrandizement; and then of decolonization. All this is easier said than done. Even where Western democratic processes, characterized by cumulative promises, Dutch-auction style, of an easier and lusher life (all militating against the maintenance of investment, however essential), have been abandoned, it is still not easy to disregard the pressure of the growing needs and accelerating expectations of a rapidly increasing population. Beyond that there is the problem of the domestic availability of technical skill and factual knowledge; and still more immediately important, the problem of how to provide from outside some of the skill and those resources to start with.

At this point, I am afraid, we are confronted with the particularistic, centrifugal empire-building attitudes of UNESCO and ILO. When I look at these important international Reports they are full of suggestions with which I am much in agreement, as for instance 'the mobilization of resources to galvanize the energies of individuals and groups so that they can tackle the obstacles to development on as big scale as possible'. *'Allons enfants de la patrie . . .'* But in fact one finds that the sociological difficulties, and especially the vitally important – indeed, in my opinion, fundamental – problem of educational planning, have not been tackled here nor has the problem of how to organize public works on a large scale. If you want to reduce the probability of feudal-type tensions developing in former tribal and small-peasant areas (which will certainly be forced upon them by the enormous pressure of the Green Revolution), the obvious solution is to create co-operatives. Of course, it is very nice to say 'let's get up and mobilize co-operatives'. We know how difficult it is to find able and honest organizers and secretaries, how often the 'co-op' is run by the feudal or tribal chiefs mostly to their own or their families' benefit. This is the truth and it must be tackled; unless we can admit these difficulties openly, the problem cannot and will not be solved.

The other two problems concern training and the supply of credit. If the Green Revolution is not to produce a potentially explosive social situation, some countervailing force must be provided to meet it; however, we do not even have the beginnings of one. Mrs Ghandi has now taken over the banks; whether or not this was popular, it was an absolute necessity, especially for the rural areas. But this must be followed up by an enormous campaign of education to make up the number of agents. Even if you have one agent for extension work to every ten villages, this would mean, in India, that some fifty thousand people have to be trained. In Africa the situation is slightly better on account of the lower density; but this itself poses terribly difficult problems, because the area to be covered is enormous, and the sub-structure needed would make the whole affair very top-heavy and capital-intensive instead of being labour intensive on a big scale. Such are the real problems, the treatment of which I miss in these Reports, with due respect to Professor Tinbergen; neither his mathematical pseudo-exactitude, nor the well-meant optimism of Mr Pearson, gives one confidence that the tremendous obstacles in the way of harmony, equality and prosperity have been realized by the Establishment.

I also miss the interpretation of what we want to do. To look at the Development Decade mainly in terms of growthmanship is surely not enough. A balance must be achieved between how much we want to pay for growth, in terms of the way in which we want to use those resources which growth itself will have created. Certainly I am aware of the soothing rationalizations of economists in this respect; increased choice, fulfilment of long-experienced needs. When one looks at some of the urban areas of the new capital cities and the surrounding slums, and the slum of the bush, one would like to know a bit more. To grow in order to grow is not enough. It will certainly not be enough if growth simply means even greater and more pervasive inequality. It would be wiser politically to have a better idea of *why* and *to what purpose* we want to grow and to discuss the problem of whether and how the ends agreed upon necessitate a modification of our ambitions for growth itself. We do not just want to grow statistically. We would use the resources created as a means to something else. A certain amount of social tension will be, in any case, inevitable because we shall, in the best of cases, lag rather stupidly behind events. We cannot anticipate events; we are not clever enough for that. But, if we refuse even to consider the problems with which we are being faced, this, to me, is the gravest possible obstacle to progress.

Let me sum up. I think that, on the whole, we have not done too badly in the First Development Decade. We could have done a lot more but we could have done a lot worse too. Most of the problems have arisen, in my opinion, from two sources. The first is that colonial liberation did not take place under very favourable circumstances; favourable that is from the viewpoint of growth. Certainly it took place favourably from the point of view of avoiding or minimizing bloodshed,[14] given the enormous revolution in power relationships which is usually connected with the fall of empires. I should have thought the amount of suffering due to this changeover was very mild, relatively speaking, though not negligible. The bloodshed in Algeria, Nigeria, Indonesia and elsewhere should prevent us from being too self-congratulatory or glib about it. But, on the whole, liberation was not too badly managed. More disturbing is that many have nurtured exaggerated hopes about what can be achieved by aid. Some of the donor countries have therefore become unnecessarily disenchanted. The Pearson Report has gone some way to remedy this by very rightly emphasizing its achievements. It is not a very deep analysis: it is a persuasive document and at the moment we need conventional persuasive documents more than anything to persuade the new-rich, like the Germans or the conservative Dutch, who are very well placed in financial matters, that they are not going to lose by giving further aid.

As to the planning processes, I sincerely hope that, with the Jackson Report, we are about to enter a new era of more conscious and more purposive planning. The Jackson Report recommends that aid should be assigned by a central planning agency on the basis of country level plans. This seems sensible. Nobody until now has been able really to co-ordinate the various agencies. And as long as multilateral aid was small there was no pressing need for it. Such co-ordination as there was, was performed by the recipient countries, through their requests. The consequence was that the weakest countries, who needed aid the most, were those where aid was least well managed. But how can the average recipient country, without technical assistance, work out its priorities? The answer is that it cannot. We have to think in terms of young administrations, expanding at a tremendous rate, modernizing the country, and thus confronted with manning the most modern institutions in social, economic and educational life. I do not believe that they can be called upon to make rational and satisfactory plans themselves. Therefore, somebody else

---

[14] Though murder has since been committed on a massive scale in a number of countries.

has to perform this task in collaboration with them. The recipient countries themselves have to make all the political decisions. The ends cannot be settled centrally; they involve the life of the nation and only the political leaders and democratic institutions in the countries themselves can really decide about them. It is the means to those ends in which they need help. But, I must say, once they are decided, the problems and the difficulties which arise ought not to be swept under the carpet, and if I have perhaps succeeded in irritating you a little to think about these things I shall be well pleased.

12

Planning Development Planning*

The central problem of development planning is, or at any rate should be, dominated by the lack of competent staff, both in the countries which most need them and in the international agencies; and by the consequential failure to use available resources to their full advantage. On the one hand, we must train better experts, or rather retrain technically competent experts to communicate effectively from a socio-political point of view; and on the other hand, we must create a sufficiently streamlined planning structure such as to avoid any unnecessary duplication — that is to say, one in which all experts and resources are utilized to the full and in which conflicts and waste are eliminated as far as possible. (Needless to say, it is unlikely that complete success in either of these aims will be achieved.)

I. MANPOWER PLANNING AND TRAINING

So far as the first problem, that of training, is concerned, the situation is less than satisfactory. True, a number of training institutes have been established by the United Nations.[1] For instance, there is the UN training agency in New York. It is, however, insufficiently staffed and badly organized and is, therefore, unable to do anything in any depth, although at

---

* Parts I and III of this chapter are taken from a memorandum prepared for the Jackson Committee in 1968; the part dealing with the Jackson Report itself is taken from my article 'Pearson and Jackson', *Venture*, January 1970.
1 The World Bank's training institute does not handle experts, but only officials or potentially important people from the less developed countries themselves. Since that is a rather different, though important, problem, I shall leave it on one side here.

this juncture nothing less will do. The African and Asian Development Institutes are also inadequate, the former having just been reported on by E.F. Jackson of Oxford University; the Report is a sorry account of how the institute has failed to fulfil even the most elementary requirements.[2] The Latin American Development Institute (ILPES) alone has done sterling work, but it has been beset with financial and political problems.[3] No systematic training of United Nations experts has been undertaken on a sufficient scale, nor of a sufficiently high quality.[4]

As a result of this deficiency, highly-trained foreign experts are sent, more often than not, to countries about which they only know very little, or nothing at all. They have little or no idea about underlying social conditions and, hence, as to what kinds of policy measures are politically feasible; nor about the relationship of their specific programmes to the Development Plan as a whole, if such a plan exists, or else to the current development of the country. Consequently they recommend what appears to them to be the best possible technical solution of the problem before them; but, quite clearly, this need not be (and more often than not, it is not) the best possible solution from an overall social and economic standpoint. Hence, there has been an alarming increase in the rate at which expert reports are being disregarded. Yet, despite the growing recognition of the shortcomings of such reports, very little has been done to remedy the situation at its source, that is the training of the experts themselves.

In order to avoid an open clash, the question arises as to whether it would not be best to organize training courses of (say) between three and four months' duration for a growing number of experts, especially resident representatives and sub-regional officers, on the basis of a syllabus worked out by academic experts in collaboration with the staff of the World Bank and the United Nations. These training courses might be conducted at the United Nations institutes, but with the

[2] E.F. Jackson, *Some Experiences of Planning in Africa*, Development Centre of OECD, Paris, 1965.
[3] Cf. the Report of the Expert Team to the Administrator of the United Nations Development Programme, 1970.
[4] In this respect, even the Jackson Report is inadequate.

help of outside academic experts, or at universities which are willing to co-operate and to contribute teaching facilities. Whether ultimately a new institute should be established or the present ones reorganized, is mainly a political question and one on which, therefore, I should not like to offer any advice.[5]

II. ORGANIZING DEVELOPMENT PLANNING: THE JACKSON REPORT

I come now to the second of the problems mentioned, that of organizing development planning. At present, proposals regarding development projects are supposed to be put forward by the recipient member countries themselves; it is on the basis of these and of the requests for aid that accompany them that a mission is sent out to the country concerned and either technical assistance or resource aid provided, whether by the UNDP (United Nations Development Programme), the World Bank, or one of the bilateral agencies. But this method of going about things makes for some serious problems.[6]

Whereas the advantages (especially the political advantages) of channelling aid through the multilateral agencies are now generally accepted, these were often offset, or more than offset, by the inability of the United Nations specialized agencies to co-ordinate their activities and to gain the acceptance and implementation of coherent and consistent development plans. The cause of this failure lay, on the one hand, in their respective specializations and, on the other, in the dependence of their secretaries- and directors-general on the mass votes of the developing countries, thus preventing a rational approach from being adopted.

There have been numerous efforts to centralize planning, examples being the establishment of the Technical Assistance Board and the Special Fund (later combined into the UNDP). All have failed. This failure was not least due to the fierce

5 This was written at a time when I was serving as economic adviser to the British cabinet. A reorganization of the present institutes at the moment would prove difficult on account of the sharp increase in nationalism.
6 The problems of multilateral aid are discussed at length in chapter 10, above.

resistance from the specialized agencies themselves. They, of course, had been established at a time when the real aim of the United Nations was regarded as co-operation among equals, a task to which they were quite well suited. In that respect, also, their reliance on and liaison with the specialized ('sponsoring') Ministries in member countries was an advantage. On the other hand, the eradication of poverty and the fostering of economic development in the less privileged areas of the world was a new concept to which they had yet to be adapted.

The very existence of the large number of independent, overlapping (and mostly ill-chosen) committees and panels seemed to inhibit the Pearson Commission from coming to grips with the problems of reorganizing the machinery of that part of the United Nations charged with the management of development aid. As has been noted,[7] it made only the rather lame recommendation that the President of the World Bank should call a conference of the heads of the United Nations agencies to discuss 'the creation of improved machinery for co-ordination'.[8]

Yet there is no time to lose. Far from progressing towards a more rational solution, the impetus now seems to be moving away from streamlining. The FAO wished to appoint separate 'ambassadors' – resident representatives – to most developing nations, thus duplicating the role of the present UNDP resident representatives.[9] This proposal was sharply and courageously opposed by the British government; nonetheless it has been at least partially put through, incredibly enough, with the blessing of the head of the UNDP. But even the UNDP representatives, with notable exceptions, are a rather weak body of men often quite unfit to help in development planning. There was much opposition to the reform and the numerous committees that were appointed in the 1960s shirked most of the issues. Finally, under strong pressure from the donor (contributing) countries, Sir Robert Jackson, a man who has held a great many British, Australian and international jobs, and, hence, regarded as a safe trouble-

7 See chapter 10, above.
8 Cf. *Partners in Development*, p. 229.
9 Written in 1968-9.

shooter, was appointed to report on the international agencies' handling of aid. This he and his collaborators (especially Miss Joan Anstee) accomplished with distinction and courage; in facing up to their difficult and displeasing task, they produced a very notable – though, perhaps, somewhat too outspoken – document.[10]

The Report rightly points to the absolute need for planning, that is, the allocation of aid to the various agencies, to be reorganized and centralized. As the Report shows, this is still done in a completely unscientific manner on the basis of 'shares'. Moreover, although much valuable work has been done and programmes evolved, the lack of effective co-ordination in most poor countries, of effective implementation and follow-up, the diffuse organization pattern at country, regional and headquarters level, inhibit both central policy direction of the programmes and an adequate degree of decentralization at the field level, channelled through one focal point. The Report suggests that UNDP and the World Bank together should take charge in order to centralize all policy decisions affecting technical co-operation and pre-investment activities on UNDP and, secondly, to decentralize as much operational authority as possible to the country level, in the interests of the realistic preparation and expeditious delivery of programmes.[11] Here, the resident representatives must play the same central role as the UNDP itself at the headquarters level, and their position must be strengthened accordingly.

It is here, however, that I have certain misgivings. The Report would concentrate basic planning at the *country* level. But it is inconceivable that the eighty or so people, sufficiently competent for the task, could be recruited.[12] Now it might be argued that there are only fifteen to twenty countries that really matter from this point of view, and that for these the required number of experts could be found. But such an argument would overlook the fact that it is precisely those

[10] Cf. *A Study of the Capacity of the United Nations Development System* (2 vols.), United Nations, Geneva, 1969.
[11] *Ibid.*, vol. 1, para. 95.
[12] Although Sir Robert tries to deal specifically with what he calls this '*canard*', *ibid.*, vol. 1, p. 41 (note 1).

remaining small, poor countries which pose the most difficult problems of all.[13] It is there that the scarcity of indigenous trained manpower is greatest; it is there that the demands of of sovereign status are the most exigent, relative to resources; it is there that the problems of national consciousness clash most acutely with the imperative of regional co-ordination in terms of the sensible regional or sub-regional division of labour.

In brief, the continued enforced neglect of these countries will further exacerbate the polarization of fate between success and failure, not only as between rich and poor, but as between the poor themselves; this latter trend has now become all the more likely, especially in the countryside, since the successful introduction of the new agricultural techniques. Hence, unless overall co-ordination is brought to bear so as to counteract these forces, the task of rural development will pose social and political problems even more acute than those raised by the prosperity of the urban minorities: and they are quite enough on any count. The question of co-ordination and planning, which should be on the basis of large sub-regions reporting to the UNDP/World Bank co-ordinating committee, I shall return to later.

The Jackson Report, commendably, does not shirk the problem of personnel. The recruiting and training of resident representatives has been defective; yet they would appear to be the obvious people to ensure continuity and coherence. The Report, therefore, proposes the establishment of a UN career development service, specially designed to reflect the needs of an operational programme, as distinct from those of the secretariat. It should be based entirely on merit and ensure adequate geographical distribution through proper selection and training of first entrants. The service would have its own salary structure and a promotion pattern enabling the outstanding members to aspire to the top posts in the organization.

A staff college is also envisaged. The calibre of resident representatives must be raised and their conditions of service

---

13 This has been recognized in the granting of special facilities at UNCTAD III to the twenty-five poorest countries.

improved. Political patronage must be eliminated. As regards project personnel, a number of suggestions are made for improving and speeding up recruitment, notably by greater use of subcontracting and by enlisting the co-operation of member governments and private organizations and firms. More systematic briefing of project personnel is also recommended, preferably through a central briefing service organized by the staff college. The Report also advocates a more liberal approach towards the employment of government counterpart staff, and the introduction of new techniques for training and fellowship programmes.[14]

This is indeed courageous: and it is right.

Whereas the Pearson Report has scored a commendable success in restoring the morale of the aid-protagonists, the Jackson Report has, for the first time, grappled with the mounting problems posed by the stultifying bureaucratization and separatism of the multilateral-aid channels. It will depend on the principal contributory countries whether this unhoped-for chance will be fully taken.[15]

III. SOME SUGGESTIONS

The problem, in my view, reduces itself, on the one hand, to the centralization of the aid-allocation and decision-making processes and, on the other, to the decentralization of planning and, further, of the bureaucratic control of field operations.

This would seem obvious enough on the basis of current experience and past mishaps; it is, however, more or less just the opposite of what is happening now. Decision-making regarding projects is undertaken mainly at the headquarters of the specialized agencies, which means that it is decentralized from the standpoint of *total* development, while being far too *centralized* from the administrative point of view. Moreover, since the majority of those in the field are

---

[14] *Ibid.*, vol. 1, para. 111 *et seq.*

[15] The only visible consequences as yet have been the resignation of two or three of the ablest officials of the UNDP, and the reorganization and enlargement of the staff (especially of higher officials) along regional lines, thus making for further duplication.

working on the country level, and since there is no sub-regional planning staff (although there are regional and sub-regional officers), this means that, apart from a very few large countries, planning is ineffectual and might be misdirected. Furthermore, the special missions to individual countries have exacerbated this weakness, since problems are viewed in the context of too narrow an horizon.

This being the case, planning, if it is to be coherent and successful, should be *decentralized* at a sub-regional level. The responsibility for this would fall to the various sub-regional offices corresponding to, but not necessarily wholly identical with, those of the Regional Economic Commissions of the United Nations.[16] Their task would be to evolve plans encompassing the whole economic and social field in their respective sub-regions. This exercise in sub-regional co-ordination, however, would also involve achieving a degree of complementarity — to be arrived at by a process of mutual adaptation — between the various national plans of the countries comprising the sub-region. The programmes thus evolved by the sub-regions would then have to be broken down into constituent national plans, and their requirements in terms of resources and (foreign) technical expertise established.

These sub-regional offices should in turn report to and be directly responsible to the UNDP and the World Bank, which will allocate multilateral resources on the basis of these plans. They must, however, be in the closest touch with the Regional Economic Commissions, on whose help, or at least consensus, the actual execution of such plans will depend. They should consist of tightly organized planning staffs working under a sub-regional resident representative of the UNDP: these latter must have been trained so as to be able to keep in touch with sub-regional governments, but also in the techniques of planning. The sub-regional offices, meanwhile, must keep themselves continually informed on planning decisions taken by the various member countries in their area; and maintain contact both with the UNDP and the World

16 The present 'regions' are wholly unsuitable for such a scheme at present. For instance, East, Central and West Africa do not constitute one coherent economic territory.

Bank as the ultimate regulators of allocations, and with the headquarters of the various United Nations specialized agencies as the providers of expert advice. But it is in these sub-regional offices that the plans themselves should be elaborated and finalized, once the central allocations have been made, in closest collaboration with the countries concerned. This sub-regional rationalization of planning might have the effect of sufficiently reducing manpower requirements such as to attract staff of the required quality, which might perhaps be supplemented temporarily by people on rotation from the universities and, possibly, from the bureaucracies of the more developed countries.

Liaison with the governments of the sub-regions would not be through the representative of the specialized agencies, but through the resident representative of the UNDP (and, of course, the World Bank), acting through the *planning offices* of the governments concerned, rather than their specialized ministries, which is now the case. This would seem to be especially advisable, since at present the specialized agencies and the specialized ministries combine with each other in trying to enlarge their programmes as much as possible, irrespective of whether they are, marginally speaking, making the most valuable contribution to the solution of the problems of the country and the sub-region as a whole.

Once a sub-regional plan has been elaborated, *all projects* which are discussed with the governments concerned should be scrutinized within the context of the plan and reported back to an Allocating Committee consisting (in the main) of the World Bank and the UNDP, who will then cross-examine the various specialized agencies in respect of the proposals made.[17] The overall planning framework may be conceived as follows:

(1) *Allocations* should be made centrally, but with the full knowledge of the sub-regional and national resident representatives of the UNDP and of the headquarters of the specialized agencies. This means, in fact, that programmes will be elaborated and allocations made from an overall point of

[17] The Jackson Report makes similar proposals, but on the basis of *countries* as planning units.

254

view. The specialized agencies would participate in, but not control, the planning of their 'special' sectors (although they would continue to supervise the execution of projects in that field).

(2) Once a project has been approved as forming part of, and as affording the maximum support to, the total plan, it should be reported back to the specialized agencies, which then recruit the necessary technical assistance staff with which to implement it. *The choice of specialists should, therefore, be in the hands of the headquarters of these agencies.* In choosing, the agencies should pay some attention to the problem of communication; that is, the selection of experts should be determined by the consideration as to whether or not they are in a position to understand the social and economic problems involved in the technical project in question, hence, whether their proposals will be appropriate to the country, its bureaucracy, and so forth.

(3) *The scientific supervision of the actual field operations,* on the other hand, should again be centralized in the headquarters of the specialized agencies, although the actual personnel management of the experts should be administered through the sub-regional offices, the latter being in constant touch with the experts and only reporting back to headquarters or to the World Bank should exceptional problems arise. In this way the present tremendous top-heaviness of the *specialized agencies* as to their personnel and administrative staffs could be avoided.

There was a moment, indeed, when one could have justifiably hoped for the advent of better things. Mr McNamara's appointment as President of the World Bank in 1969 led to a striking expansion in the Bank's activities.[18] His

---

[18] Annual average net flows received from the World Bank and its subsidiaries increased from US $353.71 million during 1960-6 to US $542.86 million during 1968-70, the principal element in this expansion being IDA loans; see Report of the Chairman of the Development Assistance Committee, *Development Assistance, 1971 Review,* OECD, Paris, December 1971, pp. 188-9, table 17. In the first year of his presidency, the World Bank Group increased its financing of development projects by 87 per cent over the previous year; see *Address to the Board of Governors* by Robert S. McNamara, Washington, DC, 29 September, 1969, p. 2.

speeches reflected not merely a clear understanding of the main problems that plague the less developed countries, but also an exceptional degree of courage for a man in his public position in discussing them openly.[19] One of his first measures was the organization of joint departments with the FAO and UNESCO for the purpose of stimulating projects in the vital fields of agriculture and education. Quite clearly he was destined to the role of charismatic leader in the ailing field of aid, especially multilateral aid, where few, if any, rivals were to be discerned.

As time passed, however, one perceived a growing reliance on mechanistic quantification on the part of the Bank, to the detriment of politico-sociological understanding – a characteristic of Mr McNamara's which had resulted in dire consequences for his record at the Pentagon.[20] Furthermore McNamara shrank from the attempt to use the opportunity opened up by the Jackson Report for rationalizing and reforming the muddle into which multilateral aid had drifted as a result mainly of ambitious bureaucratic empire-building. He did not meet the need for an overall planning of multilateral foreign aid, specifically in the fields of technical assistance and pre-investment; especially did he not coax the other agencies into a conscious co-ordination of their activities with a view to preparing the way for such overall planning, not only of multilateral, but also of bilateral, aid. Instead McNamara – probably discouraged by the UNDP's

---

[19] See especially the speech referred to above: ' . . . the Bank's efforts are not merely – or even mainly – quantitative in their goal. They are, above all, qualitative. We seek to provide assistance where it will contribute most to removing the roadblocks to development' (p. 4); 'When I point out then, that we have begun to put a new emphasis on population policy, and on educational reform, and agricultural expansion – and when I add that we are planning to give a new thrust to our activities related to the problems of unemployment, urbanization, and industrial growth – I am not choosing sectors at random. What we are trying to do is to form a framework in which each of these vital fields can be dealt with in an interrelated and mutually reinforcing manner' (p. 5).
[20] An example of the mathematical exercises indulged in is given in a paper by Joseph Buttinger: 'A Pentagon systems analysis . . . showed that the increase in American troop strength did not produce correspondingly high increases in enemy losses. This memorandum . . . predicted that "in theory", if 200,000 more Americans were put against the Communist forces, "we'd then wipe them out in 10 years"' (Cf. J. Buttinger, 'The programming of Robert McNamara', *Harper's Magazine*, February 1971).

incomprehensible rejection of the Jackson Report — claimed for the Bank the task of planning, a task which was to be performed by visiting missions; these were to be on a yearly basis to the most important countries, and less frequent ones to the rest.[21] I have given my reasons why such missions are likely to be disastrous or fruitless. The staffing of the Bank certainly does not allow of the successful accomplishment of such a heavy task. However, even if the Bank were to succeed in hiring accepted experts in the field of economic analysis (which it no doubt can), I wonder whether a *bank,* however much it succeeds in transcending its original appellation and terms of reference, and in turning itself into a *general planning agency,* i.e. an essentially political organ, could in fact win acceptance for this new role. I should have thought that these periodic visitations would provoke nationalistic resentment, which in turn might well undermine the whole operation of multilateral aid and give a stimulus to bilateralist tendencies. The future of a rational design for aid, therefore, remains in the balance. With the growing impatience and the failures of the past, this uncertainty now is lamentable. There is still time to take remedial action; but it is difficult to perceive any grounds for hope.

IV. CONCLUSIONS

To recapitulate: (1) It is essential that there should be a training programme for experts; (2) the present training institutes are inadequate; (3) whether a new institute should be established, or the training programmes, so to speak, be farmed out to outside institutes or universities, is a political question on which I am not competent to advise; (4) the planning of development should be decentralized and entrusted to sub-regional offices, reporting back to the World Bank and the UNDP; (5) the allocation of funds should be the responsibility of the World Bank and the UNDP working together; (6) the choice of experts should remain with the headquarters of the United Nations specialized agencies; (7) the actual control of

[21] I had good opportunities to witness these activities in India, Brazil, Argentina and Madagascar.

field operations should be shifted to the sub-regional offices acting through resident representatives trained according to (1) − (3), above, and only in the case of special problems arising should there be reference to the headquarters of the specialized agencies, which should, on the whole, be slimmed down.

13

The Outlook for India[*]

THE POLITICAL BACKGROUND

With the death of Nehru the last of the great charismatic leaders of British India passed away. He left the country in a dangerous situation of paralysis. The ruling party, Congress, had been formed to get rid of the British. Once that task had been performed and the princely states integrated into a new dominion, soon to become a republic, the *raison d'être* of the Congress vanished. It contained reactionaries who would make Sir Alec Douglas-Home look progressive; and — all across the rainbow to the Left — Marxists, Stalinists, Trotskyites and Maoists. To expect the spontaneous *emergence* of a coherent policy from an inchoate conglomerate was a pipe-dream on an extreme scale. Now Nehru could have *enforced* a coherent policy on and through the Congress. He might have lost a number of friends and comrades on the way; but he could have given life to a pragmatic but radically progressive social reform. He would, however, have had to fight and enforce it upon a large and most articulate section of his party. He could not face this critical decision. Most of India's present problems originate in his aristocratic ambivalence towards

* This chapter is based on notes prepared during a brief assignment to the Indian Statistical Institute in the winter of 1960; and on an article which first appeared in a Supplement to *Capital*, 30 December 1971. I am deeply grateful to the late Professor Mahalanobis of the Indian Statistical Institute for offering me the opportunity of spending a fascinating period at the Planning Unit of his Institute at the Planning Commission in New Delhi in both 1960 and 1971. I have benefited much from discussion with him and Professor Lefeber, as with the late Pitambar Pant, the late V.K. Ramaswami and M.J. Solomon. I am also grateful to Dr Wolf Ladejinsky of the World Bank and Professor Abel-Smith of the Rockefeller Foundation for advice and illumination. I alone am responsible for the opinions expressed.

the masses and the guilt-feelings to which this gave rise. He consciously forced himself to listen to all, respect all, carry all with him and he certainly performed miracles in doing so. Unfortunately it meant that he tried to reconcile the irreconcilable. The result was hypocrisy of a new and completely bewildering intensity.

The new constitution accepted the basically British compromise of 1935. It therefore left the most acutely important sectors of the economy, especially agriculture, under the states. It also left to them the taxation of land and agriculture. Now this would not have been fatal if the all-India dominance of Congress had continued and if it had meant something politically. As it was, Congress, as long as it was dominant, proved to be far more conservative in the states than in the Centre; and after 1965 it lost power in an increasing number of states. At the Centre, it became paralysed, especially after the India-China conflict. This and the Pakistani débâcle deflected vitally needed scarce resources from reconstruction to rearmament and shattered the reputation of the party leadership.

No doubt Congress had accomplished a great deal. The maladministered princely state disappeared. The land reform at least abolished the British-created feudal (zamindari or talukdari) system. All this, however, left the country woefully short of that socialist state to which Congress under Nehru had increasingly committed itself. They did little to alleviate the fate of the actual tiller; indeed it is arguable that under the new conditions they almost certainly aggravated the position of the landless agricultural labourer[1] and very likely even those with some land (up to five acres), whether or not they were doing any labouring. Distinguished statistical work tends to indicate that there has been an increase in the number living below the so-called poverty line (per capita consumption per day of one rupee – or £0.7½p).[2] This makes sense in all areas where peak-season demand for labour has not increased.[3] Rural and, even more, urban advance has

---

[1] Except in the most favourably situated areas being fully able to exploit the 'Green Revolution'.
[2] By P.K. Bardham, Indian Statistical Institute memo.
[3] Mainly Punjab, parts of U.P. and Rajasthan.

been mainly in the upper and middle-income ranges (including semi-skilled workers).

This was the situation when independent India's second prime minister suddenly died and the party bosses, instead of elevating the strong and conservative finance minister, chose Mrs Indira Gandhi, whose name and birth combined the memory of two heroes of independence. They thought that a woman in a man's country, especially a woman who had shown no keen interest in the exercise of power and political tactics, would suit their interests even better.

They little knew. Mrs Gandhi has shown herself not only devastatingly clever in tactics but also statesmanlike in conception and strategy. The break came over the filling of the presidency after the death of Dr Prasad. She took the political offensive by nationalizing great private banks (19 July 1969), forced the old bosses to oust her from Congress, and retained the majority of the Centre even if she lost most of the provincial organizations. This was a move which enabled a practical approach to the essential problem of helping the small farmer and industry whom the urban-centred banks had never catered for.[4] She organized conferences with state chief ministers in 1969 and 1970, hoping to press them for action on landownership, security of tenure and fair rents. She had no success in these efforts but created the basis for the totally unexpected landslide electoral victory. The Indians in the electoral battle (unlike the British!) did not fall for the blandishments of the Establishment, which asserted that they would take better care of the majority than the progressives. A double-tier demagogue alliance of disparate political cliques at the Centre and in the states, spiced with greed, corruption and incompetence, well displayed in the past and aggravated by amateurishness on vital points, has not been allowed to take control. The election gave her not merely a workable majority (a number of people near her did not believe that she could sustain the numbers that she held after the split); she obtained the two-thirds majority needed for constitutional change.

[4] The number of their branches increased by 42 per cent and agricultural credit by 3,000 per cent, between June 1968 and September 1970.

She was no less active in strengthening her hand in policy-making. The headship of the civil service was transferred from the Home Office to the cabinet secretariat directly under the Prime Minister. The ridiculously small and dilettante private secretariat was expanded, and strengthened, and experts drawn in. Its head became one of the ranking permanent secretaries. The overwhelming electoral victory was therefore at once a tremendous opportunity and challenge.

So much on the credit side. There is, unfortunately, a dark aspect. The election itself, because of the anachronistic and irrelevant constitution (probably the most fatal bequest of the British to India) has wrought much havoc. The Dutch auction for favours which seems inescapable at general elections of the Westminster type — in India redoubled or more by the state elections (a great number of which will come within a year and some of which have taken place) — makes sensible policy-making that much more difficult.

The Congress Party has forcibly been made much more homogeneous by the exit of the old politicking bosses. It is still a coalition, however, combining very disparate views. Mrs Gandhi, though outstanding in stature and image, has had, like the Indian Avatar Rama, to accept, indeed woo, the help of many whose sectionalism and greed will prove a heavy burden in exploiting electoral victory for faster and more balanced progress. She will have to make haste if her personal triumph is to lead to solid achievement. If her position is more dominant in fact — if not in sentiment — than her father's ever was, there is now no longer any excuse for not acting.

The obvious and increasing gap between promise and performance, between principle and reality, the extension of the crass contrast of opulence and misery into the countryside where it is aggravated by racial-caste oppression, the frustration and feeling of complete impotence, have produced a terrifying crisis of credibility. It is this which has led in West Bengal to a breakdown of law and order of a degree equivalent to open civil war. It would be surprising if it did not spread to other areas.

It was the cruellest blow to India and the government that at this juncture the catastrophe in East Bengal broke on a horrified world. The slaughter was followed by an exodus not paralleled in recent centuries (although the death toll is probably as yet not as high as it was in Indonesia). Like the Chinese incident before, the refugees will once more put an almost unendurable strain on India, however forthcoming the industrialized countries will be with their aid. This strain will be further intensified by the increase in military expenditure[5] due to the East Bengal crisis, which has escalated. The exacerbation of the internal political situation — not least in West Bengal — will also add to the burden. Yet the prime minister has not much time to lose in showing progress. The political obstacles to ordered progress are thus formidable. She will have to take on the larger and increasingly prosperous landowners, who dominate the countryside and blackmail all political parties, including the new Congress.

THE FUTURE ROLE OF FOREIGN AID

In discussing India's dependence on foreign aid, stress should be laid not so much on the actual achievement of self-sufficiency in the sense of a total ending of foreign aid but on national independence in the sense of being able to achieve a tolerable rate of growth on the basis of purely domestic resources. The total ending of foreign aid is neither probable not desirable. But it is absolutely essential, in view of the vagaries of the foreign policy of the Great Powers and the increasing demands on the resources of the United States from other parts of the world, that India should achieve self-sufficiency in the sense of being able to stand alone and yet achieve a socially tolerable rate of economic progress without aid.[6] It is therefore imperative to make the most of foreign aid in the next few years.

[5] The Bank Mission to Pakistan is said to have reported that the military dictatorship there had spent considerable amounts of its scanty remaining reserves on buying sophisticated weapons-systems (*The Guardian*, 28 June 1971).
[6] Indian poverty is much greater than in most of the other underdeveloped areas, and from a purely humanitarian point of view the Indian claim for further help is unassailable. But the distribution of foreign aid is not determined by rational humanitarian considerations alone.

Planning

My doubts as to the desirability of being without foreign aid are based on the fact that even if the Third and Fourth Plans as contemplated were fully successful, national income per head in India would still be lower than $100. This would mean that India would still be amongst the poorest nations, probably slipping behind China. There would be no reduction in international inequality.

Even more evident is the fact that, on the basis of a rate of growth of per capita income by, say, 2 per cent per annum, internal inequality in India will also persist, if not become more acute than it is at present. So long as the agricultural population is growing in absolute numbers, no real relief from inequality can be expected. An immense effort will be required if this increase is not to result in a further aggravation of the disparity of the productivity between the overcrowded rural and urban India.

Thus foreign aid will still be necessary. I have little doubt that a continuation of foreign aid will be easier and not more difficult to secure, even if the present main motivating force, the Cold-War competition, should abate. The sense of international responsibility has been steadily growing. Foreign aid should become a conscious weapon controlled internationally to combat poverty and inequality in an international framework. This does not mean, however, that the Indian government and people need not press on to render their basic development independent of foreign contributions.

EQUALITY AND PROGRESS

Even such a modest end requires a concentration of effort, the intensity of which does not seem to be fully realized. When people in India talk about the strain and stress experienced by her economic system, they seem to forget that the strain hitherto experienced was not more than an increase of the internal contribution to investment from 6-7 per cent to about 8 per cent of the national income.[7]

[7] The increase in taxation was so slight (from 6.9 per cent of the national income to 9.3 per cent, direct taxes rising only from 2.4 to 2.7 per cent – the regressiveness of taxation seems to have been accentuated) as not to merit much consideration here.

This small increment measures the internal effort brought towards the increase in national income. To regard this as the limit of effort is to accept failure in advance and condemn India to stagnation and eventual revolution.

No doubt the physical demands on the Administration, as well as on the managements of various new undertakings, were very great. This strain is in some way a measure of the failure to plan adequately the physical needs of the increased output and national income. Looked at from this viewpoint the difficulties in the coal and steel sectors represent not a strain as a consequence of planning but a stress caused by failure.

What needs to be emphasized over and over again is that far from involving any sacrifice, and more especially any sacrifice on the part of those who were already above the poverty level, the Second Plan enabled a very appreciable increase in consumption by certain of the urban classes of industrial and transport workers, and some industrialists and businessmen. Without any doubt it has also meant a very appreciable improvement in the standard of life of medium- and large-size farmers who have begun to take what might be called an 'entrepreneurial' attitude towards their work. There remain, however, large rural areas and sections of the population which have hardly been affected by the progress made. There remains the basic problem of rural under-employment which has hardly been diminished and may indeed have increased as a result of the growth of the population; and there remains urban unemployment, which is still on the increase. All this means an increase in inequality, against the professed aim of the government.

I am in no position to assert that there are many in India whose situation may have actually deteriorated, though this seems not improbable in view of the rise in prices, but it would be safe to say that a great number of people still remain pressed down to a level which, from all human points of view, may be regarded as totally insufficient. Any success-ful attempt to cope with this particular problem implies measured in conventional terms. Given the rate of increase in India's population and the character of the Indian economic system, a failure to attain a certain rate of expansion means that the degree of underemployment and unemployment increases, and with it the number of those who, despite the growth of national income, are unable to obtain income. Thus the degree of inequality in the community also increases. Only when the increase in employment at average income is greater than the growth of the population can progress towards greater equality be claimed.

The annual increase in population now is probably above eight million and will soon rise towards ten million per annum. If these people are to be cared for, the necessity of accelerating investment and growth in the organized sector is evident. Otherwise, the expansion in the organized industrial sector will show an ever-increasing sharp contrast with the continued stagnation of the rest of the economy. The relationship between the attainment of other meritorious social aims in India and the size of the Plan, and especially the size of investment in organized large-scale industry on which the hopes for an accelerated increase in the national income must be based, is thus evident.

Attempts to cope with the problem of unemployment by short-cut methods such as the dispersal of industry, or the subsidizing of cottage industries without sufficient attention to the productivity of the proposed schemes, are likely to be self-defeating and, because of the relentless increase in the population, decidedly harmful. A real reduction in inequality will only be possible if attention is concentrated on achieving the maximum increase in the national capacity to provide productive employment. Thus schemes which produce greater income more quickly will facilitate increased investment, which in its turn will permit further increases of output and investment.

This does not mean that rural industries should not be supported, or that community development projects should not try to augment the standard of life of rural populations by such means as the mobilization of the unemployed through linked public works based on schemes which might increase productivity (e.g. dams, irrigation, and drainage canals), or through handicraft centres which might represent net additions to available supplies. But it does mean that the main consideration must be the most effective and largest possible increase in the organized industrial sector of the economy.

Within the task it would seem essential to choose techniques which enable the largest possible utilization of manpower. Labour-saving devices must not be employed unless the nature of the technical task makes this unavoidable. What must be avoided is a reduction of the capacity to provide employment through using available scarce capital and management inefficiently.

This means that the problem of the less favoured areas must be tackled for the moment by efforts to increase rural productivity, rather than by forcing new industries to migrate and develop in unsuitable places, in unsuitable units. In most cases, even this might imply a fall in the efficiency of the investment which must be offset by measures increasing its total volume.

Much more attention should be paid to widening the access to education. This would promote equality of opportunity and could also accelerate growth through the creation of a background favourable to the acquisition of technical knowledge and skill. The access to education, especially technical and higher education, is still extremely limited, and (partly in consequence) the establishment of closed new privileged minorities is threatening.

Thus the popular distinction between the purely economic and the social aims of the Plan is based on a fatal misconception of the consequences of the failure to maintain a minimum rate of expansion. Any claim to the achievement of a socialist society, or even a modest progress towards the goal of establishing a socialistic or socialist community, is inseparably bound up with the size of the Plan and the contemplated rate of economic growth.

THE RELATION BETWEEN ECONOMIC AND SOCIAL ENDS

It is necessary at this stage to realize that a divergence between economic and social ends may arise when some measure of affluence has been achieved in India. There is growing un-ease in highly developed capitalist countries due to the dependence of continued high employment on continued profitability, which in its turn drives an increasingly saturated economy towards the artificial creation of wants. Only if dis-satisfaction is created can production yielding adequate profits be possible. In contrast, collective needs such as town planning, health, education, and the like are starved because they depend on taxation, and a powerful publicity machine is mobilized to appeal to immediate self-interest in fighting increases in taxation. Thus the affluent society suffers from increasing social and psychological stresses.

What is perhaps less realized, because of Professor Gal-braith's exclusive concentration on the problem of the United States, is that the problem of affluence, the problem of the creation and satisfaction of wants, in some respects is posed in a more acute form in communities which combine a low average income with grave inequality in its distribution than in rich countries. If the pattern of income distribution and production in a community undergoing a violent industrial transformation is not directed towards the desired end, but is left free to develop, there is grave danger that the emerging industrial structure will be shaped by the current anomalous, because extremely unequal, income distribution. Once the pattern of consumer goods industries has evolved, a strong vested interest among workers is created in the continuance of the anomalous distribution of income. It is feared that change would result in unemployment and distress. If a better society is to emerge from the industrial transformation, either a balance between incomes must be created at the outset or licensing of private, and the establishment of public, sector enterprises must take into account the final aim of the system.

The proposed establishment of a so-called 'people's car' factory in the public sector shows the extent of the failure to realize this simple truth. To call a motor-car 'people's car' when the production proposed is some ten thousand per year for a population of over four hundred million is, to begin with, patently incongruous. By introducing the new model, a new want is created, social pressure to obtain a vehicle widened, savings decreased, and credit control made more difficult, and an additional conspicuous social distinction is created causing disharmony. Thus, quite apart from the unfavourable implications for resource allocation and productivity, a positively harmful influence is created on the demand side.

The control of productive activity through licensing should conform closely to the desire to create a balanced socialist society if that is really the declared political desire of the country. The creation of new wants is directly hostile to saving and accumulation and thus impairs the growth of the economy. It must be kept under strict control. In particular, care should be taken now not to introduce into Indian society the social escalation of material desires which has led to such frustration in the highly developed industrial countries of the West. A better balance between work, leisure, material income, and satisfaction and between private and collective consumption might be striven for. This will not merely make India a more balanced society than now exists in the West but will hasten the day (because of a concentration of effort and the avoidance of conspicuous consumption) when a satisfactory minimum standard of life for the great multitude of the Indian people can be achieved.

In principle, progress towards a better distribution of wealth could be achieved by appropriate tax reforms. In practice, the resistance of the majority of the voters to increased taxes, even when they are not personally affected by the tax measures, has been sufficient to limit such attempts. Moreover, the efficiency of the measures has been shown to be impaired through various legal ways of avoidance or illegal types of evasion. It is exceedingly difficult to keep track, and prevent the shifting of the burden of personal taxes on to the organizations employing them so long as the organizations are privately owned. New loopholes have always been found, and the attempts to make taxation effective call for the employment of increasing numbers of able and skilled persons whose efforts should rather have been concentrated on increasing productivity and production.

In these conditions, national ownership and public accountability represent one way of securing the greater equality and increasing share of the national income devoted to collective purposes which are essential for the establishment of a balanced and satisfied community. National ownership can perform this task only if it does not result in inefficiency and waste and if it can contribute to national accumulation and investment.

In particular, the dynamism of Indian growth of population – and of production – necessarily creates a vast appreciation in land values. In the social and economic framework of India, a large part of this capital gain has been alimenting consumption. Thus the failure to acquire land near cities and development sites represents an important cause of the increase in inequality and of the insufficiency in domestic savings. Public ownership of land acquired compulsorily at pre-development-use value is an essential requirement for the success of the conception of the Plan. Land should then be leased to users for periods long enough – forty to fifty years – to enable orderly planning and give material incentives but not long enough to permit large speculative gains.

The mere fact that a proposed industrial development (e.g. the production of a small car) is to be included in the public rather than in the private sector is not sufficient to establish its desirability. While the increase in the scope of the public sector is an essential condition in the strategy of establishing a 'socialistic' society, each individual project must be carefully scrutinized from the point of view of its effect not merely on the pattern of income distribution and demand but also on the rate of growth of total national accumulation and production.

THE RELATION BETWEEN PHYSICAL
AND FINANCIAL PLANNING

A certain lack of clarity characterizes a great deal of the discussion on the requirements and implications of planning. In particular, there is a tendency to regard the problem in global monetary terms and to calculate the resources in terms of various types of finance. The outlay is calculated in terms of money, and the estimates are made, on the basis of various hypotheses regarding the growth of the national income, consumption, imports and so on, of how this outlay can be covered by taxation, savings, and the increase in cash holdings in the economy needed as a result of the expansion.

This procedure is thought to safeguard the stability of the system, avoid inflation, and secure balance. Even the experience of highly integrated and fully developed economies with flexible production structures has not borne out the hopes implicit in this attitude. In the first place, the impact of taxation on savings and consumption is not easy to forecast. Secondly, modern economies have shown themselves prone to sharp bouts of instability, due partly to changes in the demand for durable consumer goods and in the demand for stocks of commodities for working capital. The anticipation of price fluctuations of primary products has an extremely destabilizing effect, because it brings forth the fluctuations which were anticipated and thus proves self-justifying. The experience of Mr Gaitskell in Britain in 1951, when he tried to balance the nation's economic accounts by cutting social services by £40m. and was then confronted with an increase in commodity stocks of roughly £600m., shows the difficulty, in an unplanned economy, of achieving a neat global balance. A similar difficulty was experienced by India in 1958 when the unplanned increase in capital goods imports by the private sector resulted in a drain on exchange reserves.

No doubt the physical controls now in being in India can be used to prevent such strain. Nevertheless, reliance on global balance would seem to be both ineffective and liable to hinder the attainment of the professed objectives of the Plan.

In the first place, global balance is likely, in present Indian conditions, to be quite insufficient for assuring stability. The Indian economy is not an integrated system. The subsistence agricultural and small handicraft sector is only tenuously linked with the organized money economy, and remains extremely rigid. The elasticity of the economy is further limited by the lack of foreign reserves and the unfavourable outlook for the bulk of traditional exports.

The lack of detailed physical planning for each sector might in these circumstances result in awkward partial imbalances which might put a very severe strain on supplies and prices in any one sector. This could start an inflationary general rise in prices and prevent an increase in real output. The gap cannot be bridged by imports. Failure of careful and detailed physical balance in vital sectors will also result in a failure to attain the hoped-for rate of expansion, for no idle reserves in productive capacity and usable manpower are available. It is essential, therefore, to move from simple global calculations to a more detailed plan.

The economic meaningfulness of global balance is further impaired by the character of foreign finance which tends to increase rather than decrease the rigidity of the investment process. Foreign resources are more easily available for certain specific projects than for general balance-of-payments purposes. In consequence, while the need for complementary imports increases, the capacity to pay for them does not rise and a further unbalancing factor is introduced into the picture.

In these conditions, the failure to plan sectorally on a physical basis may result in the loss of valuable opportunities and depress the maximum attainable rate of expansion. Indian national income has been shown in the past ten years to be subject to the influence of the vagaries of the weather. Unless detailed preliminary physical plans are prepared well in advance and possibly beyond immediate implementation possibilities, against the chance of increased foreign aid or unforeseeable increases in harvests, such opportunities cannot be fully exploited. Not only will resources thus be wasted but incalculable harm will be done to the psychology of producers.

These seemingly self-evident propositions do not appear to be firmly grasped. Nor is the close relation between sectoral balance and the size of the Plan realized. The *Draft Outline* for instance, foresaw a rate of growth of agricultural output of over 6 per cent per annum. Yet it assumed that national income is to rise by not much more than 5 per cent per annum, although industrial output was expected to increase by about 10 per cent per annum. Unless total income rose far faster than agricultural output there is danger of an agricultural crisis which would put a stop to any ordered expansion. These relationships are either not understood or deliberately neglected.

Global planning has a further and even more unfavourable consequence. In order to be successful, it has, at least subconsciously, to pay attention to possible physical limitations. Thus the global balance must be struck on the basis of the narrowest anticipated bottleneck to be on the safe side and to avoid inflationary pressure. Hence the discussion is usually conducted with reference to the need for maintaining sound financial principles. This means restricting the Plan to the rate of the least progressive sector of any importance. Development is restricted to the rate at which bottlenecks are no longer anticipated, i.e. at which no concentrated administrative effort is needed or special responsibility is thrown on to the bureaucracy. The great advantages of this procedure are patent from the point of view of the 'planners', even though it means that the economy is held back well below the possibilities which could be achieved by an appropriate mobilization of resources (especially rural resources).

Global planning in India thus means not merely a loss of potential income but also a threat to the character of balanced social development, because it results in an insufficient provision of employment at average wages to the increase in the population, and thus increases inequality between those who are privileged to obtain employment and those whose needs both for work and income necessarily remain unmet. Once this is realized, the meritoriousness of a 'conservative' financial policy and 'sound' global resource-utilization planning vanish. They are revealed as a kind of mental laziness and lack of determined courage, implying an avoidance of exertion at the cost of perpetuating, or at least prolonging, the agonizing transition period during which Indian planning will not be able to provide a substantial equality of opportunity for the population.

The only politically sound and morally responsible strategy involves steady pressure up to the limits of physical resources. It involves hair-sharp sectoral balance and concentration of attention on the widening of supply bottlenecks as they arise. The soundness of a plan from a national point of view can be tested only by the strain it causes. A lessening of strain, the accumulation, for instance, of foreign reserves, means that the system is not being driven to the utmost of its physical capacity. It means not a success but a failure of planning. This does not mean that the strain should be permitted to make itself felt through an uncontrolled inflation. The consequences of such an inflationary process in Indian conditions would be most unfavourable both economically and socially. Savings habits are frail, and the distribution of income is very unequal. Inflation would undermine the former and worsen the latter.

Pushing the economic system to its limits means that the purchasing power created through investment, inasmuch as it is not offset by the rise in savings associated with the investment,[8] must be either intercepted by taxation of deflated by direct controls into savings or innocuous expenditure, i.e. expenditure which does not impinge on scarce resources, especially which does not burden the balance of payments but makes use of excess capacity. It means, therefore, a need for constant vigilance and great flexibility.

A further point now needs to be made with some force. Global monetary planning is based really on the principles governing budgets only superficially modified to take into account 'economic' or 'overall national income' changes. It is in essence a disjointed operation which is entirely legitimate so long as the state impinges on the economy only on the margin. Physical planning on the contrary necessarily deals with the continuous stream of the physical requirements of material, men and power needed to obtain final products. The end of a Five Year Plan does not mean nothingness. It means that the intermediate stages of the final pattern of output due in the next five years has to be prepared and partly put into being. The fact that in each of the first two Five-Year Plans a certain vacuum opened in the final year, depressing investment below the level which would physically have been maintained (especially as on both occasions the harvest was excellent), shows how incompletely this self-evident maxim has been acted upon. It is essential that the

---

[8] The fact that the increasing productivity of investment is likely to raise savings (including the increase in money holdings) does not seem to be appreciated. The efficiency of investment thus is an important factor determining the limits of save deficit financing.

Plan should be elastically rolled forward over a longish, ten-to-fifteen-year period, for otherwise the rationale of the Plan is likely to be lost sight of.

This forward planning is also essential because the exclusive concentration on a relatively short fixed period is likely to lead to imbalance and a deterioration in the quality of projects. If, for instance, regional 'balance' is striven for in each Five-Year Plan or indeed in each annual budget period, this will inevitably entail pressure for decentralizing projects in order to share them out, with attendant losses in productivity. Thus short-term budgeting, far from ensuring 'fiscal responsibility' and 'soundness', undermines the effectiveness of planning.

THE ECONOMIC SITUATION

India even at the end of 1970 had not completely recovered from the grave economic setback it had suffered as a result of the catastrophic series of failing monsoons in the mid-1960s. The index of per capita national income was still some 4 per cent below 1964-5. The damage to the all-important rate of domestic savings was worse. Having painfully risen from below 9 per cent in 1960-1 to 12 per cent in 1965-6 it fell to 7.8 per cent and has not reached 10 per cent yet.[9] The fall in the rate of investment was even sharper because of the decline of net foreign aid which, together with domestic savings, maintains it. All this limits the increase in the national income per head. And although the distribution of income, as we have said, has probably worsened, the proportion of the total in the hands of the 'rich' is not sufficient to base a determined attack on the problems of the country.[10]

[9] Source: Central Statistical Office. Some of the apparent fall is due to statistical distortion as a result of devaluation; but the weakening of investment capacity is undoubted.
[10] A clerk earning Rs. 200, or less than £15, per month is in the highest decile of the population.

Population

Long-run strategy thus seems to depend on an effective policy of birth control. According to the preliminary results of the 1971 census, the population at 547 million showed an increase of 2.25 per cent per annum in the last decade. This is 0.30 per cent a year (or more than one-seventh) higher than the increase in the previous decade. Given the improved statistics, and the impact of a better preventive health system, this result is objectively not too dispiriting. The birth-control campaign shows impressive absolute achievements — 17.3 million sterilizations up to 1969-70 and 3.3 million IUD insertions — but both are falling and, relative to the total of some 140 million women of child-bearing age (soon to reach 200 million), the effort relative to the need is insufficient. Birth control must continue to have first priority because social progress is made impossible by the pressure of the increase on the available land. Sharply rising land values and the frustration of legislation in favour of tenants clearly prove this deterioration.

Agriculture

Less than 110 million of the 547 million Indian population live in urban areas. Employment in the 'organized' sector is seventeen million. This shows the extreme urgency of the rural problem, and of agricultural employment and production in particular. Much publicity has been given to the 'miracle seeds' and the 'Green Revolution' which, it is said, have 'at a stroke' removed the threat of starvation.[11] In fact, and despite the increase of the area sown to high-yielding seeds to perhaps 30-35 million acres, only a small proportion — 9 per cent of the total arable land, and 12 or 13 per cent of the grain area — has as yet benefited. The results in wheat are

---

[11] See for example, the Pearson Report, *Partners in Development*, and Lester Brown, *Seeds of Change: The Green Revolution and Development in the 1970's* (reviewed above, chapter 6).

startling: its production at twenty million tons has doubled in the last decade. Yet (partly because of the tardier revolution in rice) the introduction of the new varieties had not affected the basic trend — what it did was to make good the grievous shortfall in the year when the monsoon failed. Output figures for the last two years did not reach the target. The per capita availability of food grain estimated in 1970 was over 6 per cent below 1965. Some of the fall was due to the halving of imports (which, incidentally, should be fully taken into account when discussing aid policy).

There can be no doubt, however, that in certain areas where water control is manageable — Punjab, parts of Utlar Pradesh and Rajasthan — the new seeds and the changes in technique and equipment that they necessitate, have brought about a rural revolution. Large profits there were for those who were in a position to profit. The second outstanding socio-political problem which has arisen is the importing into the countryside of the blatant inequality of the life in towns. For the moment mechanization — mainly restricted to tractors — does not seem to have put severe pressure on employment; and there is no doubt that tractors, by their speed and power, promote production. Indeed in some areas employment has increased and wages have shot up. But pressure on employment will undoubtedly come if further mechanization is permitted (e.g. combine harvesters, etc). Thus it is urgently necessary to discourage mechanization by taxation and direct prohibition and to put in hand structural reforms to enable the small farmer and landless labourer to participate in the 'revolution'. A beginning has been made with the nationalization of the banking system. Co-operatives are still lagging, and access to essential supplies and know-how is lacking for the small man.

The need for rural taxation and reorganization

It is equally essential to reorganize the taxation of agricultural income and land and also charge for water for irrigation. From this point of view the *holding* of the election itself (in contrast to its *result*) and the following state elections, meant a sharp setback. They reinforced the influence of the rural elite.

(1) Taxation of the larger peasant landowners must be arranged so as to provide the maximum incentive to higher production land taxes should increase with the size of the building but be based on average yields per acre by classes of land.

(2) Overpumping is now a distinct danger. Ground water levels are rising and water, if it is utilized at all (the access canals are lacking), is more often wasted than not. The establishment of a Central Ground Water Board provides a broad framework for action. The constitutional limitation on central government powers in agriculture will certainly have to be revised.

(3) Classical forms of primary education are incompatible with rural development. Modern education should be strongly vocationally based. By training agricultural, education and medical 'help' ('orderlies'), the supply of technical know-how to rural areas could be increased without increasing the risk of brain-drain.

(4) The institution of compulsory national service, at any rate for those who benefit from secondary and higher education, for the promotion of rural rehabilitation should be considered. The idea of communal work (*shramdan*) was excellent. It was the hope that it would succeed without the obligatory participation of the privileged that was naive. The national service corps is insignificant and does not command sufficient resources.

(5) Rural public works far greater than now contemplated should have direct relevance to those living at or below the poverty line. The vast autoroute investments should come later than access-canals, access-roads, communal buildings, demonstration farms.

(6) A beginning must be made with the updating of land registers preparatory both to tax reform and tenant protection. The cumulative land grabbing must be stopped.

Planning of foreign aid

Development planning should be based on the absorption of the maximum foreign aid available. As long as the present

discrepancy between national income levels persists, any endeavour to 'free India of dependence on aid' is not merely
silly but, because of its implications, also immoral. All international political efforts should be concentrated on increasing aid and on freeing it from political strings. Trade liberalization is no substitute for aid. It does not increase the investment capacity of the country to anything like the same
extent. In the case of primary products, moreover, trade
concessions (unless the export is conducted through Public
Marketing Boards) raise awkward distributional problems
since the growers of cash exports are likely to be relatively
prosperous and least worthy of aid. The import of manufactures of less developed countries on the other hand necessarily arouses antagonism in the developed countries out of all
proportion to the good it does to the exporter.

Industry

Far more effort must be devoted to fact-finding to be able to
plan effectively. The basic strategy must remain the greater
participation of the worst-off in employment and income. This
can only by accomplished by an indirect approach. A maximum surplus must be secured from large-scale industry and
the more comfortably off, and used for labour-intensive public
works programmes, especially in the rural sector.

Consequently the present schizophrenic attempt to limit
the operational scale and distribute organized industry in
penny packets all over the country with disastrous effects
on productivity must be stopped. Anti-monopoly drives of
this type are *laissez-faire* attempts to do the impossible, to
secure 'perfect' competition. They are incompatible with
effective social reconstruction. Important commissions, for
example the Monopolies and Restrictive Trade Practices
Commission, admit that the choice of managements in the
public sector has not been fortunate, and that that sector
cannot stand up to private industry as yet without being subsidized. But in spite of this, a system of monopoly control
is being pushed (much resembling British efforts) which is
inimical to mass production. Yet large-scale industry is

indispensable for efficiency; and without a vigorous drive for efficiency, increased investment will prove abortive as it has in railroads and in steel. Financial participation by the government in large-scale industry, without interference with management, rather than the suppression of large-scale enterprise, should be the proximate aim of industrial policy. Small-scale industries should be supported only if their *productivity in terms of capital* is not too unfavourable.

The transformation of the ill-conceived Monopolies Commission into an effective Prices and Incomes Board is, in my opinion, an essential prequisite for progress. In an environment of oligopoly a steadfast pressure on prices is the sole viable means of avoiding excessive profits. This is needed, however, if wage-costs are to be controlled as they necessarily will have to be.

Tax policy

Taxation — and more especially the elimination of evasion — should be the preferred means for redistributing income. The new middle and lower-middle class must be brought into the orbit of taxation along with prosperous peasants and landowners. Conspicuous consumption has increased and with it the demand to check big business by legislation. Despite the very mediocre results of the policy of imposing ceilings on land-holdings, the generalization of the policy to all wealth is propagated. It is not realized that an attempt to implement it would result in capital flight and an abrupt fall in savings.

Taxes on conspicuous consumption, especially motor-cars, should be materially increased, and a distortion of the investment programme enforced by the growing motorization of transport avoided. Taxes on wealth and income should, as in France, be based on estimated expenditure.

Given these social advances it is essential to subject wages in the organized sector (e.g. large-scale industry, government and commerce) to compulsory arbitration with statutory sanctions. It is intolerable that the semi-privileged classes, such as clerks and skilled workers, should exploit their monopoly power to the detriment of the really poor.

Planning

At the level of the Centre, the Planning Commission, before its recent reorganization, seemed to have become frozen in its technocratic projections whose socio-economic feasibility is at best questionable. It was, for instance, unreasonable to hypothesize a marginal savings ratio of 45 per cent. This explains much of the criticism of the latest Five-Year Plan. The Planning Commission in any case has been burdened with the unenviable task of reconciling the conflicting claims of the Centre and the states, and yet safeguarding overall efficiency. This would have taxed Hercules.

Until the election increasingly difficult problems of Indian development found the organ of the executive weaker and not stronger. This is obvious in the Centre-state relationship. The slogan decentralization and devolution is attractive only as long as one severely turns away from contemplating such questions as to who devolves what and on whom? How is the whole to be held together?

The most determined action is bitterly needed, based on a clear understanding of the problems faced. Unfortunately factual knowledge about India is, to say the least, scanty and ambiguous. There are legitimate grounds for disagreement on the most important and basic facts on which policy has to be based. The regrettable tendency to imitate the most affluent societies in spawning universities and institutes devoted to a duplication of esoteric research based on insufficient evidence is only too obvious and is at the moment on the increase.

Mathematical abstractions, based on unrealistic and irrelevant assumptions, seem to be used for policy advice. A vast amount of resources is spent not on obtaining solid facts but in supporting institutes dedicated to spinning complicated theories on the basis of insufficient knowledge. Consequently the manning of the central government's planning agencies has become more difficult in this strange new penury amidst plenty. This is the more regrettable as the state agencies and politicians are in no way fit to discharge the onerous task of assigning priorities. In the regional tussle for projects, effeciency goes by the board. In the event – as in Britain – the

Central Finance Ministry takes over the job of economic co-ordination, with the inevitable financial bias that is insepar-able from its effective functioning.

THE OUTLOOK

The outlook for India is therefore troubled. India's problems are, in the best possible circumstances, perplexing. The size of the country, the vastness and variety of its population, the torrent of its increase, render solutions complex and difficult to administer. The centrifugal forces of regionalism have undoubtedly suffered a setback in the election; but an insane sort of nationalism is growing on the Right, as is desperate violence of the Left. Both menace rational solutions, espe-cially as such solutions demand time. Only Mrs Gandhi can stop the fatal drift.

Administrative reorganization

A start has undoubtedly been made. A Planning Ministry has been established. It is not quite clear whether the Economic Department of the Ministry of Finance, a key portion of the administrative machine, will not come under the Planning Ministry. Nor is the latter's relation to the Planning Commis-sion fully defined. The minister has become the vice-chairman of the commission (i.e. the administrative head; the chair-man is the prime minister); the members have resigned and three new members have been appointed. It is not clear, how-ever, whether this change means that a new direction in research and action will be followed.

The budget

The budget also represents a step in the right direction provi-ded it is regarded *strictly* as a first step only. Taxation has been increased by Rs. 285 crores (£220 million). But direct taxation has not been extended widely; savings exemptions

were retained and the anomaly due to the treatment of un-
divided Hindu farming income remains. Even at Rs. 60,000
annual income (i.e. some 150 times the average of £4,000)
the increase in income tax is only 1.9 per cent. Wealth tax
has been doubled at 8 per cent but this only affects people
with a fortune of Rs. 16 lakhs (over £100,000), and above.
Tobacco, petrol and coarse cloth bear the brunt.[12] It is
unlikely therefore that the Prime Minister's plan for wage
restraint will be heeded.

The Bengal catastrophe

Public-sector saving was to have been increased from 1 per
cent to between 3 and 4 per cent. This will, after the catastrophe in East Bengal, not now be possible. Both revenue and
investment expenditure lag badly behind schedule, which
augurs ill for the immediate future.

The threat of the various centrigugal forces would in any
case have been difficult to contain. Only Mrs Gandhi can maintain some semblance of a balance; she can only do it if her
administrative and planning staff are reorganized and brought
to a full pitch of efficiency; and success depends on greatly
increased foreign aid. The East Pakistan war might lead to a
breakdown of such economic stability as the Indians were
able to preserve. Decisive action by the Great Powers, therefore, both on the diplomatic and on the aid level, is essential, and of the utmost urgency if a human catastrophe of an
unparalleled magnitude is to be avoided.[13]

---

[12] It is to be feared that this anomalous division of the burden will lead to a
further artificial diversion of resources toward luxuries.

[13] Despite her overwhelming electoral victories in 1971 and 1972 Mrs Ghandi
does not seem to be able to tackle the basic problems of agriculture, industrial
expansion and taxation. Time seems to be running out.

Index

Index

Index